The Garland Library of War and Peace

The Garland Library of War and Peace

Under the General Editorship of
Blanche Wiesen Cook, *John Jay College, C.U.N.Y.*
Sandi E. Cooper, *Richmond College, C.U.N.Y.*
Charles Chatfield, *Wittenberg University*

History of the Theory of Sovereignty Since Rousseau

by
Charles E. Merriam, Jr.

with a new introduction
for the Garland Edition by
Harold D. Lasswell

Garland Publishing, Inc., New York & London
1972

The new introduction for this
Garland Library Edition is Copyright © 1972, by
Garland Publishing Inc.

All Rights Reserved

Library of Congress Cataloging in Publication Data

Merriam, Charles Edward, 1874-1953.
    History of the theory of sovereignty since Rousseau.

    Reprint of the 1900 ed., issued as v. 12, no. 4 of
Studies in history, economics, and public law.
    Originally presented as the author's thesis, Columbia.

    Bibliography: p.
    1. Sovereignty. I. Title. II. Series: Columbia.
studies in the social sciences, v. 12, no. 4.
JC327.M5   1972   320.1'57   78-147736
ISBN 0-8240-0495-7

Printed in the United States of America

Introduction

The doctoral dissertation of the late Charles E. Merriam is of interest to historians of political theory from several points of view. The volume is an excellent reflection of the best scholarship of the 1890s, and deserves a respected place in the literature on the topic with which it is concerned. The fact that Merriam was the author is especially intriguing, since it is appropriate to ask whether we find hints of the creative role subsequently played by Merriam in initiating the Social Science Research Council, and in stressing the importance of assembling empirical data about the political process.

The dissertation was prepared under the direction of Professor Dunning, the distinguished historian, at Columbia University, whose three-volume history of political theories was for many years the standard treatment of the subject. The research reflected the exacting requirements of sound scholarship. Merriam often remarked on the utter boredom of the task of plowing through the several volumes of Bodin, or the endless proliferation of tiny points in the German scholarship of the nineteenth century. In harmony with Dunning he was fully alert to the personal and the collective factors that influence both the invention and the subsequent impact of theory.

INTRODUCTION

Merriam was cognizant of the dual methodology that is required in examining notions like "sovereignty." It is appropriate to analyze the definitional structure — later called the "syntactical" features — of a theory, and to formulate the levels of generality or contradiction among enunciated propositions. The complementary method is to examine the degree to which "explanatory" propositions are stated that are open to study by gathering data of observation.

The reexamination of the "philosophical" as contrasted with the "scientific" significance of a political theory led Merriam, as it had led Dunning, to take a dim view of the contributions of philosophy. Both of them were more than a little appalled at the brilliant minds who had contributed little more than justifications (and, in a later usage, "rationalizations") of power demands. They were hopeful of the cumulative impact of science in exposing the causes and consequences of claims to sovereignty. Merriam, at least, was confident that the claims of the "many" would be strengthened in conflict with the "few." Although his expectations were less developed at the time of thesis preparation, he also assumed that democratic nations would in the end be less disposed to war than nations that were dominated by "the few."

Some of Merriam's outlook was confirmed by his exposure to Hugo Preuss, the eminent constitutional jurist, to whom Professor Dunning sent Merriam. I was one of the last beneficiaries of the tradition that

INTRODUCTION

law and theory should be studied in Germany. When I was sent to Berlin in the twenties Professor Preuss was the prestigeful draftsman of the Weimar Constitution. Some of the drafting was intended to prevent capricious national policies in the name of romantic notions of sovereignty.

As a result of his exercise on the theory of sovereignty Merriam was permanently motivated to find a way of chastening "sovereign" claims.

Harold D. Lasswell
Ford Foundation Professor Emeritus
of Law and Social Sciences
Yale University

HISTORY OF THE THEORY OF SOVEREIGNTY SINCE ROUSSEAU

BY

C. E. MERRIAM, JR.

Sometime University Fellow in Political Philosophy

SUBMITTED IN PARTIAL FULFILMENT OF THE REQUIREMENTS
FOR THE DEGREE OF DOCTOR OF PHILOSOPHY
IN THE
FACULTY OF POLITICAL SCIENCE
COLUMBIA UNIVERSITY

New York
1900

PREFACE

THE province proper of the following study is the development of the theory of sovereignty from the beginning of the reaction against the principles of the French Revolution. In view of the poverty of English literature on the history of political theory in general, to say nothing of the particular doctrine here discussed, it has been thought advisable, however, to prefix a brief sketch of the theory of sovereignty prior to the period which is the special subject of this investigation.

The writer wishes to acknowledge his indebtedness to Professor Gierke, of Berlin, from whose works, lectures, and personal counsel he has obtained invaluable assistance; to Professor Burgess, of Columbia, whose doctrine of sovereignty first stimulated interest in the present study; and, above all, to Professor Dunning of the Department of Political Philosophy in Columbia, under whose direction all of the writer's work in the field of political theory has been conducted.

CONTENTS

CHAPTER I

INTRODUCTION

	PAGE
Classic basis of the theory	11
Mediaeval development	11
Theory of Bodin	13
Althusius and the Monarchomachs	17
Grotius	21
Hobbes	24
Pufendorf	28
Locke	30
Rousseau	33
Conclusion	36

CHAPTER II

THE KANTIAN THEORY

Sketch of the anti-revolutionary movement	39
Kant's general theory	43
Absolute character of sovereignty	45
Attack on the right of revolution	45
Limitations on sovereignty	47
Theoretical and practical sovereignty	48
Modifications made by Kant's followers	49
Fichte's doctrine of popular sovereignty	50

CHAPTER III

THE REACTIONARY THEORY OF DIVINE RIGHT

	PAGE
Clerical reaction against the revolution	52
Attack on the contract theory	54
Argument against popular sovereignty	55
Necessity of a divine source of political power	56
Character of divine authorization	58
Nature of sovereignty	59
Significance of the theory	61

CHAPTER IV

THE PATRIMONIAL THEORY

Critique of the contract theory	63
The law that might rules	64
Acquisition of sovereignty	66
Nature of sovereignty	68
Sovereignty as a property right	69

CHAPTER V

THE SOVEREIGNTY OF REASON

Historical basis of the theory	73
Reason or justice as sovereign: Cousin, Guizot, Constant	75
Relation to the theory of divine right	79
Doctrine after 1830; sovereignty of national reason	81
Modification in 1848	83

CHAPTER VI

POPULAR AND STATE SOVEREIGNTY

Historical basis of the theory	85
Conception of the State under "Naturrecht" influence	88
The Schelling-Hegel-Krause school	90
Historical school	96
Bluntschli's doctrine	99
Opposition to sovereignty of the State	103
State as a sovereign juristic person, or as an organism	108

CHAPTER VII

POPULAR AND STATE SOVEREIGNTY (CONTINUED)

	PAGE
Various uses of the term sovereignty	122
The unity of sovereignty	123
Limitations on sovereignty	124
Sovereignty as an essential mark of the State	125
Monarchical sovereignty	126
Conclusions	127

CHAPTER VIII

THE AUSTINIAN THEORY

Historical basis	130
Bentham's doctrine	131
Austin's conception of law	136
The "habit of obedience"	140
The "determinate" sovereign	141
Sovereignty as "legal despotism"	143
Criticism of Austin by Maine and others	151
The theory of "legal" and "political" sovereignty	154

CHAPTER IX

SOVEREIGNTY AND THE AMERICAN UNION

The theory of concurrent sovereignty	162
Calhoun and the indivisibility of sovereignty	168
The sovereignty of the Nation	172
The distinction between the sovereignty of the government and that of the State	179

CHAPTER X

FEDERALISM AND CONTINENTAL THEORY

Waitz's theory of concurrent sovereignty	185
The "Competenz-Competenz" doctrine	191

The doctrine of Jellinek	193
The separation of sovereignty from statehood	197
The defence of sovereignty as a characteristic of the State	202
The elimination of sovereignty	207
International law and semi-sovereignty	209

CHAPTER XI

CONCLUSION

Historical résumé	217
The tendency of the development of the theory, internally considered	221
The tendency, externally considered	222
The development in relation to the nature of sovereignty	222
Analysis of the various concepts and application to the progress of the theory	224

CHAPTER I

INTRODUCTION

THE beginnings of the theory of sovereignty are found in Aristotle's *Politics*, and the classic body of the Roman Law. In the *Politics* there is a recognition of the fact that there must be a supreme power existing in the state, and that this power may be in the hands of one, or a few, or of many.[1] In Chapter II, of Book III, appears a justification of the rule of the many, fairly expressed in the statement that "the principle that the multitude ought to be supreme rather than the few best is capable of a satisfactory explanation, and though not free from difficulty, yet seems to contain an element of truth."[2]

Among the Romans the idea of sovereignty found its clearest expression in the well-known sentence, "The will of the Prince has the force of law, since the people have transferred to him all their right and power."[3]

The renewed interest in the Roman Law in the 12th century, and the study of the newly discovered works of Aristotle in the 13th, furnished the fundamental propositions in the discussion of the theory of sovereignty, to which the struggle between Church and State gave rise. The Empire, asserting the juristic continuity of the Roman State, and

---

[1] Book III, ch. 7. Jowett's translation.

[2] Book III, ch. 11.

[3] "Quidquid principi placuit legis habet vigorem cum populus ei et in eum omne suum imperium et potestatem concessit. *Institutiones*, LI, Pt. II, sec. 6. Other expressions were, " Princeps legibus solutus est," " Error principis facit jus," " Omnia jura habet princeps in pectore suo."

claiming for its present head the attributes of the earlier Emperors, found in the same body of law which declared the ruler *legibus solutus*, the doctrine that the source of this authority was the Roman people. Hence the idea of original popular sovereignty could not be successfully contested by the State.[1] The Church, at first, under the influence of Augustine, declared through Gregory VII the State (and with it the sovereignty) to be the work of sin and the evil one. Later under the spell of "the Philosopher" Aristotle, Saint Thomas Aquinas taught that the supreme power arose from a purely human foundation—namely, the act of the people, in contrast to the God-established church.[2] The authority of the Pope, it was maintained, came directly from God; that of the Emperor from the consent of the people and the co-operation of the Church. Still later the popular argument spread from State to Church, and was used against the supremacy of the Pope himself in the great conciliar controversy.[3] So universally prevalent was the idea of original popular sovereignty that "from the end of the 13th century it was an axiom of political theory that the justification of all government lay in the voluntary submission of the community ruled."[4] Government based on the consent of the governed was the ruling theory in the Middle Ages.

[1] See Dante, *De Monarchia*, 1313.
Marsilius of Padua, *Defensor Pacis*, 1324-1326. Compare Bryce, H. E., *Holy Roman Empire*, ch. vii.; E. Friedberg, *Die mittelalterlichen Lehren über das Verhältniss von Staat und Kirche*; and above all Otto Gierke, *Johannes Althusius und die Entwickelung der naturrechtlichen Theorien*, a work which contains a wealth of material on mediaeval political theory and on the period down to the French Revolution.
Also Bezold, *Die Lehre von der Volkssouveränetät im Mittelalter* in Sybel's *Historische Zeitschrift*, xxxvi, 1876, 313-67.

[2] *De Regimine Principum*.

[3] See for basis of arguments Marsilius of Padua, and Occam, *Octo Quaestiones*, 1339-42.

[4] Gierke, *Althusius*, 78.

The conception of sovereignty, however, failed to attain a high degree of development in respect either to the essential nature and attributes of the supreme power, or to the location. A strong doctrine on the *nature* of sovereignty was hindered, theoretically, by the prevalent idea of the dominance of divine and natural over positive law, and by the idea of the so-called mixed form of state; politically by the conflict between Church and State and by the feudal condition prevalent within the State itself. The bearer of the sovereignty was declared to be the "people" (populus), but by people was understood, in spite of the frequent and sometimes striking analogies with physical organisms,[1] nothing more than the mass of the subjects. The unfolding of a complete theory awaited the development of the national State.

The first systematic discussion of the nature of sovereignty was made in France by Jean Bodin. His native land was then passing out of the last stages of feudalism, through the convulsion of civil war, into the form of a centralized state.[2] Bodin was an adherent of the nationalist party (les Politiques) which placed the interests of the State above religious or personal considerations. Reflecting the spirit of his party and the political conditions of his time, Bodin, in his masterly work *On the Commonwealth*,[3] became the framer of the theory of sovereignty upon which the French monarchy was

---

[1] Early employed by John of Salisbury in his *Policraticus*, 1159.

[2] See H. Baudrillart, *J. Bodin et son Temps*.

[3] *Six Livres de la République*, 1576; revised and translated by the author, and appearing as *De Republica*, 1586. On the theory of Bodin see: E. Hancke, *Bodin, Eine Studie über den Begriff der Souveränetät*, 1894; W. A. Dunning in *The Political Science Quarterly*, vol. xi; Adolph Dock, *Der Souveränetätsbegriff von Bodin bis zu Friederich dem Grossen*, 1897; Max Landmann, *Der Souveränetätsbegriff bei den französischen Theoretikern von Jean Bodin bis auf J. J. Rousseau*, 1896.

to rest; upon which, in fact, modern political science was to build.¹

Bodin starts with a definition of sovereignty (souveraineté, suprema potestas) as "The absolute and perpetual power of a commonwealth (la puissance absolue et perpetuelle d'une République), or in the later Latin edition, "The supreme power over citizens and subjects, unrestrained by law (suprema potestas in cives ac subditos, legibus soluta). Sovereignty is the central fact in Bodin's political theory; on it depends the definition of citizenship, the classification of forms of state, the identity of the state; it is indeed the essential and vital element in the commonwealth.²

What then is the nature of the supreme power as conceived by Bodin? It is in the first place absolute, in that it is wholly free from the restraint of law, and is held subject to no conditions or limitations.³ Indeed the very definition of law is the "command of a sovereign using his sovereign power."⁴ The sovereign must be wholly independent of any higher law-giver. Bodin enumerates nine degrees of subjection, and declares that "none but he is absolute who holds nothing of another man."

The supreme power is moreover unlimited in time, perpetual. Hence such officers as the Roman Dictators and Greek Archons were not truly sovereign, because their authority was for a limited period only. "Perpetual" is not, however, to be too broadly taken, and signifies properly

---

¹ Baudrillart says (p. 76): "Bodin est le philosophe du partie politique, son livre, considéré à ce point de vue, n'est que la politique nationale réduite en corps et formulée en système."

² "La République sans puissance souveraine, qui unist touts les membres et parties d'icelle et tout les menages et colleges en un corps, n'est plus République." I, ch. ii, p. 9, ed. 1577.

³ I, 8, 89 Fr. edit.

⁴ I, 8. "Sed plurimum distat *lex a jure;* jus enim sine jussu, ad id quod aequum, bonum est; lex autem ad imperantis majestatem pertinet."

for the life of the person who holds it ("pour la vie de celui qui a la puissance.")[1] Sovereignty is, further, indivisible in its nature; there cannot be two supreme powers.[2] It is, moreover, imprescriptible and hence cannot be effaced by the mere lapse of time.[3] As to the alienability of the sovereignty the statements of Bodin are confused. In the desire to protect the sovereign he declares that none of his rights can be in any way alienated.[4] But to avoid the argument for popular sovereignty, he asserts that the people may surrender their supreme power without any conditions whatever, so that it passes completely out of their control.[5] And finally to the aid of this abstract conception of sovereignty, comes an enumeration of nine definite rights which are the nine marks characteristic of its possession.[6] Of these the foremost is that to which reference has already been made, namely the power of "giving laws to the subjects in general without their consent."

Strongly stated as the idea of sovereignty was by Bodin, there were, nevertheless, certain limitations upon its absoluteness, some consciously, others unwittingly introduced. He by no means desired that the sovereign should be freed from obligation to any and all law, but, on the contrary, expressly

[1] It is possible that supreme power for life may not constitute sovereignty. "Si le peuple ottroye sa puissance à quelqu' un tant qu' il vivra, en qualité d' officier, ou lieutenant, ou bien pour se décharger seulement de l' exercise de sa puissance, en ce cas il n' est point souverain, ains simple officier ou lieutenant I-VIII.

[2] I, 10, " duo vero infinita ut sint, fieri nullo modo possit."

[3] I, 10 Lat.

[4] I, 10, " ea jura nec cedi, nec distrahi, nec ulla ratione alienari a summo principe posse."

[5] " Le peuple, ou les seigneurs d' une République, peuvent donner purement et simplement la puissance souveraine et perpétuelle, à quelqu' un pour désposer des biens, des personnes et tout l'éstat à son plaisir." I. viii., 89. Fr. ed.

[6] I, 10 Lat.

declares that every ruler in the world is subject to the laws of God, of nature, and of nations.[1] Less clearly outlined, but none the less omnipresent and insuperable, are the "leges imperii," the vaguely defined laws of the kingdom, which no sovereign can break through.[2] Thus the Salic law cannot be altered even by the supreme power, however absolute it may otherwise be. All these limitations are, however, ethical rather than political in character, and could at best bind only the conscience of the ruler.

The subject in which the sovereignty is vested may be, according to Bodin, one, a few or the many;[3] but the possibility of the mixed form is energetically combated.[4] The personal preferences of Bodin are strongly in favor of monarchy, but he concedes, nevertheless, that democracy or aristocracy may also enjoy the full attributes of sovereign power. The State as a whole is not regarded as the sovereign, but one element thereof is the bearer of the supreme power and the other is the object against which this power is directed. Of the Respublica itself as the bearer of the sovereignty he has only a dim idea.[5]

Such then was the the theory of Bodin. In France it became the theoretical bulwark against particularism and antinationalism; it furnished the theoretical basis for seventeenth and eighteenth century absolutism; and, in a still broader sense, became the foundation of the modern theory of sov-

[1] I, ch. 8, Fr. ed. By the lex naturæ the sovereign must keep his private contracts with his subjects. Even God is bound to keep his promises.

[2] I, ch. 8, "Quantum vero ad imperii leges attinet, cum sint cum ipsa majestate conjunctæ, Princeps nec eas abrogare nec iis derogare possit, cujusmodi est lex Salica, regni hujus firmissimum fundamentum."

[3] II, 1 Lat.

[4] Bodin distinguishes, however, between form of *state* and form of *government*. II, 1-2 Lat.

[5] On the influence of Bodin compare Gierke's *Althusius;* also Landmann and Dock. *loc. cit.*

ereignty. It was the first systematic study of the essential nature of the supreme power.

Over against the theory outlined by Bodin, and defended by his followers, stood that of the school of political writers characterized by their adversaries as the "Monarchomachs." The historical basis of their doctrine was the religious intolerance and persecution which followed the course of the Reformation, and necessitated the development of a theory of resistance for the use of the minority party.[1] Enthusiastic adherents were found in France, Scotland, Germany, Spain, and in the ranks of Jesuits and Reformers alike. The central features of the doctrine were the original and inalienable sovereignty of the people, the contractual origin of government, the fiduciary character of all political authority, and the consequent right of the people to resist and destroy the existing rulers whenever found guilty of a breach of trust. These theories, already widespread in the Middle Ages, were revived and were stated, if possible, more clearly and concisely, while their application was bolder and more sweeping than ever before. Among the writers, by far the ablest was Johannes Althusius, whose work "*Politics Systematically Considered*" (Politica methodice digesta, 1609), was easily the most scientific of his time and school.[2]

---

[1] See R. Treumann, *Die Monarchomachen*, 1895. Gierke's *Althusius*.
Weill, *Le pouvoir royal en France pendant les guerres de réligion*.
Ch. Labiette, *De la Monarchie chez les prédicateurs de la Ligue*, 1841.
The term Monarchomachs was first employed by an adversary of the school Barclaius, according to Treumann, in a book (1600), entitled: *De regno et regali potestate adversus Buchananum, Brutum, Boucherium et reliquos Monarchomachos libri sex.*

[2] See O. Gierke, *J. Althusius*. Althusius' work was long forgotten until rescued by Gierke. Prominent among the Protestant representatives of the school were George Buchanan, *De jure Regni apud Scotos*, 1579; Junius Brutus (Hubert Languet), *Vindiciæ contra tyrannos*, 1579. Among the Catholics, J. Boucher, *De justa Henrici III abdicatione*, 1591; Mariana, a Spanish Jesuit, *De rege et regis institutione*, 1599.

The theory of Althusius is permeated with the element of contract. The bond of the primary political associations is contract, tacit or express; the state is the final form in a series of contracts,[1] and the authority of the government results from an agreement, tacit or express, between the ruler and the ruled.[2] Sovereignty he defines as "The highest and most general power of administering the affairs which generally concern the safety and welfare of the soul and body of the members of the State."[3] As to the content of this power, Althusius denies that it is absolute, or supreme, since it is subordinate to the laws of God and nature, but he declares it a unit and is disposed to admit that the power is free from the civil law.[4]

The goal of the Monarchomach's effort was not, however, the determination of *what* sovereignty is, but rather *where* it is; or better, the defence of the original and inalienable sovereignty of the people.

He therefore maintains that the source of all governmental power is ultimately found in the people, which is the great political creator, the true monarch-maker. Sovereignty is essentially an attribute not of individuals, but of the whole. It is not called into being by one particular member of the society, but results from the action of all taken together;[5] it must therefore be attributed not to in-

---

[1] Family, corporation, commune, province, state.

[2] Ch. xix, p. 234, ed. 1617. Ch. ix, 114 ff.

[3] "Potestas praeeminens et summa universalis disponendi de iis quæ universaliter ad salutem curamque animæ et corporis membrorum Regni seu Reipublicæ pertinent." Ch. ix, 125.

[4] See his polemic against Bodin ch. ix, 122 ff. Here Althusius seems to confuse the sovereign monarch, as governmental agent, with the sovereign people. He denies that sovereignty is perpetual, an admission fatal to his cause. See p. 122.

[5] "Non ab uno, sed universis simul membris universalis consociationis constitui potest, sic nec singulorum, sed universorum membrorum illud esse dicitur." Ch. ix, p. 121.

dividuals, but to all.¹ But this might be conceded and yet the power of the government remain as unlimited as before. If, as with Bodin, it is possible to alienate the original popular sovereignty, then the concession may be even worse than worthless. Althusius maintains, therefore, and in this represents his school, that the supreme power was not only *originally*, but remains *permanently*, in the people.

The sovereignty is declared to be an attribute of the whole body which cannot be alienated to any of the limbs or members. The people is always the greater power, hence is always superior to the administration; and however great the power conceded, the party conceding always remains superior to the concessee.² Again, the people is immortal, whereas the rulers are merely mortal, hence the people alone are the fit subject of permanent power.³

If then, the community is the source and remains the bearer of sovereignty, all governmental power must be purely derived authority, always subordinate to the higher will of the true ruler. In the Althusian theory all government owes its existence to a contract which if not express must be presumed, and whose terms if detrimental to the people's right are to be regarded as null and void.⁴ At best, the rulers are only administrators, or temporary possessors; the people continue to hold the undisputed and unimpaired title of the owner. Hence comes the practical conclusion that if the ruler is unfaithful to the trust in his charge, he

---

[1] Universis membris et toto corpori consociato regni competit," p. 121.

[2] "Quantacunque enim est potestas quae alii conceditur, semper tamen minor est ejus potestate qui eandem concessit," p. 123.

[3] " Negari non potest, illam majorem esse, quae alteram constituit, quae immortalis in subjecto suo, populus scilicet, et alteram minorem, quae in unius persona consistit, et cum eadem moritur," p. 124. Bodin came close to this conception in his reference to sovereignty as "perpetual."

[4] The terms are " ea quae sancta sunt, aequa et justa et in Decalogo continentur," and if bad conditions are made, " illae pro nullis habenda sunt." Ch. xix, 234.

may be judged by the people, may be deposed and punished as the circumstances may¹ demand.²

These arguments of Althusius were typical of the school, though his method was far superior to that usually employed. Throughout the discussion, the doctrine of sovereignty made little advance, in respect to either its content or its bearer. "Popular sovereignty" was energetically and ably defended against that of the government, but just what this sovereignty was, or who "the people" were, found no very satisfactory answer. If the supreme power belonged to the community, its nature was not a matter of primary importance. On the other hand, when the sovereignty was attributed to "the people," even though denominated the regnum, respublica, civitas, body politic, state, by this was understood not the ruler and the ruled, but the mass of the subjects, *excluding* the governor.³ The sovereign people were not the whole State, including both subject and

---

[1] See ch. xxxviii, De Tyrannide ejusque remediis. To this end Althusius proposed the establishment of a body of "Ephors," whose special function should be the oversight of the government. See ch. xviii.

[2] In Althusius as in the other Monarchomachs a distinction is made between the tyrant "absque titulo" and the tyrant "quoad exercitium." The former was regarded as a public enemy who could be rightfully assailed by any patriotic private citizen; the latter must be treated with more formality, *i. e.*, with the sanction of a magisterial body of some kind.

[3] See Gierke, 160 ff. Related to the theory of the Monarchomachs was the doctrine of the *majestas realis* and *majestas personalis*, prevalent in Holland and Germany during the first half of the 17th century. It was held that two sovereignties, the real and personal, existed side by side in the state; the real sovereignty, that of the people as the ultimate source of political power: the personal sovereignty, that vested in the existing government. Both were genuine sovereignties, each supreme in its own sphere, "in suo ordine et genere," as the phrase ran. The tendency was, however, toward a development of the sphere of the majestas realis at the expense of the personalis. Among the leading exponents of the theory were: Kirchner, *Respublica*, 1608; Linnæus, *Juridica de majestate*, 1625; Boxhorn, *Institutionum politicarum libri duo*, 1665. See Gierke and Landmann.

government, but the governed part of the State. The idea of sovereignty vested in an entity which included both ruler and ruled, was not to be found, even in the theory of the great apostle of the school, Althusius. Popular sovereignty was the sovereignty of the sum of the subjects regarded as a person in a purely fictitious sense, and as contrasted to the government.

Between the absolutist theory of Bodin and the democratic doctrines of the Monarchomachs stood that of Hugo Grotius, as elaborated in his remarkable work on *The Law of War and Peace*, 1625.[1] His doctrine was an ingenious compromise between the popular and the monarchical ideas, and exercised a powerful influence, particularly upon Pufendorf, and through him upon the German theory of the seventeenth and eighteenth centuries.

To Grotius sovereignty signifies "that power whose acts are not subject to the control of another, so that they may be made void by the act of any other human will."[2] Clashing with Bodin, he maintains that the duration of the power does not affect its essential nature. A distinction, he holds, must be made between the power itself and the tenure of the power.[3] The sovereignty he likens to a field over which one may enjoy full ownership, the usufruct, or a temporary right only. The Roman dictator was none the less sovereign though for a limited time only, and likewise the elective king, provided only that the power be irrevocable during the given period. Further, the absoluteness of sovereignty is in no wise insisted upon by Grotius. The supreme power is, as customary, limited by divine law, natural law and the law of

---

[1] *De jure Belle ac Pacis*. There is an English translation by Whewell.

[2] Summa autem illa dicitur, cujus actus alterius juri non subsunt, ita ut alterius voluntatis humani arbitrio irriti possunt reddi, B. I, ch. iii, sec. 7.

[3] I, 3, sec. 9, "*Duratio* autem naturam rei non immutat."

nations,[1] but also by such agreements as are made between ruler and ruled. Thus an indefinite number of rights may be subtracted from the authority of the ruler; his acts may be rendered subject to ratification by a senate or other body;[2] it may even be provided that in certain cases a right of insurrection falls to the people[3] yet the sovereignty still retains its essential quality unimpaired. The key to the readiness with which Grotius admits the possibility of limitation is found in the fact that he freely concedes that the supreme power is capable of division. While unity is in general desirable and advantageous, there are cases, he says, in which the sovereignty has been actually divided; as, for example, in Rome with one ruler in the east and one in the west. In Grotius' words "Many persons allege many inconveniences against such a two-headed sovereignty, but in political affairs nothing is quite free from inconvenience."[4]

The most important element in the theory of Grotius was not, however, that of the content, but that of the bearer of the sovereign power. The sovereignty, Grotius declared, may reside either in a general subject (subjectum commune) or in a special subject (subjectum proprium); as the general subject in which the sight resides is the body, the special subject, the eye.[5] Hence, one may say either that the body sees, or that the eye sees. So the sovereignty has a general bearer, that is, the body politic, or civitas, and also a special bearer, namely the person or persons constituting the government. One may say, consequently, that the State as a whole is sovereign, or that the special

---

[1] I, 3, sec. 16.   [2] I, 3, sec. 18.

[3] I, 4, sec. 14. So a period of prescription against the sovereignty. II, 4, sec. 11.

[4] I, ch. 3, sec. 17; also sec, 20.

[5] Book I, 3, No. 7, "Subjectum aliud est commune, aliud proprium, ut visus subjectum commune est corpus, proprium oculus; ita summæ protestatis subjectum commune est civitas......subjectum proprium est persona una pluresve pro cujusque gentis legibus ac moribus." Also II, 6, sec. 6.

organ, the Government, is sovereign. Grotius here came close to the idea of State sovereignty. The theory was not developed, however; Grotius' State was a semi-artificial creation at best; and the whole concept was contradicted, as will presently appear, by the patrimonial notion.

In accordance with his theory of general and special sovereignty, Grotius could deny, as he did, the assertion of Althusius and the Monarchomachs that the supreme power everywhere and always belongs to the people, that is, the people excluding the government.[1] He could deny that all government exists for the benefit of the governed alone, and declare that it is often for the good of the ruler and ruled together.[2] Here, however, influenced by his idea of the patrimonial state, he departs from the theory of the two subjects of power, and maintains that the people may absolutely alienate their sovereignty, as an individual his control over a piece of property.[3] Reasoning by analogy from Roman private law, he considers that just as a person may legally alienate his liberty, so a people may deliver itself into slavery. He would apparently apply to a people the argument used in reference to the individual, namely that man is not a slave by nature, but he is not by nature a creature that cannot become a slave.[4] Sovereignty may be held either with full property right (jure pleno proprietas), or with usufruct only (jure usufructario). Where the sovereignty is a full property right, it includes ownership of the land and the people, and the right to dispose of all at pleasure. Hence, either the land or the people may be bought or sold like any other property.[5] Mere usufruct

---
[1] I, 3, sec. 8.   [2] I, 3, sec. 8.   [3] II, 5, 31.

[4] II, 22, sec. 11, " Ut natura quis servus non sit, non ut jus habeat ne umquam serviat; nam in hoc sensun nemo liber est."

[5] Proprie tamen cum populus alienatus, non ipse homines alienatur, sed *jus perpetuum eos regendi* quâ populus sunt," I, 3, sec. 12.

carries with it only the enjoyment of certain rights, but not the ownership proper.[1] In short, the sovereignty is treated by Grotius as property to which perfect rights or imperfect rights of all possible degrees may be held. His system is pliable enough to meet the requirements of either the democratic or the monarchic school, without completely satisfying either.

Against the theory of original popular sovereignty, with the corollaries of binding contract and reserved right of resistance, so widespread in the first half of the seventeenth century, the Englishman, Thomas Hobbes, in his *Leviathan* (1651) constructed the most complete argument for absolutism that had yet been made.[2] The historical influence under which Hobbes worked was that of the conflict between the English throne and the people. The method he followed was that of sharp definition and unfaltering deduction; his central argument, the very contract which had been the strongest defence of the popular cause. The premise from which Hobbes proceeds is that of a state of nature in which there prevails a war of all against all (*bellum omnium contra omnes*), in which there is no common power, and where every man's right reaches exactly as far as his might. Out of this anarchical condition government arises through

---

[1] Grotius subtly remarks, "distinguendam esse summitatem imperii ab habendi plenitudine, adeo verum est ut non modo pleraque imperia summa *non plene* habeantur, sed et multa non summa habeantur *plene*," I, 3, sec. 14. So the right to alienate territory does not belong to rulers who "imperium etsi plenum habent, attamen non plene." II, 6, sec. 7.

Grotius returns to his organic idea when he declares that the state remains the same state despite changes in form of *government*. There are two elements in the state, he says, one the "consociatio juris atque imperii," the other "relatio partium inter se earum quæ regunt et quæ reguntur. Hanc spectat Politicus: illam jurisconsultus." II, 9, sec. 8.

[2] *De Leviathan*, 1651, Morley's Translation.
De corpore politico, 1650.
Elementa Philosophica de cive, 1642.

the agency of a compact, the impulse to which Hobbes introduces into the "natural man," together with the tendency to keep the agreement when made.[1]

By the terms of this contract, each individual surrenders his rights to one person (physical or moral) who thenceforth becomes the bearer of the personality of all the contracting individuals. As the agreement reads: "Every one to own and acknowledge himself to be the author of whatsoever he that beareth their person, shall act or cause to be acted, in those things which concern the common peace and safety, and therein to submit their wills, every one to his will, and their judgments to his judgment."[2] This person so endowed is the sovereign, and all others in the community are subjects.[3] The characteristic feature of Hobbes' contract is, however, that the agreement is made among the future subjects, while the future sovereign remains outside the contract. The agreement is one among incipient subjects, not between incipient sovereign and incipient subject. There is no possibility of a reserved sovereignty, for the supreme power comes into existence only with the creation of the governmental person who is its bearer. Sovereignty and its subjects are created simultaneously. Sovereignty is not delegated or alienated by the people, for they were not a people until the sovereignty was created; in other words, the people never possessed the supreme power, and consequently had no right to dispose of it. Thus the authority of the ruler was protected at the point against which the Monarchomachs had directed their most effective assaults. There is an original state of nature, a contract, a sovereign as its creature, but the sovereign is the Leviathan, or mortal

---

[1] *Leviathan*, ch. xiii–xv.

[2] *Leviathan*, ch. xvii.

[3] This "person" need not however be an *individual*, but might be many individuals regarded as a person.

god, armed with the power and entrusted with the judgment of all his subjects—"bearing their person."

The extent of the sovereign power so derived is far-reaching. Hobbes asserts that, as a result of the contract made, the subjects can enter into no new agreement or covenant, not even with God; the sovereign can himself commit no breach of covenant, and hence cannot forfeit his right to the people; the sovereign can do no *injustice* (though he may commit *iniquity*); the sovereign cannot be punished; he is judge of the means necessary for the defence of the state; has the right to decide what doctrines shall be taught among the subjects; the law-making power; the judicial power; the right to carry on war; the right to appoint officers; the rewarding and punishing power. And all these rights are, as Hobbes says, "incommunicable and inseparable."[1] Further, the unity of the sovereign power is unconditionally asserted. Within the commonwealth there can be but one supreme authority. All rights are transferred by the terms of the contract to the sovereign, and there can be no room remaining for another independent authority. Even the church must be regarded as subordinate to the sovereign, since he is the vicegerent of God, and determines the validity of doctrine, even the authenticity of inspiration.[2]

Sovereignty appears, then, with Hobbes as far more absolute than in the theory of Bodin. There is no limitation in the law of God or of nature; for of these the sovereign is the final judge, while the limitations in the form of the "leges

---

[1] Ch. xviii. On the sphere of liberty left to the subjects see ch. xxi. On the concept of law as the command of the sovereign, see ch. xxvi.

[2] See ch. xxix, "As there have have been doctors that hold there be three souls in a man; so there be also that think there may be more souls, that is, more sovereigns than one in a commonwealth; and set up a supremacy against the sovereignty......And this is a disease which not unfitly may be compared to the epilepsy or falling sickness, which the Jews took to be one kind of possession by spirits in the body natural."

imperii" do not appear. In the language of Hobbes, "The sovereign power, whether placed as in monarchy, or in one assembly of men, as in popular and aristocratical commonwealths, is as great as possibly men can be imagined to make it." And further, "he who considers it too great and will seek to make it less, must subject himself to a power that can limit it, that is to a greater."[1]

Regarding the sovereignty as absolute, unified, inalienable, based upon a voluntary but irrevocable contract, the theory of Hobbes was so closely articulated that even the keenest weapon found difficulty in penetrating it. The logic was cruelly complete, and granting the necessary premises, the conclusions he drew were difficult to escape. Hobbes had designed the theory as a solvent for the political difficulties in England, and had hoped for the establishment of a strong monarchical government on the basis of the principles he laid down. But by providing for the subordination of the ecclesiastical to the political authority, he alarmed even the loyalist clergy, and hence his arguments found little support and had little influence on contemporary conditions. Theoretically, however, the work of Hobbes exercised a decided influence on the development of later political science.[2]

[1] Ch. xx. Hobbes admits that no such power has ever really existed, but denies that this affects the mathematical certainty of his conclusions.

[2] In line with the theory of Bodin and Hobbes was that of the defenders of the Bourbons in France, particularly Bossuet in "*La Politique tirée de l' Écriture sainte*," 1709; "*Avertissements aux Protestants*," 1689-91; and in Fénélon, *La Télémaque*, 1699. To the attributes of sovereignty already developed was added that of *sacredness*. The absolute and paternal character of the monarch was avowed and defended, but great emphasis was placed on the moral responsibility of the rulers. Compare the patriarchal theory of Robert Filmer in *The Patriarcha*, 1680, posthumous.

An application of the method and principles of Hobbes was made by Spinoza, but to the advantage of democratic rather than monarchic government. In the *Tractatus theologico-politicus*, 1676, the *Tractatus Politici* (posthumous) and the

The first half of the 17th century saw the completion of the theory of the Monarchomachs; the middle of the century was marked by the *Naturrecht* absolutism of Hobbes; it remained for the close of the century to state the doctrine which dominated Germany to the French Revolution and that which in England constituted the justification of the overthrow of the Stuarts. The German theory was formulated by Samuel Pufendorf; the English by John Locke.

The theory of Pufendorf was developed under the influence of Hobbes on the one side and Grotius on the other, and combined in a remarkable way the compromising theory of the one with the absoluteness of the other. In his massive work, *The Law of Nature and of Nations* (De Jure Naturæ et Gentium, 1672),[1] Pufendorf accepts the contract principle as the basis of the State, but requires two stages in the process, namely an agreement to form a civil society, the "Pactum Unionis," followed by a farther contract between the people so formed and the Government, "Pactum Subjectionis." The sovereignty so created is the supreme power in the State.[2] None of his acts may be rendered void by any other organ in the society; he is responsible to no

---

Ethica (Part IV), he found that there was originally a lawless state of nature, a compact between individuals, and a resulting sovereign government. (Tractatus theologico-politicus, ch. xvi.) But out of the nature of the supreme power itself certain limitations are deduced: thus the nature of the political power requires that it have a rational end (Tractatus Politici iii, 7); only that sphere in which acts or forbearances can be induced by rewards or punishments is a subject of the sovereign's activity (Tractatus politici, iv. 4). Again, the sovereignty is limited by the fact that it must deal with human subjects (Tract. pol. iv. 4); and lastly the power of the state must certainly be subject to some class of law: "For if the state were bound by no laws or rules, without which the state could not be a state, then it would not be a real object, but a chimaera." (Trac. pol. iv. 4). Spinoza's statement of the difference between his position and that of Hobbes is contained in his *Epistolæ* L, Opera ii, 184 (Van Vloten und Laud).

[1] See also *De officio hominis et civis*, 1673.
[2] *De J. N. et G.*, VII, ch. 6, sec. 1.

other power, free from the restraint of all human law;[1] and this power is essentially one and indivisible.[2] But on the other hand, a distinction is drawn between *sovereign* power and absolute power.[3] Absolute power gives one complete freedom to use his rights as he will, but by a supreme power is meant only that, in the same order of beings, there is none superior. Sovereignty, properly understood, Pufendorf declares, signifies not absoluteness, but merely supremacy. Again, it is frankly admitted that owing to the unfortunate frailty common to all men, there not only may conceivably, but should actually be, certain limitations placed upon the sovereign.[4] In the grant of power to the ruler, definite restrictions should be placed upon him of a character calculated to restrain his tendency to usurp all authority. With Grotius, Pufendorf maintains that the sovereignty may be held either with "full right" or in a manner more or less limited, but though limited, remains none the less truly sovereign.[5]

The elective or limited monarch is, therefore, contra Hobbes, a genuine sovereign, and not a mere agent of the constituting power. To Pufendorf it does not seem essential that the sovereign should have all power, but it is sufficient if he have the highest power; that is to say, he must be supreme, but need not be absolute. In the same conciliatory spirit, Pufendorf repudiates the misinterpeted declaration of Hobbes that the sovereign can commit no injustice, but admits that in matters pertaining to the general welfare Hobbes' proposition would be true; and this holds even though the sovereign's measures may, as a matter of fact, be contrary to the common weal.[6] Cutting away the superfluous verbiage, it would seem that the sovereign is free to follow the course

---

[1] *De J. N. et G.*, VII, ch. 6, sec. 2.
[2] *Ibid.*, VII, ch. 4, sec. 4.
[3] *Ibid.*, VII, ch. 6, sec. 10.
[4] *Ibid.*, VII, ch. 6, sec. 9.
[5] *Ibid.*, VII, ch. 6, sec. 11–14.
[6] *Ibid.*, VII, ch. 8, 1.

he chooses, although to such a statement Pufendorf would have been unwilling to assent.

Yet, notwithstanding its somewhat contradictory character, or one might say even because of it, the theory of Pufendorf became widely influential. It reconciled to a certain extent the benevolent despotism of the German states with the spirit of individual liberty, by conceding supremacy to the one, but not excluding the other from a degree of control. With some modifications his doctrine was followed by the great German expounders of political science in the eighteenth century, such as Christian Wolff,[1] J. A. Boehmer,[2] and Christian Thomasius,[3] and continued to be the dominant theory down to the time of Kant.

Locke[4] appeared on the political field as the Whig champion of the English Revolution of 1688. His theory was the accepted justification for the overthrow of the Stuarts; it later found expression in the American Revolution against England, and still remains the popular theory of sovereignty among English-speaking peoples.

Locke starts with a state of nature, which is not, however, as with Hobbes, a state of war, but rather a condition where individual rights are imperfectly secured. In order that a guarantee may be obtained, there is established a civil or political society and then a government.[5] To this end every man surrenders irrevocably to the community his natural rights in so far as is necessary for the common good—and no farther.[6] The political society so constituted establishes by

---

[1] *Fundamenta juris naturæ et gentium*, 1705.

[2] *Introductio in jus publicum universale*, 1726.

[3] *Jus naturæ methodo scientifica pertractatum*, 1740–50. *Institutiones juris naturæ et gentium*, 1754. See Gierke's *Althusius*, p. 184; Bluntschli, *Geschichte der Staatswissenschaft*.

[4] *Two Treatises of Government*, 1689. Compare Richard Hooker, *Laws of Ecclesiastical Polity*, 1593–98.

[5] Sec. 95–99. [6] Sec. 129–30.

a fundamental law the Legislature. which is the supreme governmental power. This body is then the source of law,[1] the representative of the will of the society, the "soul that gives life, form and unity to the Commonwealth."[2] It is the highest governmental representative of the political society which has given it life. The Legislature is, however, a power to protect and preserve, not to destroy; hence "it is not, nor can possibly be, absolutely arbitrary over the lives and fortunes of the people."[3]

Where the Legislature is not always in session and the Executive power is vested in a single person who has also a share in the Legislature, there, according to Locke, that single person "in a very tolerable sense, may also be called supreme."[4] So long as within the limits of the law he may be looked upon "as the image, phantom or representative of the Commonwealth." As the lowest term, then, in the series of sovereigns stands the king as the formal or *legal* sovereign, supreme while within the limits of the law. Next in order comes the legislative body, the sovereign among the governmental powers, and so far absolute, or as we might say, the *governmental* sovereign. The Legislature is, however, only a "fiduciary body," entrusted with certain powers, and hence is in a sense subordinate. Back of the Legislature stands another body, which is ultimately the true sovereign. This is the civil or political society which has instituted the Legislature, and might be called the *political* sovereign.

Between the government and the political society there is no common judge; in other words, they are in a perpetual state of nature, the essential characteristic of which is this lack of a common umpire. Hence, when the people of a

---
[1] Sec. 134–151.   [2] Sec. 212.
[3] Sec. 135. See the four specific limitations enumerated in sec. 142. Sec. 151.

political society is deprived of civil rights, it has still an original natural right, as Locke declares, "a liberty of appeal to heaven."[1] In other words, the political society has always the right to resume the sovereignty temporarily placed in the hands of the Legislature.[2] As Locke explains, "The community may be said in this respect to be always the supreme power, *but not as considered under any form of government*,"[3] because the power of the people remains latent until the government is dissolved.[4]

Locke's theory is, then, that the executive (as already qualified), is, while within the law, supreme; that the Legislature is the sovereign governmental organ so long as the government endures; and that the political society (or the majority thereof) is the *latent*, and on the dissolution of the government, becomes the *active* sovereign.[5]

As to the content of sovereignty, it is difficult to deduce anything more than the statement that it is not absolute. If the power is used for the general good it would seem to be be almost without limit. Thus Locke declares that a good prince cannot have too much prerogative, "that is, power to do good."[6] "Whatsoever cannot but be acknowledged to be of advantage to the society and people in general, upon just

---

[1] Sec. 168. "But he that appeals to heaven must be sure that he has right on his side." Sec. 176.

[2] "Though the people cannot be judge so as to have, by the constitution of that society, any supreme power to determine and give effective sentence in the case." Sec. 168. Locke denies that his theory is anarchical. The alternative is that "the people should be always exposed to the boundless will of tyranny, or that the rulers should be sometimes liable to be opposed when they grow exorbitant in the use of their power." Sec. 229.

[3] Sec. 168.   [4] Sec. 149.

[5] Locke uses the terms "political society," "government," "body politic," confusedly and confusingly; see Sec. 95, 97, 98, 99. On the three grades of sovereignty compare Ritchie, *Annals of the American Academy of Political Science* I, 385, who revives the theory of Locke in another connection.

[6] Sec. 164.

and lasting measures, will always, when done, justify itself."[1] Into further refinements of the nature of sovereignty Locke does not enter.

The next stage in the development of the theory of sovereignty was the formulation of the doctrine upon which the French Revolution was to rest. In the writings of Jean Jacques Rousseau, the theory of sovereignty of the people as developed from the basis of "natural rights" was followed out to the last extreme.[2]

Again the point of departure is the individual, again the sovereignty arises from the voluntary agreement of independent wills. In the original contract, each surrenders all to all and the product of the process is the body politic, which when passive is called the State, when active is termed the sovereign.[3] The abstraction of the element common to the individual wills results in the formation of the general will (volonté générale), which is the soul and spirit, the sovereign in the State.

The first characteristic quality of the general will is its inalienability.[4] Power, Rousseau says, may be transferred, but not will. It is impossible for any organ to exercise the sovereign will save the sovereign body itself. If the people promise to obey a ruler; the people as such ipso facto is dissolved, the State no longer exists. The State, as a State, can no more alienate its sovereignty than a man can alienate his will and remain a man. Thus Rousseau protects the people against such a loss of supremacy through voluntary act, as deemed possible by Grotius and Hobbes. By the same logic the idea of representative government is shattered, for inasmuch as the sovereign power can never be

---

[1] Sec. 158; also sec. 3.

[2] *Lettres de la Montagne*, 1764; *Du Contrat Social*, 1762; *Gouvernement de Pologne*, 1772.

[3] Contrat Social, I, 6.   [4] *Ibid.*, II, 1.

delegated, the instant a people gives itself representatives it ceases to be free.¹ There is but one possible bearer of the sovereignty, the people; but one form of State, the democratic.²

Indivisibility is a further characteristic of the sovereign power. The will, it is held, is one or not at all.³ The emanations from the sovereignty, as the legislative and executive powers, may be divided, but the general will, the sovereignty itself, is wholly incapable of division.⁴

In addition to its attributes of inalienability and indivisibility, the sovereign will is declared to be infallible. It is always right and always tends toward the general welfare.⁵ It is true that the general will may be momentarily deceived, but on the whole, its tendency is toward the right. "Merely because it is, the sovereign is always what it ought to be."⁶

And finally, the sovereign will is absolute. Rousseau declares that "as nature gives every man absolute control over all his members, so the social contract gives to the body politic an absolute power over all its members.⁷ The sovereign has unlimited control over all that affects the general welfare, and the indisputable right to judge as to what falls under this category. No rights are reserved to the individual; in fact, no guaranty of rights from sovereign to subject is conclusive.⁸ It is no more possible for the people

---

¹ III, 5.

² But Rousseau distinguishes between form of state and form of government. In one passage he seems to admit the possibility of an aristocratic sovereignty. "Le meilleur des gouvernemens est l' aristocratique; la pire des *souverainetés* est l' aristocratique." *Lettres de la Montagne*, VI.

³ II, 2.   ⁴ II, 2.   ⁵ II, 3.

⁶ I, 7. "Le souverain, par cela seul qu' il est, est toujours tout ce qu' il doit être."

⁷ II, 4.

⁸ I, 7, "Il n'y a ni peut y avoir nulle espèce de loi fondamentale obligatoire pour le corps du peuple, pas même le contrat social."

to guarantee a right to an individual as its subject, than to surrender a right to an individual as its ruler. The sovereign cannot bind itself; the will must remain free. Limits are set to the sovereign power, to the extent that it shall always act for the general good, and that it shall not discriminate between various classes of citizens,[1] but of these restrictions the sovereign is the final judge.

The sovereignty as conceived by Rousseau, stands out as absolute, infallible, indivisible, inalienable. It finds its source in an original contract and abides permanently in the body politic, the creature of the compact. Rousseau, thus, accomplished for the people what Hobbes had done for the ruler. The English writer's theory absorbed the entire personality of the State in the ruling body, the government, the bearer of the personality of all. Rousseau, by the same logic, absorbed the government in the people. The only true personality is that of the "corps collectif," as against which the government has not even a delegated power. In both cases the bearer in which the supreme power was vested was the product of contract between individuals.

Rousseau's theory became that of the Revolution,[2] and found frequent expression in the constitutions. In the "Declaration of the rights of man and of the citizen," 1789, it was asserted (Art. 3), that "the principle of all sovereignty resides essentially in the nation." In the constitution of 1791, that "the sovereignty is one, indivisible, inalienable and imprescriptible" (Tit. III. Art. 1); and, with still more alarming emphasis in the Constitution of 1793, that "every individual who usurps the sovereignty may be at once put to death by freemen" (Act 27, B. of R.); also in

---

[1] II, 4.

[2] See Janet, *Histoire*, tome ii., "Rousseau et la Révolution." "Il n' y a pas à proprement dire, d' école de J. J. Rousséa cette école, c'est la révolution entière."

Article 35, "When the government violates the rights of the people, insurrection is for the people,[1] and for every portion of the people, the most sacred of rights and the most indispensable of duties."[2]

In conclusion, on the period we have here sketched it may be remarked, in the first place, that the theories of sovereignty considered have a common characteristic, in that all alike admit the contractual basis. There is a general agreement in the postulation of an original contract as the foundation of the sovereign power. Whatever the divergence of opinion respecting the exact terms of this contract, or the effect of the agreement when made, there is a general admission of the formation of a contract at some time or other, in some form or other. The contract might be one between government and people, as with many of the Monarchomachs; or a social contract organizing the people, followed by a further agreement between people and government, as with Pufendorf; or, again, the single contract in which the sovereign and the State are created simultaneously, as with Hobbes and Rousseau. In any event, the tendency was to rest the supreme power upon a basis of popular consent. In the later period, especially after Grotius, the State and sovereignty were construed generally from the point of view of the individual, whose natural rights were combined with those of others to form the political right of the ruler. The first tendency was to derive the power of the sovereign from the people as a whole, the later from the units of which the people was composed. One may say, then, that a strongly

---

[1] Robespierre (1790) defines people thus, "La majorité des citoyens, les citoyens les moins puissants, les moins caressés par la fortune ou par l' ancien gouvernement, ces citoyens que l' on appelle peuple, que j 'appelle ainsi parceque il faut que je parle la langue de mes adversaires, parceque ce nom me paraît à la fois auguste et touchant." *Archives Parlementaires*, xii, 574.

[2] See Hélie, *Les Constitutions de la France*.

characteristic feature of the development of the theory of sovereignty during this period was the individualistic-contractualistic tendency. The emphasis on the individual came from the Reformation, the form of contract from the Roman law.

Further, a prevailing tendency of the theory, whether monarchically or democratically designed, was the movement toward the absolutist conception of sovereignty. Constitutional limitations, the laws of God, of nature and of nations must yield to the Leviathan, the mortal god of Hobbes, while with Rousseau the sovereign will of the people emerged, untrammeled by limitations, incapable of contractual restraint. In both theories, the individual, the unit, must surrender absolutely all, so far as the interest of the State requires, and of its needs the sovereign is the judge, from whose decision there is no appeal. The individualistic theory of sovereignty, based upon voluntary agreement, was one of the strongest ever constructed, since, to the fear of external force, it added the sanction of internal obligation. As Rousseau said of earlier theories, so his own changed force into right, or as otherwise expressed, "made of virtue a necessity."

Again, it is to be observed that an adequate conception of the unity and personality of the State was wanting throughout the period under consideration. As already seen, the movement in the earlier phases of the development was toward the organization of two public persons in the same State, the people on the one hand, and the Government on the other, with reciprocal rights and duties. Neither the people nor the Government constituted the whole State. Later, the State was absorbed either in people or in Government. With Hobbes, the Government swallowed up the State, and became the sole representative of its personality, so that the Government could truly say "L' État c'est moi." Or, with Rousseau, the people became the Government, and the Government was lost in the State. Hobbes saw a particular organ, the special bearer of power, but not the organism. Rousseau saw the organism as a whole, the general bearer, without organs capable of exercising sovereign power. And lastly the idea of personality, whether of the people or a part of the people, was at best of a wholly unreal and artificial character. Except where an individual was sovereign, the ruling body was a person only by the grace of fiction, persona representata, persona ficta—one in the place of many. Person was an abbreviation for a sum of individuals, and the bearer of the sovereignty not a real entity. The only real persons were individuals, all others were fictions.

The result of the individualistic development was then, the vesting of the absolute, indivisible and inalienable sovereignty in a body created by a suppositious contract and fictitiously endowed with personality.

CHAPTER II

THE KANTIAN THEORY

THE reaction against the theory of the Revolution proceeded along a number of lines,[1] which ran closely parallel to each other. To facilitate the understanding of the discussion over the doctrine of sovereignty, these different courses are here briefly indicated.

The first attack was made by the so-called historical school. The revolution emphasized the artificial, the conscious element of the life of states, and asserted the right and power of any given generation to make and unmake political institutions at will. The historical school, on the contrary, emphasized the element of unconscious growth in political forms. Language, morality, law, the State, are all the result not of any single act of men, but of a long and painful process in which many succeeding generations have participated. The State, in particular, is therefore not a contract between individuals, but is a product of tradition, of custom, of historical development. The first great champion of the movement was Edmund Burke in his *Reflexions on*

---

[1] For the period under consideration, the following general works are of service; J. K. Bluntschli's *Geschichte der neueren Staatswissenschaften*, best for the German literature, 3d ed.; Henry Michel, *L' Idée de l' Etat, Essai critique sur l' histoire des théories sociales et politiques en France depuis la Révolution*, 1895; R. von Mohl's *Geschichte und Literatur der Staatswissenschaften*, 3 vols, 1855–58; Adolph Dock, *Ueber Revolution und Restauration*, 1900; I. H. Fichte, *Die philophischen Lehren von Recht, Staat, und Sitte in Deutschland, Frankreich und England, von der Mitte des achtzehnten Jahrhunderts bis zur Gegenwart*, 1850; J. Stahl, *Philosophie des Rechts*, Pt. I.

the *Revolution in France* (1790),[1] the most effective work written against the Revolution. In Germany the movement was widespread, especially among the historical school of jurisprudence, founded by Hugo, whose first important work was a *Manual of Natural Right* (1798).[2] He was followed by the great apostle of the school, Savigny, *On the Vocation of Our Time for Legislation and Jurisprudence*[3] (1814), and later, the *System of the Modern Roman Law* (1839).

Kant formally accepted the contract theory, but by his distinction between the ideal and the real agreement damaged the revolutionary cause more than if he had directly opposed it. One might say, perhaps, that ideally he was revolutionary, but practically the reverse. Later, even the form of the contract was denied by his followers on the ground that entrance into the State was not a matter of choice for the individual, but a *necessary* step. Reason and morality demanded, it was said, that every man should enter into political and social relations. Not human will, but rational and moral necessity is the true basis of the State. So held Jakob Fries in the *Philosophical Theory of Law* (1803);[4] Ancillon, *On Sovereignty and (State) Constitutions* (1815);[5] K. S. Zachariä in his *Forty Books on the State* (1820-32).[6] Schleiermacher, *On the Idea of the Various Forms of State*

---

[1] Against the revolutionary theory see also Ferguson, *History of Civil Society*, 1764; *Principles of Moral and Political Science*, 1792; David Hume, *Essays Moral and Political*. With Burke compare Thomas Paine's *Rights of Man*; A. L. Schlözer, *Allgemeines Staatsrecht und Staatsverfassungslehre*, 1793.

[2] *Lehrbuch des Naturrechts.*

[3] *Vom Beruf unserer Zeit für Gesetzgebung und Jurisprudenz. System des heutigen Römischen Rechts.*

[4] *Philosophische Rechtslehre und Kritik aller positiven Gesetzgebung.*

[5] *Ueber Souveränetät und Staatsverfassungen.*

[6] *Vierzig Bücher vom Staate.*

(1814),[1] and the *Theory of the State;* Schmitthenner in the *Principles of Ideal or General Public Law* (1845).[2]

Another direction was taken by the group of thinkers who emphasized not the will of the individual, but the universal will, as the central point in the construction of a political system. The method was inaugurated by Schelling in the *System of Transcendental Idealism* (1800),[3] and the *Method of Academic Study* (1803). The whole "world-process" was regarded as a progressive reconciliation of necessity and freedom which finds its highest practical expression in the State. This is the realization not of the individual but of the absolute will, "the immediate and visible type of the absolute life" (das unmittelbare und sichtbare Bild des absoluten Lebens). His mystical theory was carried on by John J. Wagner in the *System of Ideal Philosophy* (1804) and *The State* (1815)[4]. The idea found its fullest expression, however, through Hegel, in the *Philosophy of Law* (1821).[5] In this Platonic, pantheistic philosophizing over the absolute and its objectification in concrete institutions, the individual man and the revolutionary theory dropped out of sight. If the State were a machine, men might hope to mend it a little, but as a "type of the Absolute" it was unapproachable. The State was now not a rational necessity (Vernunftnothwendigkeit), but a natural necessity (Naturnothwendigkeit), that is to say it was dictated not by the reason of the individual, as with Kant, but by the so-called "world-reason" as a part of the "world-process."

[1] *Ueber den Begriff der verschiedenen Staatsformen. Lehre vom Staate,* posth. published.

[2] *Grundlinien des allgemeinen oder idealen Staatsrechts.*

[3] *System des transcendentalen Idealismus; Methode des akademischen Studiums.*

[4] *System der Ideal-Philosophie: Der Staat.*

[5] *Grundlinien der Philosophie des Rechts.* Compare C. C. F. Krause, *Abriss der Philosophie des Rechts,* 1828. Fr. Köppen, *Politik nach Platonischen Grundsätzen mit Anwendung auf unsere Zeit,* 1818.

A parallel path was that taken by the religious school, which declared that purely human power was wholly inadequate to produce legitimate political institutions, and that the sanction must be sought in God. The State was held to be, not the result of a contract, but of a divine command. So held Nowald, De Maistre, Stahl. (See chapter III.)

In addition to historical tradition, the Kantian doctrine, transcendentalism, and the religious reaction came a revival of the patrimonial theory of the State. The source of authority is here property, not men. The social contract is repudiated and the foundation of political power is laid in the relations that center around the possessions of an individual or a corporation. The great champion of this anachronism was the Swiss, Ludwig von Haller.

These were the principal lines along which the assault upon the eighteenth century political theory was conducted. They all converged at one point, namely the proposition that the state was the result of a contract deliberately made by individuals. They all agree that the State is *something imposed upon* the human will, not a pure result of its own decree. The course of history, rational necessity, the world-process and the Absolute, the will of God, were so many different forms of statement for the same fundamental idea.[1]

Proceeding to the examination of the theories of sovereignty developed, we begin with that of Kant. Rousseau gave to the theory of the social contract a form adapted to the people; the deduction of the philosophic formula was accomplished by Immanuel Kant. Bluntschli says "Rousseau bore a flaming brand through street and mar-

---

[1] As already stated, these were parallel lines, but often two or more blended in the same person. The transition from one to another or the union of various theories was easily accomplished and did often occur. Or the reactionary theories might be blended with the revolutionary.

ket, Kant lighted the still lamp and candle in thousands of studies."[1] Kant gave not only to general philosophy, but also to the theory of the State, an impress which endures to the present day.

The new formulation of the contract theory is found in the work on *The Relation of Theory to Practice in Public Law* (1793); *On Eternal Peace*, 1795; and the *Theory of Right*, 1797.[2] The problem with which Kant starts is as with Rousseau, by whom he was profoundly influenced, that of the co-existence of conflicting individual wills, under some form of order.[3] This is possible only under a condition where there prevails right (Recht) or law, which is defined as "the sum of the conditions under which the will of the individual may be united with the will of all, according to a general law of freedom."[4] This is made possible in civil society, the establishment of which is the greatest problem of the race.[5] The formation of the State is effected through the medium of a contract in which the private wills are united under the general or public will.[6] Kant departs from his predecessor, Rousseau, however, by *expressly* denying

---

[1] *Geschichte der neueren Staatswissenschaften, 3te Auf., 373.*

[2] *Vom Verhältnisse der Theorie zur Praxis im Staatsrechte; Zum ewigen Frieden. Metaphysische Anfangsgründe der Rechtslehre*, as a part of the *Metaphysik der Sitten*. References here are to Rosenkranz and Schubert's edition of Kant's works, 1838.

[3] The sphere of the state is distinct from that of morality. Mere political society, Kant says, may exist among a number of moral devils, if only they are rational, V, 264. "Das Problem der Staatseinrichtung ist, so hart wie es auch klingt, selbst für ein Volk von Teufeln (wenn sie nur Verstand haben) auflosbar."

[4] "Das Recht ist also der Inbegriff der Bedingungen unter denen die Willkühr des Einen mit der Willkühr des Andern nach einem allgemeinen Gesetze der Freiheit zusammen vereinigt werden kann," VI, 33.

[5] Das grösste Problem für die Menschengattung, zur dessen Auflösung die Natur ihn zwingt, ist die Erreichung einer allgemeinen, das Recht verwaltenden, bürgerlichen Gesellschaft, V, 323.

[6] V, 207.

the real or historical existence of such an agreement. As a matter of theory, the contract is a necessary basis of the ideal, logically-derived state, but, as a matter of fact, empirically, it is in no wise indispensable, " is as such even impossible."[1] The actual historical origin of the State it is impossible to determine; it is even to be supposed, "from the nature of savage men that they would have begun with force."[2] For those already in civil society it is impossible, unnecessary, and even dangerous to enquire closely into the beginning of their State.[3] The contract is, after all, "a mere idea of the reason," not an historical fact. Its real value consists in its applicability as a criterion for the justification of law; every just law should be made as it would have been made, if in accordance with the spirit of the agreement.[4]

Out of this hypothetical contract issues the sovereign general will. This, has, however, no reality, except when vested in a physical person or persons.[5] The practical sovereignty may be located, according to Kant, in an Autocracy,[6] an Aristocracy, or a Democracy. A distinction is also made between the form of State (forma imperii) and the form of administration (forma regiminis). A form of administration or government is republican when the three classes of powers, legislative, executive, judicial, are separated; despotic when they are united.[7]

---

[1] V, 207.   [2] Rechtslehre, sec. 52.
[3] VI, 164.

[4] V, 207. " Denn das ist der Probestein der Rechtsmässigkeit eines jeden öffentlichen Gesetzes."

[5] VI, 189.

[6] To be distinguished from monarchy, " Monarch ist der welcher die *höchste*, aber Autokrator oder Selbstherrscher der welcher *alle* Gewalt hat; dieser *ist* der Souverän, jener *repräsentirt* ihn bloss. VI, 190.

[7] V, 243. Moreover every truly republican form of government must be representative. Pure Democracy cannot be representative, and is, therefore, always despotic. V, 244.

The nature of the sovereign power existing in the State is strongly suggestive of the Leviathian of Hobbes, or the "general will" of Rousseau. Kant's idea is clearly expressed: "The ruler in the State has against the subjects clear rights and no (enforceable) duties.[1] (Der Herrscher einer Staates hat gegen den Unterthanen lauter Rechte und keine (Zwangs-) Pflichten). If there were legal rights against the sovereign, reasons Kant, they must be capable of enforcement against him; but this could be accomplished only by some body able to *coerce* the sovereign. Such a body would, however, be the true sovereign, or further limited by some still stronger power. The series of limitations must end at some point, and here appears the unlimited and illimitable sovereign of the State.[2] By the use of this argument, the so-called limited constitution is made to appear as an absurdity, as a form belonging not to the domain of law (Recht), but to that of expediency.[3] No constitutional restriction or limitation can be imposed upon the sovereign, except by some stronger power, which as already seen would signify that the true point of sovereignty had not been at first detected.

Alarmed by the revolutionary excesses in France, Kant turned the full force of his powerful logic against any recognition of the right of resistance. In no case whatever is there a justification for the exercise of force against the existing government, not even the time-honored "jus in casu necessitatis."[4] He recognizes neither the tyrant "absque titulo," nor the tyrant "quoad exercitium." Whatever the title of the ruler, or whatever the character of the administra-

---

[1] VI, 165.   [2] VI, 165.

[3] VI, 166, "Also ist die sogennante gemässigte Staatsverfassung, als Constitution des innern Rechts des Staats, ein Unding und anstatt zum Recht zu gehören, nur ein Klugheitsprincip."

[4] V, 210, 11.

tion, obedience must be rendered. The end of the original contract, urges Kant, is the establishment of an association under the rule of law; but resistance and revolution are in their very nature destructive of the legal order. The welfare of the people is the supreme law, it is true, but the highest good consists in the preservation of a condition in which prevails formal law, at least.[1] The slightest attempt at revolution is, therefore, high treason, while the execution of a monarch is a crime, like unto the sin which can be forgiven neither in this world nor in that which is to come.[2] But, if imperfect men, deaf to the commands of pure reason, arise and overthrow the government, what shall be done? Whenever a revolution is an accomplished fact, says Kant, then the people are bound to render obedience to the newly-established rulers, however unjust the revolution may have been in its origin and execution.[3] The de facto Government is apparently always de jure. "Whatever is, is right," legally, though in the stormy days in which Kant wrote, it was not always easy to determine "what is." The right of resistance is, then, in the theory of Kant, absolutely excluded; the people have given up to the Government their right to judge of the general welfare, hence, they have legally no opinion; but if they could form an opinion, they would have no legal organ through which to give it expression; or if such an organ existed, that must be regarded as the real sovereign. The

---

[1] V, 209, "das öffentliche Heil......ist gerade diejenige gesetzliche Verfassung die Jedem seine Freiheit durch Gesetze sichert."

[2] VI, 168, "Scheint denjenigen ähnlich zu sein, was die Theologen diejenige Sünde nennen, welche weder in dieser noch in jener Welt vergeben werden kann."

[3] VI, 169, "Sie können sich nicht weigern derjenigen Obrigkeit ehrlich zu gehorchen *die jetzt die Gewalt hat.*" Perhaps as Suarez thought, "nam licet forte illi peccaverint, et qui primi sequiti sunt, tamen postquam res ad eum statum pervenit ut de facto a majore parte non servetur, tunc alii sine peccato poterunt." *De Legibus* iii, 19, sec. 12.

supreme power is formally, in a purely legal sense, incapable of limitation.

Nevertheless, Kant draws certain lines which the sovereign can not transgress.[1] He cannot do, it is argued, what the people itself could not do.[2] For example, he cannot interfere positively in the ecclesiastical organization, as this the people itself could not do, inasmuch as it is contrary to the purpose of the State;[3] cannot remove an officer without cause; cannot establish an hereditary nobility; for all these things the State itself could not, in theory, perform. It is conceded that in these cases the sovereign has no right to act, yet the subjects have no right to oppose; or better, they have the somewhat unsatisfactory "unenforceable right." One more refuge remains, namely, the only "palladium of the people's right," the " freedom of the pen " (Freiheit der Feder).[4] This the sovereign cannot deny, reasons Kant, without cutting himself off from the knowledge of the general will which he represents. If he does not hear the voice of his subjects, he may fail to understand what the general will really is; may even act contrary to it; in other words, put himself in contradiction with himself.[5] But this "Palladium," like all other rights, is not secure, and affords no authority to act against the ruler. It is an ideal political right, but may fall far short of practical realization.

Kant's theory of sovereignty was as absolute as that of his great predecessors, Hobbes and Rousseau. He started

---

[1] VI, 175 ff.

[2] "Was ein Volk über sich selbst nicht beschliessen kann, das kann der Gesetzgeber auch nicht über das Volk beschliessen," V, 217.

[3] VI, 175 ff; V, 217, ff.

[4] V, 216. Kant's own work, "*Die Religion innerhalb der Grenzen der Vernunft,*" was suppressed by the authorities in 1794.

[5] V, 216, "Alle Kenntniss von dem entziehen was wenn er es wüsste, er selbst beändern würde, und ihn mit sich selbst in Widerspruch setzen."

with the premises of the French Revolution, but ended with the conclusions of the Reaction. He began with the voluntary agreement of individuals, but in the end endorsed the Government of those who possessed the might. The general will, the creature of the contract, was lost in the will of the de facto ruler or rulers, occupying the place of authority. In the name of reason and logic, he secured the consent of the individual to a Government into whose origin reason must not henceforth enquire. In judging the theory of Kant, it must, be remembered, however, that he distinguishes, though not always clearly, between the *ideal* State and sovereignty and the *practical* State and sovereignty. In the idea, the State is a union formed by the voluntary agreement of individuals; here Rousseau had halted;[1] but Kant introduced, further, a practical and empirical State, the product of historical conditions, with the accompanying conflict of force and reason.

So there is an ideal sovereignty, which is the will resulting from the union of the wills of all, the rule of abstract law; and there is also the sovereignty of fact, which is a result of the combination of force and reason. There is a practical location for this sovereignty, namely, with those who have the power. But there is also an ideal location which must not be overlooked, and that is the organized community. "Every true republic is and can be nothing else than a representative system of the people."[2] The theoretical (rational) and the practical sovereign were undoubtedly confused in the writings of Kant, but he seems to have

---

[1] *Contrat Social*, I, 5, "C' est, si l' on veut, une aggrégation, mais non pas une association : il n' y a là ni bien publique, ni corps politique."

[2] Alle wahre Republik aber ist und kann nichts anders sein, als ein repräsenta, tives System des Volks, um im Namen desselben, durch alle Staatsbürger vereinigt-vermittelst ihrer Abgeordneten (Deputirten) ihre Rechte zu besorgen," VI, 192. ......so repräsentirt das vereinigte Volk nicht blos den Souverain, sondern *er ist dieser selbst.*" *Ibid.*, 193.

had in mind a gradual progress toward the realization of the ideal State and the ideal sovereignty.[1] In the meantime, especially in view of the conditions in France, the emphasis was laid upon the maintenance of the existing, time-honored, legal order. There is an ideal state of society which the race must some day reach, if its powers are to attain their highest perfection, but for that state we are not yet in readiness.

The formal absolutism of Kant's theory was in fact too strongly stated for the true spirit of his system, and his conclusions were followed by but a few thinkers such as Beck,[2] Reidinitz,[3] Schmalz,[4] Bauer.[5] A common tendency was to admit the Kantian argument in so far as it was held that there could be absolutely no right to resist the ruler, but here to raise the point that the ruler might cease to be a ruler by abuse of his power: there is then no longer a question of public law, but rather one of fact in which force must decide. Thus J. H. Tieftrunk, in an otherwise slavish commentary on

---

[1] See the last pages of the *Rechtslehre*. Also the *Idee zu einer allgemeinen Geschichte in weltbürgerlicher Absicht*, where he says, " Man kann die Geschichte der Menschengattung im grossen als die Vollziehung eines verborgenen Plans der Natur ansehen, um eine innerlich und zu diesem Zweck durch äusserlich vollkommene Staatsverfassung zu Stande zu bringen, als den einzigen Zustand in welchem sie alle ihre Anlagen in der Menschheit völlig entwickeln kann."

[2] J. S. Beck, *Commentar über Kant's Metaphysik der Sitten*, 1798.

[3] D. C. Reidinitz, *Naturrecht*, 1803.

[4] Theo. Schmalz, *Handbuch der Rechtsphilosophie*, 1807. Where one cannot obey he should, says Schmalz, " Keine Meuterei beginnen, aber allenfalls den Tod der Märtyrer zu sterben wissen," 278. " Ich weiss nicht, welch einen Grundsatz die Hölle selbst einhauchen könnte, welche für Recht und Glück der Menschen fürchterlichere Folgen haben könnte, als der dass eine Empörung gegen den Souverain je gerecht sein könne." S. 400.

[5] Bauer, A., *Lehrbuch des Naturrechts*, 2d ed., 1816, sec. 269 (1st 1807). Even Fr. v. Gentz admits the possibility of what he calls a "Total-Revolution." See "Ueber die Moralität in den Staatsrevolutionen," *Ausgewählte Schriften*, 1834, II, p. 33–60. Compare his review of Kant in the *Berliner Monatschrift* 1793, XXII, 518–55.

Kant, accepts the arguments of his master, but declares that "If a government in a State sinks so low that it perverts all right and destroys all the inalienable faculties of humanity, then the civil bond is broken by the ruler himself" and the obligation is at an end.[1] To the same effect, Heydenreichs,[2] Meister,[3] Maas.[4]

Another development of the theory of Rousseau into idealist form resulted in conclusions on the nature of the supreme power quite different from those reached by Kant. This tendency was best represented by J. G. Fichte, especially in his *Rudiments of Natural Right*,[5] 1796–97. Fichte forms the State by a series of agreements between sovereign individuals, the so-called "property contract," "the protection contract," the "union contract," and the "subjection contract."[6] Out of this complicated process comes at last the governing power, armed with full authority to protect the rights of the citizens. When this power appears, the people, as a unity, Fichte says, cease to exist; the people are no longer a people as a whole, but an aggregate of individuals subject to the government, which is not a part of the people.[7] Thus is established what is called the *positive* ruling power in the State;

---

[1] J. H. Tieftrunk, *Philosophische Untersuchungen über das privat und öffentliche Recht*, 1797–98. II, 366.

[2] K. H. Heydenreichs, *Grundsätze des naturlichen Staatsrechts*, 1795, Part II, 147.

[3] J. C. F. Meister, *Lehrbuch des Naturrechts*, 1808, sec. 613.

[4] J. G. E. Maas, *Ueber Recht und Verbindlichkèit*, 1794, p. 189.

[5] *Grundlage des Naturrechts*. There is an English translation by A. E. Kroeger, "*Science of Rights*." See also *Beiträge zur Berechtigung der Urtheile des Publicums über die französische Revolution*, 1793; *der geschlossene Handelstaat*, 1800; *rechtslehre*, 1812.

[6] *Grundlage*, II, p. 6 and ff.

[7] *Ibid.*, I, 215. "Das Volk ist gar kein Volk, kein Ganze, sondern eine blosse Aggregation Unterthanen, und die Magistratspersonen gehören dann auch nicht zum Volk."

but by its side there must be in all well-regulated political societies, also a *negative*, or checking power. Fichte proposes that for this purpose a body of ephors be chosen to supervise the conduct of the sovereign. On complaint of this board a constitutional assembly must be called to judge whether their charges against the government are well-founded; in the meantime they have the power to "suspend altogether the administration of the laws and the government in all its branches" (the Staatsinterdikt.)

But if this carefully devised check on the sovereign fails, then it appears that the people, as a whole, have always the right to rise. "The people," declares Fichte, "can never be a rebel, and the expression rebellion as applied to them is the greatest absurdity ever uttered, since the people are in fact and right the highest power, to which there is none superior, which is the source of all other power, and is responsible to God alone."[1] The supreme power rests in the last analysis with the *unorganized* people.[2]

---

[1] "Das Volk ist nie Rebell und der Ausdruck Rebellion von ihm gebraucht, ist die höchste Ungereimtheit die je gesagt wurde," etc., I, 222. In his later theory (see *Rechtslehre*, Werke, IV, 450, 1845) Fichte says that the governing power should be chosen from the teaching force of the state, as representative of the highest understanding of the time. "Soll darum einem Volke ein rechtmässiger Oberherr möglich sein, so muss es in diesem Volke Lehrer geben, und nur aus ihnen könnte der Oberherr gewählt oder errichtet werden."

[2] In this connection comes the work of P. J. A. Feuerbach, *Anti Hobbes oder über die Grenzen der höchsten Gewalt und das Zwangsrecht der Bürger gegen dem Oberherrn*, 1798. Feuerbach admits that the people have no right to judge of the conduct of the government while it is within the sphere of its proper power, but do have a right to judge whether it actually remains within the bounds set by the contract (154–55). He argues for an Ephorate, but denies that this body stands over and above the administration, "since it is not over the government itself, but only over the definite boundaries fixed by the subjection-contract, that it decides." (247.) Compare also L. H. Jakob, "*Anti-Machiavel oder über die Grenzen des bürgerlichen Gehorsams*. (1802, 2d ed.) On the whole field see Fr: Murhard, "*Ueber Widerstand und Empörung und Zwangsübung der Staatsbürger gegen die bestehende Staatsgewalt in sittlicher und rechtlicher Beziehung*," 1832.

CHAPTER III

THE REACTIONARY THEORY OF DIVINE RIGHT

THE theory of the Revolution, as has already been seen, was essentially individualistic in nature. The independent will of the isolated individual was the starting point in the interpretation of political institutions. The original contract, the nature of the state, the doctrine of sovereignty, all centred around the sovereign will. From this as a premise, the logic of the time led to the conclusion that the "people" are the only legitimate bearers of the absolute, inalienable and infallible sovereign power. The stormy scenes of the Revolution shattered, however, the prestige of the long dominant theory and there came the inevitable reaction against the principles upon which such alarming political events had rested. The Church especially, which had lost so heavily in privilege and power at the hands of the popular political party, was ready to lead a crusade against the prevalent doctrine of the day. The religious spirit which in the 16th century had invoked the spirit of rebellion, as seen in the writings of the *Monarchomachs*, was now called upon to reëstablish order and authority in the world of political theory. Hence came the ecclesiastical doctrine of the 18th and the first half of the 19th century. Politically, this movement found expression in the renewed place of authority gained by the Catholic Church in France and the states of South Germany;[1] likewise in the Holy Alli-

---

[1] See Treitschke, *Deutsche Geschichte*. Even Prussia's attitude was friendly. Compare Brockhaus, *Das Legitimitätsprincip*.

ance of 1815, between Russia, Prussia and Austria,[1] in which the three rulers regard themselves "as the agents of Providence to govern three branches of the same family, namely, Austria, Prussia and Russia," and confess "that the Christian nation of which they and their peoples are part, has no other sovereign than Him to whom alone belongs the power."[2] Throughout Europe the altar became the support of the throne, and the mediæval theory of the state rose to an approximation of its former power. In France the brilliant De Maistre, in his *Study on Sovereignty*, and *The Pope*,[3] with De Bonald in his *Theory of Political and Religious Power in Civil Society*,[4] were the leaders in the reaction.

In Germany the movement was carried on by Schelling,[5] Adam Müller,[6] Friederich Schlegel,[7] J. J. Wagner,[8] and by

---

[1] To this union the Pope was not invited.

[2] Art. ii: "Les trois Princes alliés ne s'envisageant eux-mêmes que comme délégués par la Providence pour gouverner trois branches d' une même famille; savoir l' Autriche, la Prusse, et la Russie; confessant ainsi que la nation chrétienne, dont eux et leurs peuples sont partie n' a réellement d' autre souverain que celui à qui seul appartient en propriété la puissance," etc.

[3] *Étude sur la Souraineté*, 1794–96; *Considérations sur la France*, 1797; *Essai sur la principe générateur des constitutions politiques et des autres institutions*, 1807; *Du Pape*, 1817.

[4] *Théorie du pouvoir politique et réligieuse dans la société civile*, 1796; *Essai analytique sur les lois naturelles de l' ordre sociale*, 1800; *Législation primitive*, 1802; *Pensées*, 1817. Compare Lammenais, *Essai sur l' indifférence en matière de réligion*, 1817; Chateaubriand, *Génie du Christianisme*, 1802; L' Abbé Thorel, *De l' origine des sociétés et l' absurdité de la souveraineté des peuples*, 1807.

[5] *System des transcendentalen Idealismus*, 1800; *Methode des akademischen Studiums*, 1802.

[6] *Von der Nothwendigkeit einer theologischen Grundlage der gesammten Staatswissenschaften*, 1819.

[7] *Vorlesungen über die Philosophie des Lebens*, 1828; *Philosophie der Geschichte*, 1829.

[8] *System der Ideal-Philosophie*, 1804; *Der Staat*, 1815.

the great Protestant theorist, Stahl,[1] in his *Philosophy of Law*.

By the Catholic wing of the school a connection was found between the principles of the Reformation and those of the Revolution. It was maintained that the root of all the political evil of the time was to be found in the triumph of the ecclesiastical revolution of the 16th century with the individualistic principles there involved. The same false idea, it was declared, lay at the basis of Protestantism and of popular sovereignty, namely the revolt of the individual against authority; in the one case applied to the Church, in the other, to the State. In the first instance, the result was a revolution in the ecclesiastical world; in the other the overthrow of political institutions. De Maistre asserted that "The great enemy of Europe—the father of anarchy—is Protestantism: it is born rebel, and insurrection is its natural state."[2] De Bonald denounced in unmeasured terms the "atheistic theory of the religious and political sovereignty of man," as "the principle of all the evils which afflict society."[3] The Catholic element aimed at the restoration of authority in the Church to the position held before the assaults of the Reformation and eighteenth century Liberalism; and, also, at the establishment of the same authoritative principle in the State. With the first object the Protestant leaders could not agree, but with the second, and that which concerns the discussion here, they were in hearty accord.

It was generally agreed that the purely human foundation

---

[1] *Philosophie des Rechts*, 1830–33. See also Baader, *Grundzüge der Societäts-Philosophie*, 1837; C. C. F. Krause, *Abriss der Philosophie des Rechts*, 1828; K. F. Göschel, *Zerstreute Blätter*, 1832–37.

[2] *Reflexions sur le Protestantisme dans ses rapports avec la souveraineté*.

[3] *Essai analytique sur les lois naturelles*, 32. Lammenais, *Essai* (5th ed., 1819–23) I, 345: "La même doctrine qui detrône Dieu, détrône les rois, détrône l' homme même."

for political power had, in the events of the recent Revolution, been shown to be utterly unstable and inadequate. It was, therefore, a pious duty to combat the exaggerated importance which had been attached to human will and reason as factors in the formation of political institutions. The theory of the social contract was accordingly repudiated and denounced, and the artificial, purely voluntary formation of government was represented as utterly contrary to the true nature and character of men. "The Tower of Babel," says De Maistre, "is the naive image of a mass of men who assemble to create a constitution;"[1] and even more emphatically, "not only does the creation not belong to men, but it appears that our power, unassisted, does not extend to changing for the better established institutions."[2] Stahl maintained that the State was never the pure product of design, or of conscious effort on the part of men,[3] and he emphasized the numerous historical factors found in its formation. The theory of the establishment of the State by any contract, simple or complex, was abandoned by the leaders of the new crusade.

The most apparent form of the despised doctrine, that of the sovereignty of the people as a result of a contract, was assailed with the greatest vigor. De Bonald identified popular sovereignty with atheism and materialism.[4] If the people is, as declared, legitimately sovereign, then, said he, all laws

---

[1] *Étude sur la Souveraineté*, 238. See 227, "Le plus grand fléau de l' univers a toujours été dans tous les siécles, ce qu' on appelle philosophie."

[2] *Essai sur le principe générateur des institutions politiques*, 53.

[3] *Philosophie des Rechts* (3d ed., 1870, II, 171) : "Niemals ist der Staat das Werk der Wahl und Absicht; nie ensteht er durch Ubereinkunft der Menschen dass sie vorher ausser dem Staate nunmehr zusammenkommen um ihn zu errichten; niemals geht seine Grundform von ihrem Nachdenken aus."

[4] "Peuple a sa racine dans le mot populare, ravager, dévaster, et de là vient que, dans le grec, multitude est synonyme de mauvais, de méchant."—*Essai analytique*, 9. See also 55.

made by them must be just; but justice rests upon a broader and deeper basis than this.[1] Everywhere in the school is seen the bitterest antagonism to the idea that the people by their own voluntary act can constitute themselves as a sovereign political power. "Democracy," says De Maistre with his usual vigor, "is an association of men without sovereignty." The "general will" is disposed of with the argument that "the law is so little the will of all, that the more it is the will of all the less it is law, so that it would cease to be law if it were without exception, the work of all who owe it obedience."[2]

It was agreed that a purely human authority could afford no secure basis for political power. The source of political authority must be sought somewhere outside of human society. As Bonald aptly said, the fulcrum could not be found in men themselves; it must be located at a point outside.[3] The merely human will, the human reason, were regarded as in themselves insufficient to afford a legitimation of political power. No human being has control over the life of another; therefore no one can give such power to another. The authority necessary to the State, therefore, cannot be derived from any man or combination of men. Sovereignty, it was held, cannot be explained upon the ground of reason, but must rise to that of faith. "Government," says De Maistre, "is really a religion; it has its dogmas, its mysteries, its ministers."[4] "Everything shows us the cradle of sovereignty surrounded by miracles, and the divinity intervening in the foundation of empires."[5] Religion, says De

---

[1] *Législation primitive*, Oeuvres, III, 21.

[2] *Étude*, 346–348: "La loi est si peu la volonté de tous, que plus elle est la volonté de tous, et moins elle est la loi; en sorte que elle cesserait d' être loi, si elle était, sans exception, l' ouvrage de tous ceux qui devraient lui obéir."

[3] *Essai analytique*, 57: "L' athéisme place le pouvoir suprême sur les hommes dans les hommes mêmes."

[4] *Étude*, 247.   [5] *Ibid.*, 199.

Bonald, gives what cannot otherwise be found, " a reason for the power to command, and a motive for the duty to obey."[1] Stahl found in the divine origin of sovereignty a basis which he regarded as in no other way attainable.[2]

The source and sanction of all political power were placed, then, by these theorists, in God, the Creator, the only power from whom authority could be legitimately derived. Here was a point outside of, and above, all human will or reason; here the real fountain of the sovereign power. Here was an explanation and justification for the control of one man over another. With this argument the whole contract theory may be overthrown, since the establishment of Government is no longer considered as a matter of voluntary agreement among men, but a condition of existence imposed by the Divine Ruler. Sovereignty is something given by God, not made by man. To Rousseau's question as to how the will of one shall be reconciled with the general will, the religious school responded that the relation in question was the will of God. Political faith was substituted for political reason.

It was not declared, however, that the human will had no part whatever to play in the establishment of the sovereignty. The supreme power comes, it is true, *from* God, but *through* the agency of men, his instruments. " To say that the sovereignty does not come from God, because men are required to establish it, is to say he is not the creator of man, because we all have a father and a mother."[3] The power comes originally from God, who has implanted in man the impulse without which the state would be impossible.[4]

---

[1] " Une raison au pouvoir de commander, et un motif au devoir d' obéir." —*Essai analytique*, 23.

[2] *Philosophie des Rechts*, II, 176: " Von sich selbst kann kein Mensch obrigkeitliche Gewalt über andere Menschen haben, auch nicht die Sämmtlichen über die Einzelnen."

[3] De Maistre, *Étude*, 179.

[4] De Bonald, *Essai analytique*, 110; Stahl, *Philosophe des Rechts.*, II, 176.

The nature of the divine authorization is stated by Stahl, who declares, "Not merely the state in general, but everywhere the particular constitution, and the particular persons in power are sanctioned by God."[1] But even here the influence of men is not wholly excluded. The persons in power may, it is argued, hold by *divine ordinance*, though not by *divine appointment*, in the narrower sense of the term. Thus, though marriage is an institution of divine ordination, said Stahl, it is not commanded that "a maiden shall marry Jacob or William, but when she actually marries Jacob, then the matrimonial tie to him is the ordinance of God."[2] So in the state God does not directly appoint the persons who are to hold the sovereign power, but when once in place these individuals are to be regarded as possessing his sanction, whether the officers are selected by the conscious act of the community or in some other way.[3] While it was denied that the people are themselves the immediate cause of sovereignty, it was admitted that they are at least the ultimate basis of the supreme power, the material out of which it is formed. The argument was not intended to show that the particular persons in possession of power are immediately and directly appointed by God, but rather that there could be no legitimate political power, as such, established without the sanction of God. From this vantage point the contractual argument of the popular sovereignty school could be resisted and the force of the revolutionary movement could be broken by

---

[1] *Phil. d. Rechts.*, II, 177: "Aber jene göttliche Institution bedeutet wieder nicht bloss dass der Staat überhaupt Gottes Gebot ist, sondern auch dass überall die bestimmte Verfassung und die bestimmten Personen der Obrigkeit Gottes Sanktion haben."

[2] *Ibid.*, II, 178, 179.

[3] "Nur die Basis des Staates als solche bedingt, beschränkt, influirt die anstaltliche (verfassungsmässige) Autorität, nicht aber ist er selbst das Subjekt der handelnden herrschenden Macht."—*Ibid.*, II, 143.

the general denial of the possibility of any humanly constructed sovereignty.

The divine right theory was applied in the support of the institutions that existed before the Revolution and whose past had been of such a character as to indicate their divine ordination.[1] France, Prussia, Austria, Russia, were ruled by monarchs whose power was given and held by the grace of God, not of man. The nature of the theory did not require, however, that it be applied to the defence of monarchical institutions, but logically permitted its use in defence of the people against whom it was now invoked. As Milton had said long before, the divine right of the people is as legitimate a conclusion from the given premises as the divine right of kings. So, in the present crisis, it was maintained by Baader that the Government and the people exist alike by the grace of God, and that so far as subject to his law they are equally justified.[2] The Government as well as the people may be guilty of revolution.

The nature of the sovereignty derived from God was not subjected to very careful analysis, but so far as considered was usually regarded from the absolutist point of view. Stahl looks upon sovereignty as "the first causal supreme power, which, conditioning and including all organs, either positively determines, or at least negatively limits them,"[3] and holds that the power of the State is *formally* absolute,

---

[1] From De Maistre's "on peut dire en général que tous les hommes naissent pour la monarchie," to the scientific defence of monarchy by Stahl.

[2] *Grundzüge der Societäts-Philosophie*, pp. 15, 21 : " Sind Regenten und Völker gleich berechtigt, so lange sie diese organische Einheit unter sich erhalten, als von Gottes Gnaden constituirt sich zu nennen. Offenbar kann der Regent so gut ein Revolutionär sein als das Volk." Compare also the works of Lammenais, *Le livre du peuple*, 1838, in which he defends the inalienable sovereignty of the people. 35. See the volume by Leroy-Beaulieu, *Les Catholiques libéraux*, 1885.

[3] *Phil. d. Rechts*, II, 190 : " Die Souveränetät ist sonach die erste ursächliche und oberste Gewalt, die alle Organe und Verrichtungen bedingt und umschliesst, sie alle entweder positiv bestimmt oder doch wenigstens negativ begränzt."

although materially subjected to restraint.[1] By De Maistre, the absolute character of the sovereignty is sharply accentuated. Every kind of sovereignty is absolute in its nature, he asserts—there is always in the last analysis an absolute power which may with impunity do wrong, which is, therefore, from this point of view, despotic in the strongest sense of the term.[2] France, he says, has covered herself with ridicule and scorn, only to place on the throne in the end, a little b, in the place of a big B.[3] He compares the sovereignty of the ruler in the political world to the infallibility of the Pope in the spiritual. Both stand for that necessary power, "from which all others are derived, which governs and is not governed, which judges and is not judged."[4] Somewhere in the search for authority we must reach a final term in the series, and that point is in the ecclesiastical world the Pope, in the political, the sovereign. Despite these emphatic declarations of De Maistre his sovereignty is, however, really capable of limitation. It appears that the power is absolute only "in its legitimate exercise," and that "legitimacy consists not in this or that class of conduct within the circle, but in not going outside the limits."[5] The supreme power may be restrained within its proper limits, without detracting at all from its full legitimacy.[6]

---

[1] As by the action of the estates. *Philos. des Rechts*, II, 192. It should be said that Stahl is far more systematic and scientific in his methods than the others of this school, who were in general inclined to vigorous polemic rather than to calm reasoning.

[2] *Étude*, 293.   [3] *Du Pape*, 213.

[4] *Du Pape*, 2: "L' infaillibilité dans l' ordre spirituel et souveraineté dans l' ordre temporel, sont deux mots parfaitement synonymes. L' un et l' autre expériment cette haute puissance qui les domine toutes, dont toutes les autres dérivent, qui gouverne et n' est pas gouvernée, qui juge et n' est pas jugée."

[5] "La légitimité ne consiste donc pas à se conduire de telle ou telle manière dans son cercle, mais à n' en pas sortir."—*Du Pape*, 221.

[6] *Du Pape*, 222. Compare *Étude*, 322.

But what power can be safely trusted with the duty of holding in bounds the political sovereign? Clearly no other political power is competent to perform such a task as this. The limitation must therefore be sought outside the state— in the church. The most natural and least dangerous form of restraint would be "some sort of intervention on the part of spiritual power;"[1] that is to say, in a revival of the mediæval relations between Church and State.

The significance of the theory of this school in so far as the *nature* of sovereignty is concerned is but slight. The supreme power was generally regarded as absolute, but the limitations imposed by the law of God were solemnly emphasized. De Maistre even demanded the restoration of the Papal oversight of the secular power.[2] In any event the sovereign was not to be the final interpreter of divine and moral law for all his subjects.[3] God who gave the power must be also able to limit it.

With regard to the *source* of sovereignty, the theory of the school was of more importance. Its argument was directed against the prevalent individualistic theory of the origin of the State. The overwhelming tendency of the theory was to emphasize the unconscious growth of institutions in contrast to their deliberate and voluntary construction. De Maistre was an admirer of Burke, and went so far as to compare the body politic to a plant.[4]

---

[1] *Du Pape*, 343–44.

[2] The later catholic movement is not here discussed. See literature cited in Ferd. Walter's *Naturrecht und Politik im Lichte der Gegenwart*, 1863. The study of Thomas Aquinas was recommended by the Pope (1879), in the Encyclica Aeterni Patris.

[3] There was a tendency to admit a right of resistance in extreme cases. De Bonald, *Penseés diverses*, Oev. 1817, VI, 137; Stahl, *Phil. d. Rechts*, II, 541; De Maistre, *Étude*, 298.

[4] *Étude*, 363.

The theory of Schelling was close to pantheism.[1] Stahl was a disciple of Schelling and Savigny, imbued with the spirit of the historical school. The religious reaction was really only one phase of the general movement away from the excessive individualism of the Revolution, and its full significance appears only in the light of this general tendency. Kant attacked popular sovereignty by accepting (ideally) its premises, but in practice rejected its conclusions. The religious school met the revolutionary movement by absolutely denying the possibility of the creation of a sovereign power by human beings. It appealed from a human contract to the divine command. On its critical side, the school denied the sovereignty of the people. Constructively, it favored the sovereignty of the monarch, though this was a temporary, rather than a necessary, tendency of the theory. There is nothing in the theory that political power comes ultimately from God, to render legitimate the claims of either king or people. It is as easy for the democrat to say that the voice of the people is the voice of God, as for the royalist to assert that the king rules by the grace of God. Historically, the teaching that all political power is of divine origin has been employed to arouse as well as to suppress rebellion. It is a sword that may cut either way. In the years following the Revolution, however, it was undoubtedly used, and effectively used, in support of the reaction against the democratic movement.[2]

[1] Compare Baader, *Evolutionismus und Revolutionismus*, 1834.
[2] This would not apply of course to America, where the democracy and the church were found in close alliance. Here it did not occur to the clergy that declarations such as those prefixed to the state constitutions were at all in conflict with the progress of the church.

CHAPTER IV

THE PATRIMONIAL THEORY

It has already appeared that the theory of Kant, though holding to the necessity of a contract ideally, had in practice virtually repudiated it, and made force the basis of the State and of sovereignty. From another point of view a theory of sovereignty ostensibly based upon might was reached by the school of which Ludwig von Haller was the great representative. Born a Swiss patrician, Haller three times felt the force of the revolutionary spirit, once in Switzerland in 1798, again in 1821, and once more while under Charles X in 1830. He abandoned the Protestant Church in 1821 and attached himself to the Catholic, and was thoroughly imbued with the spirit of the anti-revolutionary crusade.[1] From 1816 to 1834 appeared the six volumes of his work, *The Restoration of Political Science, or the Theory of the Natural-Social condition opposed to the Chimæra of the Artificial-Civil*,[2] presenting one of the most elaborate political systems constructed in the nineteenth century. Quick to see the vulnerable points in the revolutionary theory, Haller directs his keen and searching criticisms against them with remarkably destructive effect.[3] He first denies that men ever existed in the alleged "state of nature," urging against such a supposition

[1] See Bluntschli's *Wörterbuch*, B. IV. Mohl, *Geschichte und Literatur der Staatswissenschaften*, B. II, an excellent sketch. Dock, *loc cit.*

[2] *Restauration der Staatswissenschaft oder Theorie des natürlich-geselligen Zustandes der Chimäera des künstlichen-bürgerlichen entgegensetzt.*" Band VI, 1825, Band V, 1834. See also *Handbuch der allgemeinen Staatenkunde*, 1808.

[3] See the first eleven chapters of Book I.

the natural social impulse implanted in man by God. But, granting such a condition as claimed, he denies that the rights of individuals would have been any less secure than in the so-called artificial state. He enquires into the nature of the contract: what motives would induce men to enter it, who are the parties thereto, and who excluded? If a contract is actually made, to whom is the Government to be entrusted, to the weak, the strong, the wise? If there is representative Government, then what guarantee exists that the deputies will remain faithful? Against the Government of the State there will be after all no guaranty possible, and even in the artificially-constructed contract State, the liberties of the subjects must depend in the last resort on the good will of the ruler.

Against the theory of the "artificial" origin of society, Haller places the "natural" order of things. The true state of nature, he says, has never ended.[1] In all times and places men are found in social relations; into these they are born, and out of them they never depart. The social nature of men is a fundamental fact from which we must proceed, which we need not artificially construct. Within the circles of social relations, authority is built up in a perfectly natural way. It is universally true, Haller maintains, that there are found among men those who are weak and those who are strong; and, moreover, a tendency on the part of those who do not have power to attach themselves to those who have—the desire of the powerless for the protection of the powerful.[2] Out of these facts is deduced the law which underlies the new *Restoration of Political Science*, that "natural superiority is the basis of all authority, need is

---

[1] I, 327: "Ja! Der Stand der Natur hat niemals aufgehört, er ist die ewige unveränderliche Ordnung Gottes selbst." *Cf.* Ferguson, *History of Civil Society.*

[2] Fr. Ancillon, *Ueber den Geist der Staatsverfassungen*, etc., 1825, s. 13: "Die Ungleichheit ist die Quelle aller Gewalt."

the basis of dependence or servitude;¹ the stronger rules, must rule, and always will rule."² The control of a father over his children, of a teacher over his pupils, a general over his soldiers, a ruler over his subjects — all these arise from the natural superiority of one over another. Equals will not obey equals; the root of authority must be sought in a state of inequality. "The relation between the weak and the strong we may call a contract," says Haller, "but could as well say, 'there is a contract between man and the sun that he will allow himself to be warmed by it, or between him and the frost that he will clothe himself better.³'" It is a universal law of nature, even among the birds of the air and the beasts of the field, that the stronger shall rule.⁴ The extent of this power is not always the same, but depends on the degree of the necessity on the one hand, and that of the superiority on the other. As these elements vary, so the authority varies; as they endure, so the authority endures.⁵

On this basis the State becomes, in the theory of Haller, an association not at all different *in kind* from any other form, as for example, a family, a church or a school. All have essentially the same unifying bond — the necessity of the weaker and the opportunity of the stronger. The difference is one of *degree* only. Wherever in the long series of human associations we find an individual or a corporation

---

[1] "Natürliche Ueberlegenheit ist der Grund aller Herrschaft; Bedürfnisse der Grund aller Abhängigkeit und Dienstbarkeit."—Haller, *Restauration*, I, 342.

[2] "Der Mächtigere herrsche, herrschen müsse, und immer herrschen werde." —*Ibid.*, 361.

[3] I, 346.

[4] Haller is even careful to point out that man does not rule *all* the lower creation; certain insects, for instance, "behaupten ihre ihnen von Gott gegebene Freiheit."—I, 350.

[5] I, 350: "Die Natur und das Masz dieser Herrschaft sind sogar der Art und dem Grade jener Ueberlegenheit oder dieses Bedürfnisses auf das genaueste angemessen."

"serving no one but God," there appears the state, which Haller defines as "no other than an independent, social union, existing for and through itself."[1] He expressly denies that it possesses any peculiar political (*staatlich*[2]) character, and also that it has any particular purpose as a state. There are two classes of states, it appears, the Monarchy (Fürstenthum) and the Republic. Any individual who is better endowed than others, is more powerful, and is wholly independent as a ruler (Fürst), is the head of a monarchy.[3] A republic is a society (Gesellschaft or Corporation) similarly gifted and likewise independent.[4] In either case, it is not the command over others, but the fact that one is himself free from the command of another, which is the distinguishing mark of the state. The *aliis imperare*, says Haller, is only the *genus proximum*, the *nemini parere* is the *character specificus*.[5] Independence is, then, the characteristic mark of the state, and this independence is, in Haller's theory, the equivalent of sovereignty.[6]

The method in which the sovereignty may be acquired is

---

[1] "Sie ist nichts anders als ein selbständiges, d. h. für sich selbst und durch sich selbst bestehendes geselliges, Verband, vollendete und geschlossene Menschen-Verknüpfungen, unabhängige Dienst- oder Societäts-Verhältnisse."—I, 449.

[2] I, cap. 16, 17. "*Staatlich*" is one of the many German words difficult to render into English, except by a phrase. It means having the character of a state, or the quality of a state.

[3] "Ein Fürst ist nehmlich nichts anders als ein begüterter, mächtiger und eben dadurch unabhängiger Mensch (homo locuples, potens, nemini obnoxius)."—I, 459. There are three classes of monarchies, the patrimonial, the military, and the theocratic. See II, cap. 26.

[4] "So sind die Republiken wieder nichts anders als mächtige, begüterte, unabhängige Communitäten (civitates liberæ, sodalitia, nemini obnoxia)."—I, 460.

[5] I, 461.

[6] "Die Ausdrücke Unabhängigkeit, vollkommene Freiheit, politische Freiheit fürstliche oder höchste Gewalt, Souveränetät, Majestät, Machtvollkommenheit, u. s. w., sind im Grund alle gleich bedeutend, und drücken höchstens verschiedene Seiten der nemlichen Sache aus, je nachdem sie aus diesem oder jenem Gesichtspunkt betrachtet wird."—I, 467.

worked out by Haller with considerable care. Sovereignty is by no means an inborn right, he says, but one which must be acquired by the individual or the corporation. Theoretically, at least, the way is open to all.[1] There are three courses indicated by which sovereignty may be attained. First, by personal ability and effort, as when an individual slowly expands his power over lands and people, until at last he reaches the status in which he owes obedience to none. Or the acquisition of the supreme power may be the result of agreement with or gift from the former possessor; for sovereignty is looked upon as alienable; as a subject has a right to alienate his own goods, the sovereign has certainly a right to dispose of what is his own.[2] It is impossible, however, to receive sovereignty at the hands of the people as a pure gift from them. They may help him and support him in his efforts to attain independence, but cannot confer it of themselves; they may enter his service, may choose him for leader even, but cannot be regarded as giving him the sovereignty.[3] This would be, he thinks, too serious a concession to the popular theory. In the third place independence may be a gift of fortune, as when a great empire falls and its parts become independent, and therefore sovereign. Or, finally, by a combination of all three methods, by individual effort, the help of others, and the above-mentioned fortune.[4]

[1] But "*non cuivis datum est adire Corinthum.* So ist Jeder befugt und Niemanden verboten reich zu werden wenn er kann. Aber nicht Jeder hat Mittel und Gelegenheit dazu."—I, 469.

[2] See the defence of property right in II, cap. 25.

[3] "Das ist aber desswegen keine Königswahl, kein willkührlich gegebenes Amt, sondern blosse Hülfsleistung. Man ist desswegen doch Herr und nicht Diener.— I, 475. So Jarcke, a disciple of Haller, says a sovereign may be elective, but the "Wahl eines souveränen Fürsten war in der Wirlichkeit nichts anderes, als *Anerkennung eines Rechts oder einer schon vorhandenen, überlegenen Gewalt.*"—IV, 34.

[4] I, cap. xix.

Sovereignty is, then, in the theory of Haller, the result of superior force, however acquired. But it is by no means absolute or unlimited in nature. Haller distinguishes between power (potentia) and the abuse of power [1] (vis) and claims as one of the advantages of his system as against what he delighted to call the "pseudo-philosophic," that it did not leave the supreme power without a limit. Every individual, he declares, has something of his own, as life, honor, capacity, which is held as truly by the grace of God as is the power of the greatest sovereign.[2] There are also a number of methods by which absolutist tendencies may be held in check. First of all, a careful observance of the law of mutual obligation between the members of the society contributes to this result. In the second place, Haller allows the unqualified right of resistance.[3] By the exercise of force in case of an abuse of power, one only recovers what is his own, and of this primary right no sophistry can deprive him.[4] Self-defence, declares Haller, is not only a right, but even a duty.[5] Again, the weak, when oppressed, have the right to call in to their aid stronger individuals from some neighboring State, and thus protect themselves against the rapacious ruler. And as a last resort, there remains the not always available remedy of flight or separation from the State. But Haller admits that there is after all no human law capable of restraining the sovereign. He is bound only by the divine law under which the power is held.[6]

---

[1] We must distinguish "die natürliche Macht oder Ueberlegenheit (potentia), von der schädlichen Gewalt (vis), die Herrschaft welche die Natur giebt von ihrem Missbrauch welcher der Menschen Schuld ist."—I, 375.

[2] I, cap. 15; see also II, cap. 39.   [3] I, cap. 15.   [4] I, 402.

[5] I, 410: "Sie ist sogar gewissermassen Pflicht, und wurde zu allen Zeiten mit Recht als eine Tugend anerkannt."

[6] II, cap. 27. In general the same principles which apply to the monarch apply to the majority in a Republic. See VI, cap. 8; cap. 16; cap. 19. The majority rules because it is the stronger.—VI, cap. 8.

Sovereignty is regarded, thoughout, as a right to rule, which is on a par as to its origin, nature, extent, with any other class of property. It is in every sense of the word a private right, exercised by a private person or corporation for a purely private purpose. A war is the sovereign's own private war,[1] the treaties concern his own property, the officers are his personal servants, law-giving is an expression of his private will.[2] "The time will come," said Haller, "when we will write no special public law, but will treat it only under natural right in general, along with the theory of the service-and-social relations."[3]

On the surface Haller's sovereignty is based upon force—in contrast to the "natural right" upon which popular sovereignty rested. In last analysis, however, the basis proved to be not force, but an assumed "natural right" to property. Thus Haller asserts that a son inherits the sovereignty of his father. But this child is not possessed of superior force, for he may enjoy no marked ability, mental or physical, but because the right to rule is property to which the son as heir has a clear right. A right, however, under what law? Haller could not say by the law of the state, for that is the expression of the ruler's own will, and this very right to rule is in question. But with his usual unflinching logic Haller meets the issue squarely enough; one after another he rules out, as inadequate to explain the succession, the presumed capacity of a race long accustomed to rule, the permanence of governmental policy, the preservation of public peace.[4] These all

---

[1] II, cap. 28. [2] II, cap. 32.

[3] "Die Zeit wird kommen wo man kein besonderes Staatsrecht mehr schreiben, sondern dasselbe nur in dem natürlichen Recht überhaupt, bei der Lehre von den Dienst- und Societäts-Verhältnissen abhandeln und höchstens auf deren Modification durch höhere Macht und Freiheit beiläufige Rücksicht nehmen wird."— II, 59.

[4] II, 457.

arise out of attempts to compromise with the pseudo-philosophic system, and are all alike incorrect. Whence comes the right to rule then? "According to the mere law of nature or of God, which commands to give to each one his own'"[1] Property, the right to rule, the state, are based upon a natural law suspiciously like that against which the earlier polemic of the work was arrayed.

Political sovereignty rests not on popular consent, not on expediency, not on force, but on a natural, God-given, universally prevailing right to property. Property, Haller asserts, existed before human law, and may yet exist without it. "Property does not arise from the State, but on the contrary, States or Governments from property."[2] The State, it seems, is first founded on a property right, really existing before the State; and then, in the case of succession of sovereignty, all the ordinary property rights *under* the State are predicated of what is properly an original and pre-civil right.

The influence exercised by Haller was important, especially among those conservatively inclined.[3] Probably his ablest expounder was C. E. Jarcke, in his miscellaneous writings, 1834–37, and his *Prinzipien-Fragen*, 1852. He endorses Haller's fundamental theory, and declares the sovereign power the strongest in the State, but points out that it is not the only power.[4] Another able advocate of

---

[1] II, 463: " Nach dem blossen *Naturrecht* oder dem göttlichen Gesetz, welches jedem das Seine zu lassen gebietet ist jeder Mensch vollkommer Herr über sein eigenthumliches Vermögen." Haller expressly declares that another prince later born, who is not even the next heir, may possess in a higher degree the capacity to rule (II, 458),—a complete surrender of his earlier position.

[2] II, 54. *Cf.* Jarcke, iii, 73.

[3] A. Müller desired that Haller's *Restoration* should be taught in all the schools in Germany.

[4] C. E. Jarcke, *Vermischte Schriften*, publ. 1839, vol. III of Works; *Prinzipien-Fragen*, publ. 1854, vol. IV. See III, 45, 57; also IV, 31, 155.

the patrimonial theory was found in Romeo Maurenbrecher, in his work on *The Ruling German Monarchs and the Sovereignty*, 1839; and his *Principles of German Public Law*, 1837.[1]

The theory of Haller went hand-in-hand with that of the religious reactionaries. The sovereignty was based upon the right to property, which was either a natural or a divine right. In either case, the people were no longer the source of the sovereign power,[2] and the *status quo* was preserved.[3]

---

[1] *Die deutschen regierenden Fürsten und die Souveränetät*, 1839; for defense of the right to rule as a property right, see 176, 313. *Grundsätze des deutschen Staatsrechts*, 1837. See also Ludwig Thilo: *Grundriss eines Systems des Naturrechts*, 1839; *Die Volkssouveränetät in ihrer wahren Gestalt*, 1833.

[2] It is to be observed that in the preface to Book IV, Haller suggests a new classification of States into spiritual and worldly. In Book V (1834), he formally states that the Restoration of Political Science is to be found in the Catholic Church. "Monarchical only in its cause, origin and outer form, but on the other hand republican in its spirit, ultimate purpose and in the determination and exercise of its power, it mediates between and reconciles both the monarchial and the republican principle." * * * And so will accomplish the complete restoration of political science." See esp. V, 376.

[3] An interesting study of the nature of sovereignty from a psychological point of view was made by Gottfried Duden: *Ueber die wesentlichen Verschiedenheiten der Staaten und die Strebungen der menschlichen Natur*, Cöln, 1822. His theory attracted little attention and is now almost forgotten. He lays down as fundamental propositions: 1st, that no power can work at all against its basis as a whole; 2d, that any power directed against a part of its basis can work only self-destructively; 3d, that these are the only limitations of which the supreme power admits (I, 12, 13). He then inquires into the nature of this basis upon which the supreme power rests. He finds it made up of various elements, such as the struggle to exist, the fear of a higher being, the desire for freedom, the feeling of weakness, desire for the esteem of fellowmen, even the wish to rule. The combination of these various elements forms the *foundation* on which the supreme power rests. It is not, however, sufficient to consider these elements "alone, for they must be regarded in relation to the ruler who is to utilize them. (Jede Herrscher-Gewalt componirt sich aus dem Willen des Herrschers und den dafür in Anwendung gebrachten Mitteln."—III, 65.) The relation between the government and these elements is like that between soul and body, or a tool and the power using it (III, 60). The nature of the supreme power depends

upon the nature of these motives, in their relation to the capacity of the ruler to apply them. The ruler cannot act counter to *all* the motives of obedience, and in so far as he opposes *any* contracts the basis of his own power. Duden even attempts to show the relation between the historical development of forms of state and the predominance of one or another of the forces considered; as the case of theocracy and the fear of a higher being (III, 20). Duden wrote also *Die Nord-Amerikanische Demokratie*, 1837, in reply to De Tocqueville.

CHAPTER V

THE SOVEREIGNTY OF REASON

An interesting development of the theory of sovereignty grew out of the conditions in France after the restoration of the Bourbons.[1] The political practice and the political theory of this period were alike the result of a compromise between the old order and the new. Much as the ultra-royalists might desire to bring about a complete restoration of the pre-revolutionary political status, such a consummation had been made impossible by the indelible events of the last quarter of a century. On the other hand, unwilling as the Revolutionists were to sacrifice their democratic principles, the memory of the Terror was still too fresh to permit the full recognition of their liberal ideas. France was not ready to recognize either an absolute king or a constituent convention as supreme. A compromise of some sort was an imperative necessity. The form which it took was the Charter of 1814, which provided for a monarchy with a responsible ministry and a bicameral legislature, one house being appointed by the King, the other based upon a very narrow electorate; in short, a constitutional monarchy was

[1] See H. Martin, *Histoire de la France depuis 1789; Les constitutions et les principales lois politiques de la France depuis 1789*, par Deguit et Mounier; Lebon, *Das Staatsrecht der französischen Republik;* Michel, *L' Idée de l' état*, 1895, 3ème Ed., 1898; Janet, *Histoire*, II, 727-39; Treitschke, *Historische und politische Aufsätze*, III, 43-427; E. Cossé, *Du principe de souveraineté*, 1882.

established.¹ Royer-Collard termed it the alliance of legitimacy with national liberty.²

But even though the charter had been so devised as to mediate between the claims of the old regime and the new, what had become, in the process, of the absolute and indivisible sovereignty which had been recognized by both Bourbon and Revolutionist? In whose hands was this ultimate and indivisible power placed? Did the King Louis XVIII hold it now, as the crown had held it before the Revolution, or were the people still the real sovereign, and was he only their creature, their agent? Governmental *powers* might be divided by the terms of the charter, so many to the king, so many to the people; but how could it be possible to parcel out the indivisible sovereignty, to limit the absolute authority itself? Long accustomed to a clearcut definition and location of the supreme power, it was not easy for France to answer this question satisfactorily by any repetition of phrases about the division or balance of constitutional powers.

To meet this difficulty arising out of the peculiar character of the political conditions, theoretical as well as practical, there was framed by a group of thinkers known as the *Doctrinaires*, a compromise theory of sovereignty.³ Since

[1] " Louis, par la grâce de Dieu, roi de France, . . . nous avons volontairement et par le libre exercice de notre autorité royale, accordé et accordons, fait concession et octroi à nos sujets, tant pour nous que pour nos successeurs et à toujours de la Charte constitutionelle qui suit."—Preamble to Charter.

[2] " La Charte n'est autre chose que cette alliance indissoluble du pouvoir légitime dont elle émane avec les libertés nationales qu' elle reconnaît et consacre." (1820), *Vie*, II, 16. *Cf.* Chateaubriand, *Réflexions politiques*, 1815; *De la monarchie selon la charte*, 1816.

[3] The Doctrinaires believed in and supported the charter as a *finality;* the Liberals, headed by Constant, looked upon it as a transition stage between monarchy and republicanism. *Cf.* Martin, IV, 234; Block, *Dictionnaire général de la politique*, article, *Doctrinaires;* Guizot, *Mémoires pour servir à l' histoire de mon temps*, I, 156 ff.

neither the people nor the king could, under the existing conditions, rule alone and unlimited, the supreme authority was taken out of the hands of both, and placed above the reach of any human aspirant. The true sovereign, it was maintained, is really reason, justice, abstract right. Here alone can the seat of the supreme power be found.

The most able defender of this theory was the brilliant and versatile Cousin.[1] He begins by raising the question, "What is sovereignty?" and is ready with the reply that sovereignty is the same as absolute right. Hence, to ask, whence comes sovereignty? is equivalent to asking, whence comes right (*droit*)?[2] The next step, then, is to enquire into the sources of this principle itself. Three theories have been defended, says Cousin, namely, force, will and reason, each of which has been declared to be the final source of right, and consequently of sovereignty. Of these, the first is clearly impossible, since mere force cannot create right; there is no relation between the principle of force, as such, and that of abstract right. Nor can *will* be regarded as the foundation of right, declares Cousin. Right or law is not merely the expression of naked will alone, but rather the result of another and anterior principle. Will, in and by itself, stands for nothing, says Cousin; it has not the force of a principle.[3] Pure will, whether it be of one or of many, individual or general, cannot be considered as the true basis of the supreme power. The "general will," merely as will and nothing else, is incapable of constituting abstract right. The only principle which can create right and ulti-

---

[1] *Cours d' histoire de la philosophie morale au dix-huitième siècle*, 1839–40; given in 1819–20. Compare his *Cours de philosophie*, 1828.

[2] "Et d' abord qu' est ce que la souveraineté? C' est le droit. La souveraineté absolue, c' est le droit absolu."—*Cours d' histoire*, II, 297.

[3] "La volonté, encore une fois, n' a pas force de principe parce qu' elle ne représente rien par elle-même."—*Ibid.*, 299.

mately sovereignty, which as already defined is "absolute right," is, as Cousin argues, the *reason*.[1] This "reason," however, cannot be other than infallible if it is to produce right and supremacy; and, therefore, the mere human reason is excluded. Absolute power, it is held, can belong to infallibility only.[2] Not only is this reason not the possession of any individual human being, but it is also denied by Cousin to the general reason (la raison générale). If sovereignty does not belong then to force, to will or human reason, individual or general, of whom can it be predicated? The absolute reason, answers Cousin, is alone infallible, is therefore alone the source of absolute right and of sovereignty. It follows, then, that for fallible men, sovereignty is really unattainable. Louis XVIII. cannot possess it, for he is certainly liable to error. The French people cannot be infallible, and must, therefore, abandon the claim to sovereignty. The absolute reason is alone infallible, is the only true sovereign. This absolute reason is not to be found on earth; hence, there is really no sovereignty over which to dispute. There are, nevertheless, certain principles of reason to be found among men, and these are especially exemplified in constitutional government which is the first where the absolute reason has been truly represented.[3] Cousin's solution of the problem of the location of

---

[1] "La raison est donc le vrai, le seul principe du droit et de la souveraineté."—*Cours d' histoire*, II, (300).

[2] "Le pouvoir absolu, c' est-à-dire sans limites n'appartient qu' à l' infaillibilité."—*Ibid.*, II, 301.

[3] "Il est le premier où la raison absolue ait été vraiment représentée; jusque là tous les éléments du gouvernement étaient des pouvoirs purement humains (315) . . il est le gouvernement même de la raison, dont il a promulgué les principes éternels."—*Ibid.*, 318. Cousin demands that the rights to person, liberty, property, industry, *etc.*, be respected, and accords a right of resistance when they are denied.—*Ibid.*, II, 337-54.

Cf. Revue des Deux Mondes, 1851, x, 1–46; *Des principes de la révolution française et du gouvernement représentatif:* "dans une nation tout est fait pour

the sovereignty was its utter elimination from the category of political science.

To a similar end reasoned Guizot.[1] He denied that the so-called "popular sovereignty" of the Revolution was really what it had professed to be, and declared that it was merely the rule of one faction of the people over a weaker part. He announced his hostility to the theory of popular sovereignty on the one hand, and that of divine right on the other, seeing on either side only the rule of usurpation and force.[2] He therefore declared his belief in the sovereignty of the reason, of justice, of right.[3] Here alone is to be found the ruler truly legitimate—the only point at which absolute and unlimited power can be placed.

In a similar spirit argued the great leader of the Constitutionalists or Liberals, Benjamin Constant. He declared his opposition to the two principles, that of divine right and that of the *unlimited* sovereignty of the people, and asserted that the only true sovereignty is justice. He conceded the sovereignty of the people in the sense of the supremacy of the general over the particular will, but denied emphatically that this power could be regarded as without limit.[4] With the word "absolute," said Constant, neither liberty nor peace

---

la nation. . . elle n'est obligée que devant elle-même et la souveraineté de sa liberté ne s'arrête que devant la souveraineté de sa raison" (14).

[1] *Du gouvernement de la France depuis la Restauration et du ministère actuel*, 1821. *Du gouvernement représentatif et de l'état actuel de la France*, 1816; *Histoire de la civilisation en Europe* 1828–30, 8th ed. 1864.

[2] *Du gouvernement de la France*, 201.

[3] *Ibid.:* "Je crois à la souveraineté de la raison, de la justice, du droit . . Nul homme, nulle réunion d'hommes ne les possède et ne peut les posséder sans lacune et sans limites." *Cf. Histoire*, 252 ff., where all absolute power is declared to be illegitimate but where royalty is defended.

[4] *Principes politiques*, 1815; *Réflexions sur les constitutions et les garanties*, 1814–18, in *Cours de politique constitutionnelle*, 1872; *De la résponsabilité des ministres*, 1814–18.

nor prosperity is compatible. There can be no sovereignty but a relative or limited one. "At the point where the independence and the existence of the individual commence, there the jurisdiction of the sovereign ceases.[1] The supreme power is always limited by individual liberty in such forms as personal liberty, religious liberty, industrial liberty, inviolability of property, the freedom of the press. These are rights which no power can attack without destroying its own title to legitimacy. The sovereignty is practically restrained, he holds, first of all by the force which guarantees " all known truths," by opinion, and in the second place, and more precisely, by the distribution and balance of powers.[2] Constant's division of governmental powers includes the representative, the executive, *i. e.*, the ministers, the judicial, and then above all a fourth power, the royal. The crown appears as a neutral power (pouvoir neutre), holding the balance among all others,[3] constituting the force necessary to produce a stable constitutional equilibrium.[4]

---

[1] "Il est faux que la société tout entière, possède sur ses membres une souveraineté sans bornes. *La souveraineté n' existe que d' une manière limitée et relative.*"—*Principes*, 9.

[2] *Principes*, 16 : " Elle sera garantie d'abord par la force qui garantit toutes les vérités reconnues, par l' opinion."

[3] The prince is : " Un être à part, supérieur aux diversités des opinions, n' ayant d' autre intérêt que le maintien de l' ordre, et le maintien de la liberté, ne pouvant jamais rentrer dans la condition commune, inaccessible en conséquence à toutes les passions que cette condition fait naître et à toutes celles que la perspective de s' y trouver nourrit nécessairement dans le coeur des agents investis d' une puissance momentanée."—*Principes*, 21. Constant emphasized greatly the sacredness of individual liberty and the necessity of adequate guarantees therefor. Compare Daunou, P. C. *Essai sur les garanties individuelles que réclame l' état actuel de la société*, 1819; Madame de Stael, *Considérations*, 1818; Coffinières, A. S. G., *Traité de la liberté individuelle*, 1828.

[4] See in opposition to absolute power, C. G. Hello, *Du régime constitutionnel*, 2d ed., 1830 (1st, 1827). He declares: "Je combats le pouvoir absolu de la même manière que l' athéisme : je le nie : avant de soutenir sa légitimité ou ses

THE SOVEREIGNTY OF REASON

The theory of the sovereignty of reason, defended by the "Doctrinaires" was obviously adapted to the constitutional compromise of 1814,[1] with the inherent difficulty about the location of the supreme power. Unable to find the ultimate authority, either from a legal point of view or as a question of fact, the advocates of the new regime simply declared that the concept of sovereignty must be stricken out of political science. Their answer to the question of sovereignty was that there is no question to answer. It was, perhaps, as good a generalization as possible from the unsettled and confused political conditions which then existed in France. Cousin said, "Every age aims at a philosphy to represent it;"[2] and this was the political philosophy which represented the times in France.

Between this doctrine and the position of the "Theocrats" there was at bottom very little difference. Both denied the creation of sovereignty by imperfect men, and found the supreme power outside of and above human agencies. The theological school opposed to the human will the divine will. The Doctrinaires declared for abstract and abso-

---

avantages prouvez-moi qu' il existe."—p. 147. Of the king he says: "Le monarque n' est plus un homme mais *une chose, une abstraction, une intelligence*, qui occupe le centre de la machine, comme un sanctuaire."—*Ibid*., p. 153.

[1] With Cousin and Guizot compare the leader of the Doctrinaires, *Royer-Collard*, more of an orator than an author. See *La vie politique de M. Royer-Collard*, by de Barante (1861). *Cf.* the speech of 1820 (p. 33): "Voulez vous (au contraire) faire la société avec l' élément moral, qui est le droit. Le souverain est la justice, parceque la justice est la règle du droit. Les constitutions libres ont pour objet de détrôner la force, et de faire régner la justice." Compare Lanjuinais, J. D. de., Oeuvres, II., *Constitutions de la nation française*, 1819. "Il est remarquable que notre môt souverain ne signifie litéralement que supérieur, et non supérieur, tout-à-fait, absolu, et non supérieur sans limites."—p. 13.

[2] *Cours de philosophie*, 1828: "Quand tout autour de nous est mixte, complexe, mélangé, quand tous les contraires vivent et vivent très bien ensemble, il est possible à la philosophie d' échapper à l' esprit général . . . tout siècle aboutit á une philosophie qui le réprésente."—*Ibid*., Leçon. xiii.

lute reason or justice. The application of the ideas was, however, decidedly different. The Theocrats understood that although the source of sovereignty was to be found in God, there was an earthly agent capable of exercising authority by divine right. God was, indeed, the only true sovereign, but he had a human representative, who might possess power unlimited save by his personal responsibility to the Divine Author. There was no desire to eliminate the sovereignty, but on the contrary, a decided tendency to emphasize its importance in human society. The theory was used practically in the defense of the old regime against the arguments of the democratic, revolutionary party. The Doctrinaires, however, were partisans neither of the pre-revolutionary nor of the revolutionary regime. They endeavored to place the origin of sovereignty outside of and above men, not, like the Theocrats, for the purpose of supporting an existing government by a claim of divine right, but to avoid the question of human sovereignty altogether. The sovereignty of reason was not invoked primarily against people or against king, but in order to make possible a modus vivendi between these two parties in the State. Divine right meant the monarch's right against the people; the sovereignty of reason meant the right of both king and people, but the exclusive authority of neither.

The life of the compromise Charter was, however, of short duration, and the agreement between the old order and the new was shattered by the July Revolution of 1830. The Chamber of Deputies declared that "the universal and pressing need of the French people called to the throne Louis Philippe;" the monarch was no longer ruler "by the grace of God," as in the Charter of 1814.[1] It now be-

[1] "Selon le voeu et dans l' intérêt du peuple français, le préambule de la charte constitutionnelle est supprimé, comme blessant la dignité nationale, en paraissant octroyer aux Français des droits qui leur appartiennent essentiellement."—Declaration of the Chamber of Deputies, Aug. 7, 1830.

came necessary to accommodate the former theory to the new conditions, particularly with reference to the newly-manifested power of the nation. The balance between people and king had inclined in favor of the former. Lerminier asserted in his *Philosophy of Right*, (1832), that the July Revolution had made the earlier position untenable: "either legitimacy or national sovereignty must give way; eclecticism is no longer possible."[1] He, therefore, declares that "sovereignty, mélange of reason, justice and will, which represents at once what the nation believes, thinks and wishes, is in the people and nowhere else."[2] Sismondi defended the sovereignty of reason, but by reason understood not the abstract, absolute reason, but the national reason. The national sovereignty, he said, belongs to the national reason,[3] which is, however, different from public opinion, in that the latter is often hasty, passionate, capricious,[4] while the former is calm and deliberate.

Sovereignty for the philosophers of the July monarchy belongs to the intelligence, the reason of the community as a whole, the emphasis still being placed on the *reason* rather than on the *general will* of the earlier days. There is always evident the effort to limit in some way the supreme power, and to prevent the identification of absolute-

---

[1] *Philosophie du droit*, 204.

[2] "La souveraineté, mélange de raison, de justice et de volonté qui représente à la fois ce qu' une nation croit, pense et veut, est dans le peuple et pas ailleurs." —*Ibid.*, 200. Compare Laferrière, M. F., *Cours du droit public et administratif*, 2nd ed., 1841.

[3] J. C. L. Sismondi, *Études sur les constitutions des peuples libres*, 1836. "La souveraineté nationale appartient à la raison nationale, à cette raison éclairée par toutes les lumières, animée par toutes les vertus qui se trouvent dans la nation." —*Ibid.*, 132.

[4] *Ibid.*, 133: "La raison nationale est quelque chose de plus relevé que l' opinion publique, car celle-ci, quoique en général clairvoyante, est souvent aussi précipitée, passionnée, capricieuse."

ness and arbitrariness.¹ The nation is, however, recognized as sovereign, not the King, nor reason in the abstract. By "nation" is understood, now, the organized people.² The national reason is found to be embodied in the Government, and nowhere back of that can a higher power be found. Said Guizot (1842): "If one maintains that there exists, or ought to exist, in the bosom of society, two powers, one ordinary, the other extraordinary; one constitutional, the other constituent; one for working days, the other for holidays, he says what is unheard of. The Constitutional Government is the organized sovereignty of society." So reasoned the Duc de Broglie, "To appeal from the sovereignty founded and regulated by the charter to any other sovereignty, is to appeal to numbers, to brute force; it is to pretend to organize disorder, even; to bring nothingness into existence." ³ The nation is regarded as sovereign, but only as organized within the constitution or charter. It is no longer declared, as in 1793, that "insurrection is the most sacred of rights and the most indispensable of duties;" nor is "people"

---

¹ D. Serrigny, *Traité du droit politique des Français*, 1846, I, (76) distinguishes between "un souverain absolu" and "un souverain arbitraire": one consults reason, the other caprice only. *Cf.* Jouffroy, H., *Catéchisme de droit naturel*, 1841, 144. Berriat-Saint-Prix, *Commentaire sur la charte constitutionnelle*, 1836, says, p. 34: "la souveraineté du peuple se concentre parmi les gens éclairés," *Cf.* Euv. Bavoux, *Philosophie politique*, 1840, 2 vols., who defends the limited sovereignty of the people, II, 432, 435: "La souveraineté nationale a pour limites la morale, la justice et les droits de chaque individu." Gimet de Joulan, *Philosophie de la politique*, 3 vols., 1843-46, declares in favor of national sovereignty, but finds that "le peuple et la nation ne sont qu' une même chose, c'est-à-dire, l' universalité des citoyens, quel que soit leur rang."—II, 123. *Cf.*, Hepp, G. P., *Essai sur la théorie de la vie sociale et du gouvernement représentatif*, 1833.

² 19 August, *Moniteur*, 1811.

³ *Écrits et discours*, III, 131 (1842). See also Thiers, *Moniteur*, 1041 (1840): "La souveraineté nationale à notre sens, c' est la souveraineté du roi et des deux chambres faisant la loi, exprimant la volonté nationale; je n' en conçois pas d' autre;" Massias, N., *De la souveraineté du peuple*, 1833, 98: "La souveraineté réside dans le peuple agissant régulièrement par ses pouvoirs constitués."

longer used in the sense in which the term was employed by Robespierre. The sovereign is not the *will* of the *people* at large, but the *reason* of the *nation* as embodied in the constitutional authorities. The theory was stated with a conservatism corresponding to that with which the constitutional structure was erected, and the narrow basis upon which it still rested.

After the revolution of 1848, the democratic idea was expressed with greater clearness. Article I of the new constitution declared that the sovereignty rests with the general body (universalité) of the citizens." Lamartine[1] in his proclamation to the electors said: "Every Frenchman of full age is a citizen; every citizen an elector; every elector is sovereign. The law is equal, absolute for all. There is no citizen who can say to another: 'You are more sovereign than I.' Contemplate your power, prepare to enter into possession of your kingdom." The idea of the sovereignty of the nation or the people was again restored and found general acceptance, though no new discussions of a scientific nature appeared.[2] By the socialistic element the doctrine of popular sovereignty was used in support of its economic propositions, while with others the sovereignty of reason was interpreted to mean no sovereignty at all, absolute individual liberty or anarchy.[3]

---

[1] Lamartine, *Histoire de la révolution de 1848*, II, 196.

[2] See Berriat St. Prix, *Théorie du droit constitutionnel français*, 1851; De Barante, *Questions constitutionelles*, 1849. Pierre Leroux (Socialist) argues that "la souveraineté est la puissance qui de Dieu descend dans l' esprit humain et se manifeste par le peuple: c'est-à-dire par l'unité indivisible de tous les citoyens, véritable image de Celui dont elle découle."—*Projet d'une constitution démocratique et sociale*, 1848, art 19.

[3] See Proudhon, *De la justice dans la Révolution:* "C'est donc à la justice qu' appartient la direction du pouvoir; de sorte que l'ordre dans l'être collectif comme la santé, la volonté etc. dans l' animal n'est le fruit d' aucune initiative particulière; il résulte de l'organisation:"—I, 118. "La justice est pour les êtres intelligents libres la cause suprême de leurs déterminations. Elle n' a besoin que d' être expliquée et comprise pour être affirmée par tout le monde et agir." Compare Paul de Flotte, *La Souveraineté du Peuple*, 1851.

On the whole, the progress of the French theory during this period offers little of importance in the development of the conception of sovereignty. The political conditions were too unsettled and uncertain, too much lacking in definiteness, to render easy the development of a precise theory in regard to the nature of the supreme political power. It was difficult to say who was sovereign; if possible to determine, it was hardly desirable. France seemed to fear its own logic. What the publicists were most anxious to avoid was unlimited, absolute power in the hands of either king or people, the despotism of the Bourbons and that of the Revolution. Whatever the theory, the possibility of the return of either must be prevented. In pursuance of this object, it was asserted by the Doctrinaires that the only true sovereign was reason or abstract right, which no human authority could possess in unlimited measure; by the Liberals that political power could never be absolute, but must always respect individual rights. After 1830 it was said that the people were sovereign, but only the *reason* of the people, not their passing opinion or unenlightened will; or again that the people are sovereign, but only as a nation, in its organized capacity; that there is no " people " back of the ordinary government, There was everywhere evident the desire to curb or check in some way or other the absoluteness of the supreme power.

The greatest modification on the radical theory of the Revolution consisted then, in the fact that *reason* was substituted for *will* as the basis of genuine authority. The sovereign rules not merely because he wills to rule, but rather by virtue of the fact that his command is reasonable; the sovereign is not the will of the moment, but the calm and enlightened reason of the nation. So far as legal limitation is concerned, however, there is none. Whether the general will does or does not correspond to the general reason, the will is likely to rule.

CHAPTER VI

POPULAR AND STATE SOVEREIGNTY

WE have noticed the theory of Kant and his immediate adherents, that developed by the leaders of the religious reaction, the doctrine of Ludwig von Haller, and the theory of the sovereignty of reason or justice as developed in France. The next step is to trace the progress of political theory in the German States from the sovereignty of the "people" to that of the "State." The popular theory had been so greatly prejudiced by the revolutionary excesses committed in its name, that its acceptance was hardly possible in Germany, notwithstanding its earnest advocacy on the part of the many liberals.[1] Yet, on the other hand, the theory of the sovereignty of the ruler or governor alone, was also apparently no longer tenable. Neither the solution proposed by Kant, nor that of the religious school, nor that worked out by Haller and Maurenbrecher was able to win for itself a permanently predominant position. The supremacy of reason or justice was regarded as too general a proposition to satisfy the desire for a definite bearer of the supreme power, the human agent or agents of this ideal sovereign.

There was, moreover, an urgent constitutional demand for a doctrine of sovereignty in harmony with the conciliatory and compromising character of the political conditions. The great problem of the middle years of the nineteenth century[2] was the establishment of a political status, reconciling

---

[1] *Cf.* especially K. v. Rotteck, *Lehrbuch des Vernunftrechts*, 1829–35.

[2] In the Southern German states under Napoleonic rule much earlier. On the

the old ante-revolutionary régime with the new. It was agreed that the king could not govern arbitrarily and alone. There must be organized a legislative body or bodies whose consent must be obtained to important measures of state; there must be a body of responsible ministers surrounding the monarch; there must be an organic law, a constitution, in which the limits of the royal activity should be indicated, and within which the ruler should remain. This constitution might be granted (octroyirt) by the monarch himself, formally at least out of pure good will, however menacing the actual conditions might be; but when the fundamental laws were once laid down, to them he must conform. This was the principle underlying the constitutional movement which swept over Germany after the reaction against the Revolution had spent its force, and the liberal spirit dared once more to lift its head. To the Germans, however, none of the contemporary liberal systems appeared to be satisfactory, thoroughly discussed though they were in the course of the long and exhaustive political debates. Neither the system of English Parliamentary government, nor any of the numerous French models at hand, nor the presidential form of the United States was adapted to the German needs. A new system must be framed, suitable to the conditions, theoretical and practical, which were peculiar to the German states.

Nor were any of the theories of sovereignty accompanying the systems that have been here mentioned able to establish a position in German political science. As a consequence we find that in Germany there was raised above the absolute monarch of earlier times, not reason or justice in the abstract,

German constitutional development see the excellent work by H. Treitschke, *Deutsche Geschichte im neunzehnten Jahrhundert*, B. II–V. Compare also, R. v Mohl, *Geschichte und Literatur des allgemeinen konstitutionellen Staatsrechtes;* v. Rönne, *Staatsrecht der Preussischen Monarchie;* Geo. Meyer,' *Lehrbuch des deutschen Staatsrechtes;* F. Stœrk, *Handbuch der deutschen Verfassungen;* Treitschke, *Historische und politische Aufsätze*, III.

nor the people as conceived by the contract theorists, nor any Convention or Parliament representative of the people. As the new bearer of the sovereignty, German political theory advanced the State itself, regarded either as an organism or as a juristic personality, or as both an organism and a juristic person. Such a consummation was impossible from the German point of view, however, until the State had become something different from the personal property of an individual, or, on the other hand, the purely artificial creation of a social or political contract or series of contracts. A necessary prerequisite to the adoption of the theory of the sovereignty of the State was the development of a new doctrine in regard to the nature of the State itself. "State," in the sense of the revolutionary doctrine, was artificially formed, wholly a product of human will, and in the heat of conflict had been too often the name assumed by a mere fraction of the people. As a fiction, the State could not become the holder of the supreme power; it must be something more real, more definite, something less dependent, moreover, on the voluntary action of the individuals composing it. The nature of the theory directed against the doctrines of the revolution has already been noticed in the preceding chapter. It is now proposed to follow the course of the development of the idea of the State as a real organism and a person; to show how the State thus newly conceived obtained recognition as the bearer of the supreme political power in the face of the opposing doctrines; and, finally, to show the nature of the sovereignty conferred on the State, and the relation between the new concept of State and that of sovereignty.

The idea of the State as an organism is almost as old as political theory itself.[1] Plato compared the State to a great man, and drew an analogy between the functions of the indi-

---

[1] See Jellinek, *System der subjektiven öffentlichen Rechte*, 34; Jos. Held, *Staat und Gesellschaft*, I.

vidual and those of the State. The Romans personified the fiscus and made it a bearer of rights. The mediæval writers, such as John of Salisbury and Marsilius of Padua developed elaborate comparisons between the various members of the human body and corresponding parts of the State. The mediæval political theory was in fact filled with anthropomorphic ideas of a likeness between the organic functions seen in the individual man and those apparent on a larger scale in the larger life of the State. Yet the political society was never regarded as itself a reality, but merely as a very close imitation of one. As has been already shown, with the wider development of the contract theory, in spite of its highly artificial character, the organic and personal analogies continued to live and flourish. Althusius in his *Politics* discussed the organic nature of the State at some length and based his theory of sovereignty thereon. Hobbes compared the commonwealth to an "artificial man, though of greater stature and strength than the natural." Grotius developed the idea of the sovereignty of the state as an organism, with the two bearers of power, the general and the special. Pufendorf was elaborate in his exposition of the theory of what he called "moral persons" (personæ morales),[1] of which the State was one, as were also the family, the corporation, the commune, the church. Rousseau's State though formed by the agreement of individuals, was regarded, none the less, as a "moral and collective body" (corps moral et collectif). In general, however the personality of the State under the contract theory was merely a short form of expression for the legal relations of a number of individuals; the State was

---

[1] "Persona moralis composita constituitur quando plura individua humana ita iter se uniuntur ut qui vi istius unionis volunt et agunt pro una voluntate unaque actione, non pro pluribus censeantur."—*De Jure N. et G.*, I, 1-13. Moral persons are subdivided into simple and complex: the simple again into public and private; the public again into political and ecclesiastical; the political into general and special.

more of a machine than an organism, rather a convenient fiction than a real person. This very fact gave the advocates of monarchy and of monarchical sovereignty an important dialectical advantage, the measure of which was the difference between the awe inspired by a real, and that by a fictitious ruler. The king was tangible and visible; the people merely a vague fiction.[1]

But on the basis of the purely individualistic idea alone, it was exceedingly difficult to arrive at the concept of the State, either as an organism or as a real person. This difficulty was, moreover, not a superficial, but a fundamental one, since the eighteenth century theory regarded the State not at all as a result of any organic growth, but, on the contrary, as the conscious construction of human will. The contract by means of which the State came into existence was not looked upon as an organic process, but as the most complete contrast thereto. If, indeed, the revolutionary school had looked upon political institutions as the result of an organic development, it would have been no longer revolutionary, but, on the other hand, evolutionary. Had Rousseau been in harmony with Schelling's idea of the "world process," he would never have written the Social Contract; had his disciples been convinced that the existing political system was the result of a slow historical development and could be altered only in the same way, there would have been no hand raised in revolt against the king. In short, the essence of the eighteenth century political theory was the exaltation of the influence of human will in the world of politics, and the corresponding degradation of historical or organic growth. If the theory had been other than purely

---

[1] Thus Horn in opposition to the popular theory argued that the only subject of rights is an individual, that all so-called collective persons are only sums of individuals, possessing no real unity; that therefore the only true ruler must be an individual, *i. e.*, a monarch. See Gierke, Althusius, 191.

artificial, it could never have become, as it did, the rallying cry in the struggle for civil and political liberty.

With the reaction against the eighteenth century political theory came the development of a doctrine of the organic and personal nature of the State, which was impossible under the dominance of the revolutionary ideas. As has already been shown, the essence of the reactionary theory was the emphasis on the natural in contrast to the artificial element in the development of forms of political life. On every hand, the doctrine of popular sovereignty was assailed by the variously worded argument that the State is not made by man, but is imposed upon him from without, or is the unconscious unfolding of some element implanted in the depths of human nature. It is now necessary to trace the progress of the new idea of the State which grew out of that body of doctrine by means of which the theory of the revolution was met and its progress checked. In this discussion we are, as already stated, limited to the field of German thought—the most fertile soil, however, for the development of political theory in the nineteenth century.

The organic idea of the State was already contained in the abstract philosophy of Schelling and his school. To Schelling the State was not, as with Kant, merely an institution for the purpose of securing rights, but rather a part of a great "world process," one of the forms in which the Absolute found expression. He termed the State, therefore, an "*organism*," a result of natural rather than artificial or conscious construction.[1] A similar idea was given expression by a follower of Schelling, J. J. Wagner, in his *System of Ideal Philosophy* (1804).[2] Here it is again denied that the State is

---

[1] See *Vorlesungen über die Methode des akademischen Studiums*, 1802, 10th lecture, 235. (3rd ed., 1830.)

[2] *System der Ideal-Philosophie*, a work of late unnoticed, so far as the writer's knowledge goes. "Person" is used here not "in its highest philosophic and

a mere organization for the purpose of upholding the rights of individuals, or their welfare, and the declaration is made that it is an organism, a living organization;[1] and that the State must also be regarded as a person. Person, he says, is a unity of perception and will, and wherever, among a number of men, this is found, there is a personality;[2] so the family, the community, the State.

A far more powerful presentation of the new idea was found in the political theory of Hegel, who was in general inclined toward an idealization of the State. In his system the purpose of the State is broadened from the Kantian conception to that of the "realization of the moral idea."[3] The individual has reality only as a member of the State; his destiny is to lead a so-called "universal" life, that is, in accordance with the universal will of the whole, not with his own particular will. Hegel asserts that the State must be regarded as an organism, but by organism is understood the "development of the idea to its dis-

---

moral significance." *Der Staat*, 18. "Eine aus Vielheit zusammengeflossene Persönlichkeit heisst juristische (moralische) Person."—*Ibid.*, 19.

[1] "Ist in der That jeder einzelne Staat auf seiner Weise ein Organismus und in der Summe aller Staaten, die waren, sind, und sein werden, ist auch die Totalität der Idee nach der unendlichen Vielheit ihrer Nuancen dargestellt."—Sec. 27.

[2] "Person ist Subjekt, also Einheit von Erkenntniss und Wille und diese ist allgemeiner Charakter der Menschheit; wo also unter der Vielheit der Menschen sich solche Einheit gestaltet, da ist Persönlichkeit."—*Der Staat*, 4. Sovereignty (Majestät) "is the true reason or self-knowledge of the whole, and where individuals honor a sovereignty, they then loose voluntarily their private-perception (Privat-Erkenntniss) in the state-perception of those who have the sovereignty," —*Ibid.*, sec. 66.

[3] *Grundlinien*, Sec. 257: "Der Staat ist die Wirklichkeit der sittlichen Idee." "Der Staat an und für sich ist das sittliche Ganze, die Verwirklichung der Freiheit."—Sec. 258. "Es ist der Gang Gottes in der Welt, dass der Staat ist."—Sec. 258. See Bluntschli, *Geschichte*, on Hegel's practical influence on Prussian officialism. With the *Grundlinien* compare the *Encyklopädie der philosophischen Wissenschaften*, 1817.

tinctions."¹ The State is, moreover, not only an organism in this dialectical sense, but is also a personality, and that of the very highest kind.² Person is with Hegel that which "has its basis and cause in itself" ("was seinen Grund und seine Ursache in sich selbst habe"), or, in the juristic sense, a subject of rights. This quality the State possesses as truly as—even more truly than the individual. Further, and here Hegel makes a decided advance on the previous theory, to the State belongs the attribute of sovereignty.³ Under feudal conditions, argues he, not only was the monarch not sovereign, but even the State as a whole could not claim this power. The political functions properly belonging to the State, were partly in the possession of corporations or communities, partly the private property of individuals, so that the State was "rather an aggregation than an organism."⁴ The essence of the sovereignty of the State under the new conditions is found in the fact that the functions and powers of the body politic are not exercised for their own sake alone, that is, as governmental rights; nor are they the private property of individuals, but they are rooted in the unity of the State itself.⁵ In this sense, the State is the sovereign personality. Popular sovereignty expresses an idea which is true only when one regards the State externally as one among others, as when one refers to

---

[1] Sec. 269: "Der Staat ist Organismus, dass heisst Entwickelung der Idee zu ihren Unterschieden. Diese unterschiedenen Seiten sind die verschiedenen Gewalten."

[2] See *Grundl.*, sec. 35-36, on personality and the capacity to hold rights. ("Rechtsfähigkeit.")

[3] Sec. 278-79.

[4] "Nicht etwa nur der Monarch nicht, sondern der Staat nicht souverän . . . das Ganze daher mehr eine Aggregation als ein Organismus."—Sec. 278. See the comparison of the state with the nervous system in sec. 263.

[5] "In der Einheit des Staats als ihrem einfachen Selbst ihre letzte Wurzel haben."—Sec. 278.

the people of Great Britain as sovereign. Internally, the people are sovereign, in that very general sense in which by "people" is understood "the *whole State*, including monarch and what is *ordinarily* meant by "people," but not at all in the sense of "people," as contrasted with their ruler as rulers.[1] In general, when one speaks of the "people" as a particular part of the society, we are to understand "the part that does not know what it wills."[2]

After all, however, Hegel's sovereignty of the state, internally considered, is intimately related to sovereignty of the government in earlier theories. He idealizes the State, but he is also a worshipper of "constitutional" monarchy,[3] which he regards as one of the greatest political products of the new spirit of the modern world,[4] and as decidedly superior to either aristocracy or democracy. Hegel maintains, accordingly, that personality in general has existence only in so far as it finds expression in an individual.[5] The State would, therefore, be a pure abstraction, unless it were made real and "objective" in some way. This concrete bearer of the State's personality is then not "individuality in general," but a definite and specific individual, namely the monarch.[6] It is in the king that the formerly abstract idea

---

[1] "Volkssouveränetät kann in dem Sinn gesagt werden, dass ein Volk überhaupt nach Aussen ein selbstständiges sei und einen einzigen Staat ausmache."—Sec. 279. The "Volk" in a republic may also be regarded as sovereign. See sec. 328.

[2] "Das Volk insofern mit diesem Worte ein besonderer Theil der Mitglieder eines Staats bezeichnet ist, den Theil ausdrückt, der nicht weiss was er will."—Sec. 301.

[3] Constitutional monarchy as seen in the German states during the period of reaction, not as seen in the English system, which he denounces as "a loosely-connected mass of positive rules."

[4] Sec. 273.

[5] Sec. 279: "Die Subjektivität aber ist in ihrer Wahrheit nur als Subjekt, die Persönlichkeit nur als Person."

[6] "Dieser absolut entscheidende Moment des Ganzen ist daher nicht die Individualität überhaupt, sondern ein Individuum, der Monarch . . . Die Persönlichkeit des Staats ist nur als eine Person, der Monarch wirklich."—Sec. 279.

of the State becomes real and concrete; without him the community possesses, says Hegel, personality only in the abstract. The duties of the monarch may not be extensive; he may have " only to say yes, and to put the point on the I,"[1] but this one fact, that in him the State becomes real and personal, constitutes, nevertheless, the great distinction politically between the ancient and the modern world. This position of the monarch is moreover not derived or granted, but "absolutely original with its possessor."[2]

Hegel thus rescued the State from the origin which the revolutionary theory had imputed to it. He declared it to be an organism, he attributed to it personality, and he held that the sovereignty must rest with the State as thus organically and personally conceived. But by the emphasis laid upon the monarch as the "personification" of the State, attention was diverted from his proposition of State-sovereignty, and the immediate effect of his teaching was in practice similar to that of those who openly taught the sovereignty of the monarch. The State was sovereign in the abstract, but practically statehood and sovereignty found expression only in the person of the king. The concessions made to the popular argument by both Hegel and Kant were like those of the Patricians to the Plebeians at Rome, always accompanied by a saving clause. Moreover, the conception of the State, either as organism or as personality, was at best stated in terms so highly abstract, so purely dialectical, as to prejudice its ready and easy acceptance. Nevertheless, the Hegelian doctrine was influ-

---

[1] " Er hat nur Ja zu sagen und den Punkt auf das I zu setzen."—Sec. 279. "Dieses 'Ich will' macht den grossen Unterschied der alten und modernen Welt aus, und so muss es in dem grossen Gebäude des Staats seine eigenthümliche Existenz haben."—Sec. 279.

[2] *Ibid.:* "Nicht ein Abgeleitetes sondern das schlechthin aus sich Anfangende zu sein."

ential in the determination of the course to be taken by political theory, and the weight of his argument ultimately fell on the side of the sovereignty of the State.[1]

The idea that the State in some way constituted an organism or a personality continued to find recognition among political theorists. Frequently the term "moral person" was used; sometimes in the sense of the earlier theory as opposed to the "natural," sometimes with a new significance.[2] Especially Krause[3] in his philosophy defended the personality of the State, but in terms so vague, so general, so all-inclusive that the force of his argument was dissipated. Everything, he held, that is "united in common origin, language, science, art, Gotteinigkeit, morality" is a person. The family, the community, the Church, the State and all humanity were moral persons.

The Schelling–Hegel–Krause school was able to develop a theory of the personality of the State and of its organic nature, and thus to make headway against the so-called

---

[1] Especially influenced by Hegel was Troxler in his *Philosophische Rechtslehre*, 1820. He declared against the sovereignty of government and of people (111) and in favor of that of the Nation. "Selbstherrlich und eigenmächtig ist nur die Nation, nur sie ist die Quelle der Majestät und Souveränetät. Unterthan und dienstbar dagegen ist die ganze politische Persönlichkeit und sie mit allen ihren Kräften und Gliedern ist nur Mittel und Werkzeug" (p. 118). J. E. Erdmann, *Philosophische Vorlesungen über den Staat*, 1851, defends State Sovereignty. "The sovereignty may be as little separated from the state as the round form from a bullet (p. 36), but "in the King, is the State or the People *I*" (p. 171).

[2] Ancillon, *Ueber den Geist der Staatsverfassungen*, 1825, p. 309: "A State is a moral unity. It is *moral* in so far as all the individuals of which it is composed are rational and free men." Schmitthenner declares the state to be a moral or ethical *organism.—Grundlinien*, 287. So Waitz, *Grundzüge*, I, 5, says the state is a *moral* organism in contrast to a merely *natural* organism: "in ihm walten sittliche Ideen, er ist kein natürlicher, ein ethischer Organismus." Röder, K., *Grundzüge des Naturrechts*, 1846, pp. 45–6, refers to the "so-called moral, mystical, or juristic person."

[3] *Abriss*, 1828, p. 169: "in gemeinsamer Abstammung, Sprache, Wissenschaft, Kunst, Gotteinigkeit, Sitte und Recht verbunden ist."

"artificial" theory of the Revolution. Their results, though often mystical and obscure, or stated in a most abstract and purely dialectical form, cannot be neglected in the study of the development of the theory of sovereignty.

Another step in the direction of the sovereignty of the State was taken by the leaders of the "historical school," although they by no means contemplated such an end. The spirit of historical investigation was hostile to the contract theory of the popular school, but the same spirit was certain ultimately to reject the pretensions of the reaction. In the very nature of the historical method, it contained the germ of a development which was likely to end in some recognition of the popular theory against which it was at first directed.

Savigny, the leader of the school, maintained that law finds its source in the "common consciousness of the people,"[1] that the whole legal system is a growth corresponding to the various periods through which the life of the people passes. In like manner the State is generated by the gradual unfolding of a principle latent in the community. As Savigny says, "the State originally, and according to nature, arises in a people, through a people, and for a people."[2] But what is meant, he asks, by people? In answer he enumerates four different meanings of the term (*Volk*) : first, the natural whole (Naturganzes) in which the State really arises, in which its existence is perpetuated, and in which choice and will are out of the question ; second, the sum of all the individuals living in the State at the same time ; third, the same individuals with the exception of the Government, that is, the *ruled* in contrast to the ruler or rulers ; fourth, in republican States, that particular organized assembly of individuals in which,

---

[1] *System des heutigen römischen Rechts*, 1839. I, sec. 7.

[2] *Ibid.*, sec. 10: "Der Staat ursprünglich und naturgemäss in einem Volk, durch das Volk und für das Volk ensteht."

according to the constitution, the highest power really rests.[1] He points out that great confusion arises from the fact that the ideal right of the people as a whole (1) and the historical rights belonging to the Roman people (4) are often transferred to or claimed by, the sum of the subjects over against their rulers (3). But even if class two, the sum of the individuals living, could be regarded as sovereign, they must first be organized in some form, and although one generation is organized, that single generation cannot be looked upon as sovereign, but all those of the past and those yet to come must also be considered.[2] The "people" in the general sense of the term can possess no political power. They must first be organized in the State, in which they first obtain the personality and the capacity to act.[3] But, on the other hand, it is difficult to see how a Government can exist without the people as its basis.

Stahl concedes that the State is a product of popular will, though he admits neither the doctrine of popular sovereignty, nor even that of State sovereignty.[4] This popular will is not the combined will of individuals, but "rather a power which determines the will, a consciousness of moral necessity."[5] It is the basis of the State, but not itself capable of becoming the bearer of the power which belongs to the political administrator or ruler. The State is, with Stahl, a "political person," that is, it has the capacity to act and to rule.[6] In this sense it is admitted to be distinct from the monarchy; but, nevertheless, Stahl refused to recognize the so-called

---

[1] *System*, sec. 10.   [2] *Ibid.*, sec. 8.

[3] *Ibid.*, sec. 9; the State is the "leibliche Gestalt der geistigen Gemeinschaft. In ihm zuerst enthält das Volk wahre Persönlichkeit, also die Fähigkeit zu handeln."

[4] *Philosophie des Rechts*, II, 2, 143.   [5] *Ibid.*

[6] II, 18: "Enthält die Fähigkeit Subjekt des Handelns und Herrschens zu sein."

State-sovereignty, as an authority over and above both prince and people. This he regards as impossible, since the supreme power must be attributed to some *definite* organ, to which the other organs are subordinated.[1] The question is, urges Stahl, who is the head of the State? And to answer this by saying the State itself, would hardly be satisfactory.[2] Since Stahl is unwilling to accept either popular sovereignty, monarchical sovereignty, or state sovereignty, he is forced to speak of a State as a political person, distinct from the ruler, yet existing only in and through the ruler.[3]

In intimate relation to the theory of the historical school stood that of L. H. Warnkönig in his *Philosophy of Law*, 1839.[4] Here the proposition that the people are to be regarded as sovereign is repudiated as by Stahl and Savigny. Right, law, the State, are based upon the *Volks Ueberzeugung*, or popular opinion,[5] which is at any given moment the real power. When this basis alters the whole body of legal and political institutions changes, including the sovereignty itself.[6] This underlying power is not, however, the real sovereign in the organized State, and is not to be confused with the reigning ruler or rulers.[7] It operates

---

[1] II, 536: "Sondern nur einem bestimmten Organ, einem lebendigen Wesen zukommen, dem dann die anderen Organe untergeordnet sind."

[2] "Die Frage ist eben wer das Oberhaupt des Staates, wer das Centrum in den Funktionen des Staates ist, und da kann man doch nicht antworten, der Staat." —*Ibid.*, II, 536.

[3] II, 19.

[4] *Rechtsphilosophie als Naturlehre des Volks*. Compare *Zeitschrift für die gesammte Staatswissenschaft* 1851, VII, 219, 473, 622.

[5] S. 209: "Sie ist die Ursache der in einem gegebenen Zeitmomente wirklich existirenden souveränen Gewalt, diese ihre Wirkung."

[6] *Ibid.*

[7] It is "keine im Staate als wirklicher höchster Wille befehlende Person, und demnach mit der eigentlichen regierenden Souveränetät nicht zu verwechseln." —*Ibid.*, 209. See Puchta, C. F., *Cursus der Institutionen*, 1849 (9th ed., 1881), see. II, 25, who bases the state on the "Volksgeist."

outside of legal forms, and only when regular or orderly change is impossible, and extra-legal action has become an imperative necessity.

The tendency of the historical school was at the outset conservative, even reactionary, as seen in Burke, in the doctrines of De Maistre and of the Germans. Experience, tradition, history were invoked to conjure away the spirit of revolution.[1] The reaction itself, however, rested upon so uncertain an historical basis, that the power called in to aid remained to imperil those who had summoned it.[2] The very method used to refute the prevailing revolutionary theory necessarily resulted in a recognition of the forces attacked. If unconscious growth, not deliberate choice, were the originating power behind all political institutions, if the State were really a product of an unending process, extending through many generations of men, then it could hardly be produced by any one individual, or even by a ruling class. It must be the result of the labors of a whole community, a people. Law, the State, sovereignty must be evolved, even though unconsciously, by the concurrent action of a great mass of individuals forming a unity, a whole; and in so far the "people" must be looked upon as the supreme power, or at least its source. Toward the recognition of the sovereignty of the State as a whole the full development of the theory of Savigny and Stahl ultimately tended.

Toward the middle of the century there began a movement toward a theory of the State as an organism, not in the formal sense in which it was discussed by Schelling and his school, but in the sense in which the term is used in natural science. The theory of the State became really one of the natural sciences (*Naturlehre*). The organic idea was in the air; history was organically discussed,

[1] De Maistre denounced Rousseau as "the mortal enemy of experience."
[2] On the influence exerted by the German writers, see *Treitschke*, IV, 7.

the representative system, it was thought, must be organically regulated, the relation between the governmental powers must be organic, the relations between ruler and ruled, the theory of sovereignty itself, must be treated by the natural-science method.[1] Moreover, somewhat the same forces, social, economic and political, which in France culminated in the Revolution of 1848, were operating in Germany to bring about the recognition of the sovereignty of the people in a new and different form.[2] The natural-science method of the time and the democratic political tendencies were combined in the theory which held to the sovereignty of the organic State.

Prominent among the leaders of this movement was J. C. Bluntschli, with his *Psychological Studies on the State and the Church*, 1844, and the *General Theory of the State*, 1852.[3] The State, Bluntschli asserts, is an organism, "the organization of the State is the image of human organism."[4] He even progresses so far in the analysis as to be able to assert with confidence that the "State and the Church together constitute the organism of humanity, but each in a different manner; the State representing masculinity, the

---

[1] *Cf.* Mohl, *Geschichte u. Literatur;* Heinrich Leo, *Studien und Skizzen zu einer Naturlehre des Staates*, 1833; Franz, K., *Vorschule der Physiologie der Staaten*, 1857.

[2] French Constitution of 1849, Art. I.: "La souveraineté réside dans l' universalité des citoyens français." H. v. Gagern, in his inaugural address as President of the National Convention in Frankfort in 1848, said: "Unser Beruf und unsere Vollmacht liegen in der Souveränetät unserer Nation," though the sovereign nation might have reference to a strong union of the German States rather than to the French conception of the politically organized people, contrasted with the government.

[3] *Psychologische Studien über Staat und Kirche. Allgemeine Staatslehre.* Here, 6th ed., '86. See also his earlier work, *Das Volk und der Souverain*, 1831 (*Für Gebildete*).

[4] *Psychologische Studien*, 22.

Church femininity."[1] Part VI. of the Studies contains a description of the sixteen fundamental organs of the body politic, in which the analogy of the human body is carried out to limits that are absurd, if not worse.[2] Later, the organic character of the State is defended in terms a little less enthusiastic than those first used. The State, Bluntschli maintains, is an organism, though not a natural growth merely, but in a higher sense a moral and spiritual organism. He enumerates three marks of an organism which he holds are also to be found in the State, namely: the union of material elements and vital forces; the possession within the whole of special organs performing various functions; the growth from within outwards.[3] In these respects, says Bluntschli, "the organic nature of the State is apparent."

The State is, moreover, a person, in the sense of public law, that is, it can "acquire, create and possess rights,"[4] but only in the later stages of development is this personality fully recognized. In earlier times the prince or the head of the State alone is a person. Bluntschli regards the organic nature and personality of the State as not at all unreal or artificial, but as actual and real; thus he departs from the traditional doctrine of the *Naturrecht* school.[5]

---

[1] *Ibid.*, 39: "Staat und Kirche bilden beide dem Organismus der Menschheit nach, aber wiederum in verschiedener Art und Richtung, der Staat die Mannheit, die Kirche die Weiblichkeit."

[2]
$$\begin{aligned}
\text{Männlicher Geist} &= \text{Regiment.} \\
\text{Verstand} &= \text{Rath} \\
\text{Gedächtniss} + \text{Geruch} &= \text{Inneres} + \text{Aeusseres.} \\
\text{Sprache} &= \text{Herrscher.}
\end{aligned}$$

See tables, 226–28. See Bluntschli's own statement as to how the work was received.—*Allgemeine Staatslehre*, I.

[3] *Allgemeine Staatslehre*, 6te Auflage, 1886, erster Theil, 18ff: "Der Staat ist keineswegs ein lebloses Instrument, nicht eine tote Maschine sondern ein lebendiges und daher organisches Wesen."

[4] *Ibid.*, 23: "Person, im rechtlichen Sinne, ist ein Wesen, dem wir einen Rechtwillen zuschreiben, welches Rechte erwerben, schaffen, haben kann."

[5] But the state is "kein Naturgeschöpf, und daher nicht ein natürlicher Organismus."—*Ibid.*, p. 18.

Under this conception, then, to whom belongs the sovereignty? Bluntschli expressly denies the sovereignty of the people (*Volks-souveränetät*), the sovereignty of the nation (*National-souveränetät*), the sovereignty of right or justice, and that of the monarch alone. The true sovereign is, he holds, "the State as a person."[1] Sovereignty is not something before, or outside, or above the State; it is the power and majesty of the State itself. It is the right of the whole; and, as certainly as the whole is stronger than any of its parts, so certainly the sovereignty of the whole State is superior to the sovereignty of any member of the State."[2] It is even admitted that, "if party disputes had not introduced confusion," the sovereignty of the State might be called the sovereignty of the "people," understanding by people "the politically organized whole."[3] Bluntschli does not, however, attempt to deny the sovereignty of the monarch as the head of the political organism. This he freely concedes, but as already indicated, places the whole organism above any of its parts and therefore the State above even its most effective organ.[4] There can be no peace, he says, between the sovereignty of the people and that of the Prince, but "between the sovereignty of the State and of the Prince there is the same harmony as between the whole man and his head."[5]

[1] *Ibid.*, 572: "Inwiefern der Staat als Person erscheint, insofern kommt ihm ohne Zweifel Unabhängigkeit, höchste Ehre, Machtfülle, oberste Autorität, Einheit, d. h. Souveränetät zu."

[2] *Ibid.*, 572: "So gewiss das Ganze mächtiger ist als irgend ein Theil des Ganzen, so gewiss ist auch die Souveränetät des ganzen Staates, der Souveränetät eines einzelnen Glieds im Staate überlegen." [3] *Ibid.*

[4] *Ibid.*, 575: "Ausser dieser dem ganzen Staats-oder Volkskörper selbst inwohnenden Souveränetät gibt es aber noch innerhalb des Staates eine Souveränetät des obersten Gliedes des Hauptes, die Regenten-oder, da sie in der Monarchie am klarsten hervortritt, die Fürstensouveränetät." See also 583–85.

[5] *Ibid.*, 576: "Die nämliche Harmonie wie zwischen dem ganzen Menschen und seinem Kopf."

By Bluntschli then the organic character of the State was emphasized in the meaning of natural science, though without neglecting the "spiritual" elements in the body politic. Nor was the personal nature of the State neglected. Yet on the whole, the impression left is that of the State as an organism like those whose existence natural science considers. The recognition of the sovereignty of the State was really won by an approach from another direction, that of juristic personality, rather than organic nature.[1]

On the other hand, the personality of the State and its claim to sovereignty were not left in undisputed possession of the field. As already seen, the great champion of the patrimonial theory, von Haller, refused to raise the State above the grade of a private society, in respect to either its essential nature or its purpose.[2] A similar doctrine was defended by Romeo Maurenbrecher, who argued the patrimonial cause with some ingenuity.[3] He denied that the State

---

[1] Compare an expounder of Krause, Ahrens, *Das Naturrecht, oder die Rechtsphilosophie* (2te Aufl., 1846–50); *Cours de droit naturel*, 1837, I, 199: "Die Lebenskraft der Souveränetät liegt in der Nation als Gesammtpersönlichkeit, gestaltet sich aber in besonderen Organen, bleibt jedoch die Macht." In *Cours de droit naturel*, II, 363, he defends the sovereignty of the nation in the organic sense. *Cf.* Fröbel, J., *System der Socialen Politik*, 2te Aufl., 1847, II, 2: "Der Staat ist die souveräne Gesellschaft," and *Ibid.*, p. 7: "Staat und Demokratie sind also gleichbedeutende Begriffe." See also Schäffle, A., *Bau und Leben des socialen Körpers*, 1875–78, I, 663–71; Rohmer, Th., *Lehre von den politischen Parteien*, 1846; *Deutschland's Beruf in der Gegenwart und Zukunft*, 1841.

[2] Karl Vollgraff, *Die Systeme der praktischen Politik*, 1828–29, declares that the Germanic-Slavic peoples have lost the characteristics necessary to constitute them into a state (III, 76): "um eine souveräne Nation wie Athener und Römer zu sein, muss man erst sittlich ein Staatsvolk, eine moralische Person sein, einen sittlichen Willen haben. Hier ist es die sittliche Staatsfähigkeit, welche souverän macht. Da aber diese Fähigkeit allen modernen Völkern abgeht, so sind sie auch nicht souverän." *Cf.* III, 80. He suggests the substitution of "*Stat*" for *Staat*. See sec. 160.

[3] *Die deutschen regierenden Fürsten und die Souveränetät*, 1839; *Grundsätze des deutschen Staatsrechts*, 1837.

could possess a "moral personality," but admitted that it might have a "juristic personality," though in this case the capacity would be limited to *private* rights only.¹ Yet even though he declares that sovereignty is something objective, something one may acquire, possess, lose, though he declares that it is, especially in German public law, a "pure personal right of the ruler,"² the influence of the new theory is apparent. He concedes that the monarch is an organic member ³ of the community, and in no way a being outside the State, or over it, or under it, or by the side of it, but by this concession. The real cause of contention is practically removed, and the patrimonial principle is given up. Maurenbrecher declares: "I hold the ruler bound to a constitutional exercise of the governing power, while I hold that he is the owner of the latter (*i. e.*, the governing power) as much as do those who concede the sovereignty, substantially to the State, but the exercise of it to the monarch as his private right."⁴ The distance between the theory of

¹ *Die d. reg. Fürsten,* 285. *Grundsätze,* sec. 58: "The people without the rulers forms no unity." He speaks of rights of the State as "those which the monarch possesses and acquires not for himself alone, but for himself and for the sum of all other members of the State in common," as domains and other State property (*Die d. r. F.,* 184); to be distinguished from the rights of the "people," which are held *against* the crown.

² "Etwas gegenständliches das man besitzen, erwerben und verlieren kann. Insbesondere fasst das deutsche Staatsrecht als das Privatrecht ihres Inhabers auf. . . Sie ist und bleibt vielmehr das reine personelle Recht des Regenten, s. g. jus privatissimum."—*Grundsätze,* sec. 145.

³ *Die d. r. F.,* 181 : "Nach dem patrimonialen Princip der Monarch nur im Staat steht, also seine Stellung nicht zum Staate, sondern innerhalb des Staates hat, er selbst *ist ein organisches Glied des Ganzen.*"

⁴ *Die d. r. Fürsten,* 176. Maurenbrecher argues for the sovereignty of the ruler from Article 57 of the Vienna Schluss Acte: "Since the German Union consists of sovereign rulers, the whole power of the state (Staatsgewalt) must in consequence of the principles herein contained, remain united in the head of the state." See p. 81 ff.

popular sovereignty and that of patrimonial is being rapidly reduced, but is not yet completely covered.[1]

On other than patrimonial principles the sovereignty of the State is denied by another group of thinkers. Here the Hegelian distinction between internal and external sovereignty appears, as also that between the power of the State in the abstract and in the concrete. It is admitted at the outset that the State possesses a personality, and that as one among many States it may rightly be regarded as sovereign; that is to say in international law it is to be regarded as independent and self-sufficient, a sovereign community.[2] But waiving the question of international relations, the proposition that the State is sovereign cannot be conceded.[3] France might be termed a sovereign power in respect to England or Russia, but not in the public law of that State taken by itself. The essence of the State, considered apart from other States, is the relation between the ruler and the ruled. There must be those who govern and

---

[1] It is admitted that the people (Volk) are the real holders of the supreme power in a Republic. See 45, *Grundsätze*. Compare Thilo, *Die Volkssouveränetät in ihrer wahren Gestalt* (1833). There are two wills in the state, the monarch's will (Fürstenwille) and the people's will (Volkswille). The mingling of these two wills is the state-will (Staatswille).—*Ibid.*, p. 156.

[2] Zoepfl, *Grundsätze des gemeinen Deutschen Staatsrechts*, 5th ed., 1863, I, 98. Sylvester Jordan, *Versuche über allgemeines Staatsrecht*, 1828, calls the independence of a state from all others its sovereignty (234), the power of the ruler, Staatsgewalt or Machtvollkommenheit. "The sovereignty of the state belongs to the ruler and the people together, since both in the eye of international law constitute only one unity, only one moral person" (237). Weiss, K. E., *System des deutschen Staatsrechts*, 1843, 453, distinguishes between Volk in international and national sense. *Cf.* F. A. Schilling, *Lehrbuch des Naturrechts*, 1850–63, Pt. II, 56 ff.: Sovereignty of state is correct only "für die Verhältnisse eines Staats nach aussen hin."

[3] The question of sovereignty from the international side will be discussed in the later chapters on the theories of sovereignty which grew up out of the controversy over the nature of the "federal state." So far as possible the present chapter is confined to the internal side of sovereignty.

those who are governed, those who command and those who obey. Without this condition and these classes, the State would be impossible. The supreme power, therefore, belongs not to the ruler and the ruled, but to the individual or class whose function it is to command. The ruler is sovereign, not those who are ruled. "Sovereignty" (*Staatsgewalt*), says Zoepfl, is, objectively considered, the sum of the governmental rights, or regalia belonging to the ruler, as such; subjectively, ... it appears as the condition in which one possesses the right to rule in a definite territory, and consequently as the right of the ruler in the sense in which every possession over which no higher can be conceived, operates as a right. In this latter relation the power of the State (*Staatsgewalt*) is called preferably, sovereignty, suprema potestas."[1] As the right to rule, then, sovereignty belongs, not to those who are to obey, but to the governmental, the ruling, power. Sovereignty is, in other words, regarded as a force, not of the State, and therefore to be attributed to the State *as a whole*, but as a force or relation *in* the State, and hence the attribute of the ruling power[2] in the State. Prussia, for example, might be sovereign in respect to England and France, but internally, not the State, Prussia, but the ruling power, the king, is sovereign. In the ruler alone the idea of government, command, authority, which is inherent in the idea of a political society, finds concrete form, Aside from him, there is no bearer or holder of

---

[1] *Grundsätze*, I, 83.

[2] *Grundsätze*, I, 98. Schleiermacher, F., (*Die Lehre vom Staate*, Werke, III, 8: Ueber die Begriffe der verschiedenen Staatsformen, 1814), emphasized the relation between ruler and ruled as the essence of the state. *Cf.* p. 21: "Staat ist wo Gegensatz von Obrigkeit und Unterthan ist." *Ibid.*, p. 13: The state is really neither the ruler nor the ruled, but the *relation* between them. At the same time he treats the state as a "Naturerzeugniss, φύσις," and proposes to consider it as an organism.—*Ibid.*, p. 2.

the supreme power.¹ Against him, the State has no other organ through which to act,² With this later school, the theory of the sovereignty of the State seemed deficient in that it ascribed a share in the sovereign power to that part of the State which must necessarily be ruled. The existence of a State, it was argued, implied the existence of a ruling class and a ruled class. Now only the rulers, the governors, can properly be regarded as bearers of the supreme power, for to say that the governed share in the sovereignty would be manifestly contradictory. One cannot rule and be ruled, cannot be both sovereign and subject.³ Therefore, the State, which includes both governor and governed, cannot be made the holder of the sovereignty; but this must be attributed to a particular part of it, namely, that which rules or governs.⁴

Attention has been called to the sovereignty of the State

---

[1] "Der Staatsherrscher ist also das Subjekt in welchem der in der Staatsgewalt liegende Gedanke der Herrschaft personificirt, d. h., äusserlich erkennbar und handlungsfähig dargestellt wird."—Zœpfl, *Grundsätze*, I, 97.

[2] *Ibid.* Zœpfl declares (I, 108) that "between the so-called rights of the State and the rights of the state ruler there is never any essential difference." Compare Jordan, *Allgemeines Staatsrecht*, 235: "In staatsrechtlicher Hinsicht —der Regent (summus imperius, rex) Souverän genannt wird." The people are only the supports (Stütze) of the sovereignty—*Ibid.*, 237. Stahl, *loc. cit. Cf. Das monarchische Princip.*, 1845; Schmitthenner, *Grundlinien*, 268.

[3] This, was, however, precisely the proposition upon which Rousseau's system rested. "Chaque individu, contractant pour ainsi dire avec lui-même, se trouve engagé, sous un double rapport; savoir, comme membre du souverain envers les particuliers, et comme membre de l'état envers le souverain."—*Ibid.*, I, 7.

[4] See Zœpfl, *loc. cit.* Compare Weiss, K. E., *System des deutschen Staatsrechts*, 1843, 455, 511; Schilling, F. A., *Lehrbuch*, II, 192. The sovereignty cannot belong to the state, but may fall to a monarch, an aristocracy, or a democracy.—*Ibid.*, II, 59. Compare the more recent argument by Max Seydel, *Grundzüge einer allgemeinen Staatslehre*, 1873, 4. He denies that the state is either organism or personality. "Staat und Herrscher sind so zweierlei wie Eigenthum und Eigenthümer." The will of the governor is a will *over* the state, not *of* the state. See also Bornhak, *Preussisches Staatsrecht*, I, 63 ff.

as developed first out of the philosophy of Schelling and his school, and second from the natural-science point of view assumed by Bluntschli.[1] It now remains to show the development of the theory of State sovereignty from the side of the more strictly *juristic* personality of the State. It is perhaps needless to say that the various view points were not always so clearly distinguished as in even the rough classification here given.

Not until the ideas of the organic and personal nature of the State were somewhat sharpened and the field limited to that of juristic usage was the conception of the State as sovereign able to make wide conquests.

The nature of legal or juristic personality, that is, the capacity to bear legal rights and duties, has been, during the present century, the subject of an animated discussion among German jurists. Two great parties have long divided the authorities on jurisprudence in general, the so-called Romanists and the Germans;[2] one following closely the paths marked out in the Roman law, the other emphasizing the importance and value of the elements contained in the native law of the German States. The Roman school, the first to

---

[1] In addition to the literature already cited the following works are of service: Otto Gierke, *Johannes Althusius*, for the earlier period (to 1800); *Das deutsche Genossenschaftsrecht*, 3 vols., 63–81; *Die Genossenschaftsrechtheorie*, 1887; *Deutsches Privatrecht*, I, 1895; J. K. Bluntschli, *Die neueren Rechtsschulen der deutschen Juristen*, 1839; H. Preuss in *Archiv für Offentliches Recht*, II., on *Die Persönlichkeit des Staates*; also, *Gemeinde, Staat, Reich*, 1889; Bernatzik, *Kritische Studien über den Begriff der juristichen Persönlichkeit der Behörden insbesondere*, 1890, in *Archiv für öffentliches Recht*, V.; Zitelmann, Ernst, *Begriff und Wesen der sogenannten juristichen Personen*, 1873; Krieken, A. T. v., *Uber die sogennante organische Staatstheorie*, 1873. Rehm, H., *Allgemeine Staatslehre*, 1899; Jellinek, G., *System der subjektiven öffentlichen Rechte*, 1892; Jos. Held, *Staat und Gesellschaft*, '61–'65.

[2] *Cf.* Bluntschli, *Die neueren Rechtschulen*, especially ch. vi, *Der Streit der deutschen und der romanisirenden Schule*; Bierling, *Zur Kritik der juristichen Grundbegriffe*.

feel the inspiration of the historical method, filled with distrust of the speculative spirit as exemplified in the results reached by the Naturrecht-theorists, refused to recognize the real and actual personality of the State. But the historic method did not lead to the exclusive acceptation of any one system of law, however well adapted to the needs of the people for whom and by whom framed. Attention was consequently turned to the development of the native, as well as the adopted, principles of law. Thus arose the German school. In general, this party, resting upon the earlier German notions, declared in favor of the real personality of the corporation, and against the "personification" theory. The discussion was in great part confined to the field of private law, but in so far as it involved the concepts of public law must be here noticed.

What then, was the Roman idea of juristic personality, especially that attributed to the State? Among the Romans, the State, as a whole, never appeared as a distinct personality, but was always the sum of the Roman citizens (populus Romanus) *en masse* or later the emperor. Such it was originally, and such the concept continued to be.[1] It was only in the later period that the *fiscus*, the treasury of the State, was personified, and became a subject of legal rights and duties.[2] The State was a person, as the Roman conceived it, but with a two-fold limitation—first, that it became such only by virtue of a fiction; secondly, that its legal personality was limited to those cases involving the property relations of the community as a whole.[3] This fiction theory

[1] This is the position taken by Gierke in his *Das deutsche Genossenschaftsrecht*, III, 43.

[2] Gierke holds that "persona" was never applied to the state.

[3] The people had first the ærarium; later, the Senate the ærarium, and the Princeps the fiscus; later the two were blended in the fiscus, which was, however, distinct from the private property of the ruler (res privata Principis). Savigny, II, sec. 88.

survived in that of the natural-right school, and the "fiscus" was always a troublesome factor in the public law of the monarchical State.

It was this Roman form of personification theory which was held by the great leader of the historical school, Savigny. There are two classes of persons, he declared, the natural and the artificial; the natural person, and the only natural person, is the individual man; the artificial person is something outside of the individual, but possessing the capacity to hold legal rights and duties.[1] The artificial person might be a "foundation," a corporation, a community, a city, a State. "The greatest and most important of all juristic persons, says Savigny, "is the fiscus, that is, the State itself, conceived as the subject of private law relations."[2] To the State there is accorded then only a fictitious personality, of a different grade from that which is recognized as belonging to the endowment or corporation.

Savigny was followed by Puchta,[3] Brinz,[4] Windscheid,[5] who defended the same proposition as to the real or actual

---

[1] *System d. h. römischen Rechts*, II, 60: "Ich gebrauche dafür lediglich den Namen der juristischen Person (welcher dann die natürliche Person, das heisst der einzelne Mensch entgegengesetzt ist), um auszudrücken dass sie *nur durch juristischen Zweck* ein Dasein als Person hat."—Sec. 85. Savigny objects to the use of the term "moral person" in this connection.

[2] *System*, II, sec. 86.

[3] See *Zitelmann, loc. cit.;* Puchta, *Vorlesungen*, 1847, I, sec. 25–27.

[4] Brinz, *Lehrbuch der Pandekten* (Here 2te Auf., 1873), I, sec. 60.

[5] Windscheid, B., *Lehrbuch des Pandektenrechts*, 1862 (here 7th ed., 1891), sec. 57: "Die s. g. juristischen Personen sind persönlich gedachte Nichtpersonen; dass sie als Personen gedacht werden, beruht auf einem dem Menschennatur inwohnenden Zuge." Böhlau, Hugo, *Rechtssubjekt und Personenrolle*, I, 1872, 22, holds that "not juristic," or "fictitious" but *the role of a person* (Personenrolle), is the correct contrast to the so-called physical person, that is the person absolutely." Mohl, R., *Encyklopädie* (2te Aufl.), 71, denominates the state an organism, but not in the sense of natural science, *Cf.* p. 41: "Die Vergleichung des Staats und seiner Anstalten aber mit dem Organismus des menschlichen Körpers und seinen Bestandtheilen ist eine blosse Spielerei."

existence of the juristic person. Much of the controversy had a bearing upon private law only, but its influence was soon felt in the field of public law as well. If the State were only an artificial personality, then the tendency was as in the preceding century and centuries, toward the recognition of the king or the government as the real and visible representative of something in itself invisible, and unreal.[1] The earliest and the most successful defenders of the sovereignty of the State were those who regarded it as a real and natural existence, not as a purely artificial construction of jurisprudence.

It is now in order to follow the development of the new theory of the real juristic personality and with it the sovereignty of the State. The proposition, that the State is a juristic person, a real person and a sovereign person, was early defended by Karl Göschel,[2] of the religious reactionary school (1835). The State has juristic personality, he maintains, in that it has a will, enabling it to become, as a whole, the bearer of rights and duties.[3] The State, the juristic person, is also sovereign, though it is pointed out, using the organic analogy, that no one member is either wholly subject

---

[1] The controversy was long, and involved a great variety of problems. It is referred to here only so far as necessary to show the nature of the forces operating to develop the various theories of sovereignty.

[2] *Zerstreute Blätter*, Band II, *Politische Glossen*. Gierke, O., *Genossenschaftsrecht*, refers to B. I, but not to B. II, which states the idea much more strongly, and moreover strikingly supports Gierke's own fundamental theory. "Als integrirender Körper ist der Staat so wenig ein unwirklicher Begriff oder Phantom dass er vielmehr überall seine Realität beweist. Jedes Blatt in der Geschichte handelt von Staaten als lebendigen, vielgegliederten Einheten."—*Ibid.*, 114.

[3] "Dem Staate kommt die juristische Persönlichkeit so gewiss zu, als seine Glieder, den in ihrem Kreise geltenden und von da aus auf das Ganze einwirkenden Willen unbeschadet, zugleich ein Wille verbindet, der mehr und mehr allen eigen wird, 'quasi contraxissent'; erst durch diese Einheit wird die Vielheit zur Totalität, welcher Rechte und Pflichten zukommen."—*Ibid.*, II, 114. In B. I, the State is termed a "moral person."

or wholly sovereign, as no part of an organism is always a merely passive subject, but both acts and is acted upon. Personality, he says, consists essentially in active and passive exercise of will, in right as well as in obligation. The State, therefore, the organism, the person, has sovereignty over the body, as the head is sovereign over the body but as the head is not the whole body, but only its chief organ,[1] so the State is only the highest of organs.

The juristic idea was again advanced by E. Albrecht (1837), in a review of Maurenbrecher, the defender of the patrimonial theory.[2] He exalted the State as an institution "which stands above the individual, which has a purpose in no way merely the sum of the individual interests of the ruler and the subjects, but which constitutes a higher common interest."[3] In so far, then, as there exist these higher interests to which no individual person can lay claim, in so far must we here attribute to the State itself a personality, in the juristic sense.[4] A distinct exposition of the new doctrine was first made by Beseler in the *System of German Common-private Law*, 1847.[5] By person is now understood "whatever is a subject of rights.[6] First among these rights is the time-honored privilege of holding property, long accorded to the State, but it is by no means limited now to this narrow field. Pre-eminent among juristic persons formerly termed moral or mystical persons is the State, "which brings together the people in an organized unity."[7] This he holds

---

[1] Göschel, *op. cit.*, II, 121.

[2] *Göttingsche gelehrte Anzeigen*, II (1837).   [3] *Ibid.*, 1492.

[4] *Ibid.:* "Die Persönlichkeit, die in diesem Gebiet herrscht, handelt, Rechte hat, dem Staate selbst zuzuschreiben, diesem daher als juristische Person zu denken." But the right of the monarch to exercise the power of the State is his private right (1513).

[5] *System des gemeinen deutschen Privatrechts*, 1847. See also *Volksrecht und Juristenrechte, 1843; Erbenverträge, 1835.*

[6] *Ibid.*, sec. 56.   [7] *Ibid.*, sec. 56.

is particularly clear from the side of international relations, but is also true when viewed from that of purely internal affairs.

The juristic idea failed, however, to make rapid progress, until the constitutional changes after 1848 had made evident the necessity for a new interpretation of sovereignty in its relation to monarchy. Most influential in determining the new course of the theory was C. F. von Gerber.[1] While it may be true, he says, that the State is an organism,[2] as jurist, one is primarily concerned with its legal character and status. Considered from this point of view, the State appears to him as "the highest juristic personality which the legal order knows; its capacity to will has the richest equipment which the law (*Recht*) can give. The power of the State to will is the power to rule; it is called sovereignty (*Staatsgewalt*)."[3] The personality of the State, it is argued, is a presumption necessary to any theory of public law; without it no scientific system is possible.[4] This will of the State is, moreover, not a fiction, but something existing in and for itself, a true reality. Again, it is not a mere abstraction, having no existence except in so far as embodied in a monarch or ruler, but is to be found in the whole "constitution of the State with all its institutions."[5] The State

[1] *Grundzüge eines Systems des deutschen Staatsrechts*, 1865. Compare the earlier work *Ueber öffentliches Recht*, 1852.

[2] "D. h. eine Gliederung, welche jedem Theile seine eigenthümliche Stellung zur Mitwirkung für den Gesammtzweck anweist."—Beilage I to 2te Auflage, 1869. See also Beilage II, *Die Persönlichkeit des Staates*.

[3] "Die höchste rechtliche Persönlichkeit welche die Rechtsordnung kennt; ihre Willensfähigkeit hat die reichste Ausstattung erfahren, welche das Recht zu geben vermag. Die Willensmacht des Staates ist die Macht zu herrschen, sie heisst Staatsgewalt."—*Ibid.*, sec. 1.

[4] *Ibid.*, sec. 1, 2.

[5] Sec. 7: "Sie ist auch nicht bloss eine geistige Substanz welche auf die Entschlüsse des Monarchen bestimmend einwirkt, sondern die ganze Staatsverfassung mit allen ihren Institutionen ist darauf berechnet."

itself is declared to be the sovereign. The monarch has the right to represent the community, to exercise its political power, but does not, as Maurenbrecher maintained, constitute the State nor possess its full power—the sovereignty. Accepting neither the claim that the monarch is merely an officer, nor the proposition that the supreme power is his personal, private right, Gerber maintains that in monarchy is incorporated the supreme power of the State, but that the king holds this authority only as an organ of the State.[1] The will of the ruler has force only so long as he remains within the limits set by the constitution.[2]

The classic presentation, however, of the theory of the sovereignty of the State, conceived as an organism, and as a really existing juristic person, has been made by Otto Gierke. The works in which his theory has been developed are the historical treatise on *The German Association Law* 1868–81; *The Fundamental Concepts of Public Law*, 1874; *The Theory of Association Law*, 1887.[3] The problem was approached by Gierke from the side of the German, rather than the Roman legal ideas. In an elaborate investigation

---

[1] "Das Monarchenrecht ist hiernach ein Recht der Organschaft für den Staat." —*Ibid.*, sec. 7. "Es setzt die Existenz des Staates voraus, hat in ihm seine Stätte." *Cf.*, also sec. 25. Gerber says in sec. 28: "the territorial-ruler (Landesherr) has exchanged his former position as a bearer of rights (Rechtssubject) outside the people (Volk) for the position of the highest organ of will (Willensorgan) *in* it (the people)." See Gerber's use of the term Sovereignty as an attribute of the whole state power (Staatsgewalt).—*Ibid.*, sec. 7.

[2] See Joseph Held, *Systeme des Verfassungsrechts der monarchischen Staaten Deutschlands mit besonderer Rücksicht auf den Constitutionalismus*, 1856. *Staat und Gesellschaft*, 3 vols., 1861–'65, with extended observations and elaborate bibliography on sovereignty. See esp. B. I, II, 512, 516, 521, 535.

[3] *Das deutsche Genossenschaftsrecht*, 3 vols., 1868, 73, 81; *Die Grundbegriffe des Staatsrechts und die neuesten Staatsrechtstheorien;* in the *Zeitschrift für die gesammte Staatswissenschaft*, XXX, 1874; *Die Genossenschaftstheorie und die deutsche Rechtssprechung*, 1887. Compare also *Johannes Althusius*, and *Deutsches Privatrecht*, I.

of the development of the native German law of association or society law (Genossenschaftsrecht), he obtained a mass of material with which to build, and as a result of his labors, drew conclusions as to the nature of the State and of public law often directly opposed to those deduced from the body of the Roman Law.[1] His theory is based throughout upon the German idea of *association law*, combined with the modern theory of organic development and evolution.

Gierke lays down as a fundamental proposition the historically established fact that " man everywhere and at all times has borne a double character, that of an individual as such and that of a member of a community (*Gattungsverband*)."[2] This fundamental social fact the Romans overlooked in their theory, and as they were never able to conceive of man in a double character, the person was consequently regarded as absolute and indivisible. They had the absolute State on the one hand, the absolute individual on the other. The State was unlimited in the field of public law, the individual in that of private; but there was no series of associations connecting the State and the individual.[3] The Romans formed no association of any kind, except in a fictitious sense, because they could not think of the formation of a new person from a number of personalities as its constituent elements. Their State was not a person, differing from the sum of the individuals who formed it, but the mass of the Roman people, considered as a sum of citizens, whose total constituted the body politic. Their juristic persons, so-called, were

---

[1] Compare O. Bähr, *Der Rechtstaat*, 1864, 32, also 45: "Der Staat ist der juristisch entwickelte Begriff für die Genossenschaft der Nation, und Staatsrecht ist nichts anders, als eine Art des Genossenschaftsrechts."

[2] "Der Mensch überall und zu allen Zeiten die Doppeleigenschaft an sich trug ein Individuum für sich und Glied eines Gattungsverbandes zu sein."—*Grundbegriffe*, 301.

[3] *Genossenschaftsrecht*, III, 36 ff.

never real, but only acted in place of, played the role of, a person. On the other hand, the German idea of the nature of personality is, Gierke explains, wholly different. In contrast to the Roman notion, personality is considered as, in the first place, not absolute, but wholly *relative*; secondly, as *capable of division;* and lastly, as *delegable*.[1]

With the acceptance of this theory, comes the possibility of the real existence of an association as distinguished from the sum of its members. Its basis is no longer necessarily a fiction, a supposition, an hypothesis, but the result of a combination of portions, so to speak, of the personalities of its various members (*Willensplitter*).[2] All true "collective-persons" (*Gesammtpersonen*), it is urged, are produced in this way. The many really become one, not in the purely artificial sense of the Roman law, or of the contract theory, but in the sense that a new and different person has actually been created out of what might be called the "social element" of its constituent members. A State may contain for example a million citizens, yet it is not the sum of these million persons, but a new person formed from the social element, the "universal" side of the million individuals. The new personality is, nevertheless, as real and as actual, as little a fiction, as the personality of any one of its citizens. As Gierke says: "The more we conceive of the organism of the individual socially, the more easy it becomes to explain the society organically."[3] With Gierke, the State and the individual are not the only persons, but between them is a long chain of unions and associations of various kinds, all shaped from what we have called the social element or

---

[1] *Genossenschaftsrecht*, II, 36–37.

[2] *Ibid., II, 36–7.*

[3] "Je mehr sie den Organismus des Individuums gesellschaftlich auffasst, um so leichter das gesellschaftliche Gemeinwesen organisch erklären."—*Grundbegriffe*, 286.

material found in every individual. Thus there is the private corporation, the city, the commune, and "out of this chain of personalities the State does not come."[1]

The State is distinguished from all other persons, however, through its possession of power in a superior degree. It is limited by no like power above it, and is superior to that of all other classes of collective persons.[2] "A will corresponding to such power is distinguished from every other, as a *sovereign will*, absolutely universal, determined only through itself." The essential element of the State is, then, the supreme or sovereign power, the characteristic which marks it out from every other person, individual or collective. The sovereignty is, moreover, not only *in* the State, but it is also *of* the State; the organism, the personality, as a whole is supreme, not any one of its members.

This political condition and theory, Gierke points out, has been the result of a long and tedious development.[3] At first the personality of the State was identified with that of the ruler, and the State was only latent in the king. In the city State and in the feudal State (*Landestaat*), the idea of the community, as something apart from the government, first grew up. Out of the feudal State came the absolute State, as in France, in which "State" was identical with "authority" (*Staatsobrigkeit*). Here was emphasized the unity of the State, but not its community (the "einheitlich" but not the "gemeinheitlich" side). Finally, came the modern constitutional State (*Rechtsstaat*, but not the Kantian *Rechtsstaat*) in which the State appears as something outside of its govern-

---

[1] "Aus der Kette der Personen tritt in allen diesen Beziehungen selbst die intensiv und extensiv höchste Persönlichkeit, selbst der Staat nicht hieraus." *Genossenschaftsrecht*, II, 41.

[2] "Dessen Macht nach oben hin durch keine ähnliche Macht beschränkt und nach unter hin jeder ähnlichen Macht überlegen ist."—*Grundbegriffe*, 304. See also *Genossenschaftsrecht*, II, 831.   [3] *Ibid.*, II, 831 ff.

ment, as something above even its highest organ. The monarch, says Gierke, is now not the only expression of the State, as in earlier times, nor is he absolute, as in the later period; he has become the chief organ of the State. One may call this privileged position of the ruler "monarchical sovereignty," but it is not to be forgotten that it is a superiority, not over the State as a whole, nor against right in the abstract, but merely against the other limbs or members of the State.[1]

The germ found in the theory of Grotius thus finds its full development in the theory of Gierke. The State has become a living reality, a juristic person in the strongest sense of the term, with no trace of fiction in its ancestry. Moreover, this legal person, this organism, has become as a whole the bearer of the supreme power, the *subjectum commune* of Grotius; while the monarch is the *subjectum proprium* of which Grotius spoke. The State is not swallowed up in the government, nor is the government rendered wholly subordinate, as with Rousseau, to the will of the artificially united people,[2] but there is given recognition both to the organism as a whole and to its special or particular organs.

Among the many supporters of the sovereignty of the State, both the conception of organism and that of person have been frequently employed. Some have declared for the one, some for the other, some for both. Thus Fricker earnestly protested against the application of the idea of juristic personality to the State, declaring that a recognition of its organic character alone is amply sufficient.[3]

---

[1] " So ist dagegen nichts zu erinnern, wenn man nur daran festhält, dass diese Souveränetät (soweit sie nicht überhaupt blos Repräsentanz der Staatsouveränetät) weder dem Staat noch dem Recht, sondern lediglich den übrigen Staatsgliedern gegenüber begründet ist."—*Grundbegriffe*, 326.

[2] *Cf.* Gierke's criticism of Grotius and the whole "Naturrecht" school in his *Johannes Althusius.*

[3] *Zeitschrift für d. ges. Staatsw.*, 1869, 36.

But on the other hand, Krieken favored the recognition of the juristic personality of the State, and saw nothing useful in the conception of organism.[1] On the whole, it is probably true that the idea of the State as a juristic personality appealed most strongly to the publicists, and was most effectual in bringing about the recognition of the sovereignty of the State. The community as a whole may be recognized as a possible or actual bearer of legal rights and duties, that is to say, as a juristic person, without reference to its organic nature, and without reference to its moral or ethical personality. For juristic purposes, the State is held as much a person as any other bearer of rights and duties. The organic idea appears clearly, however, when it is maintained that this personality is real and actual, and in no sense of the term hypothetical or fictitious.[2] After all, the answer to the question whether the State is sovereign, as a juristic person, or as an organism, or whether it should be regarded as both, was not very clearly given. There seemed to be a connection between the organic and the personal idea, but it was more often tacitly accepted than carefully explained.[3]

---

[1] A. T. v. Krieken, *Ueber die sogenannte organische Staatstheorie*, 1873, 135.

[2] Into the more recent discussion over the nature of the state this discussion does not go. The purpose is to bring the discussion down to the point where the juristic personality of the state and its sovereignty are united.

[3] With the supporters of the sovereignty of the State are Hermann Schulze, *System des deutschen Staatsrechts*, 1865; Adolph Lasson, *Princip und Zukunft des Völkerrechts*, 1871, who holds (p. 124) that "the State is a person in full earnest. It is as much a person as any living, growing man." "The state is not a fiction, but merely an *abstraction*, as is person in general."—*Ibid.*, 129. "The recognition of the state as a *moral* person is necessary to the overthrow of the theory of popular sovereignty."—*Ibid.*, 139. *Cf.* Lorenz v. Stein, *Verwaltungslehre*, 1864, (2nd ed., 1869), I, 5: "Der Staat ist eine – die höchste materielle— Form der Persönlichkeit." "The legislature is the will of the personality, the ruler its "I" the administration its action."—*Ibid.*, I, 9. See also Zachariä, H. A., *Deutsches Staats-und Bundesrecht*, 1841 (3rd ed., 1865–67), I, sec. 50: "Grund

und Quelle der Gewalt ist und bleibt der Staat, als dessen Repräsentant der Herrscher fungirt;" "Nur das organische Gemeinwesen selbst (die Anstalt des Staates) die Quelle aller öffentlichen Macht sei."—*Ibid.*, see 68. *Cf.* Grotefend, G. A., *Politische Skizzen*, 1866, 43: "Wenn daher der 'Constitutionalismus' nichts ist, als die Anerkennung der Persönlichkeit des Staates und die Darstellung desselben als eines zu bestimmten Daseinszwecke organisch gefestigten Ganzen," *etc.;* Waitz, Geo., *Grundzüge*, 1862. Beilage, II. Das Königthum und die verfassungs-mässige Ordnung, 129–152.

CHAPTER VII

POPULAR AND STATE SOVEREIGNTY (CONTINUED)

It is now necessary to observe more closely the nature of the sovereignty, the location of which was the centre of so much discussion during this period. At the opening of the century an impetus toward a stronger conception of sovereignty was given in the Rheinbund Act of 1806, which recognized the "plénitude de la souveraineté"[1] to certain states which had up to this time possessed only the so-called *Landshoheit* nominally at least under the sovereignty of the Emperor. The rights included under sovereignty were mentioned in the Act as legislation, supreme jurisdiction, police power, conscription, and the taxing power.[2] By the newly created states their *souveraineté* was interpreted in the broadest sense of the term, externally and internally, as indicated by the almost immediate alterations made in their fundamental laws. The old "estates" were brushed aside, as in Bavaria, Wurtemberg, Hesse; and constitutions granted, as in Westphalia, 1807, and Bavaria, 1808.[3] The rulers also gave up the former feudal rights held by one in the territory of another, so far at least as relations of public law were concerned. The new sovereignty proved to be also a barrier

---

[1] See G. Meyer, *Staatsrecht*, sec. 36.

[2] Rhein-Bund-Acte, Art. 26–27. "Législation, juridiction suprême, haute police, conscription militaire ou recrutement et impôt" were the "droits essentielement inhérens à la souveraineté." The "mediatized" territories retained their "proprieté patrimoniale et priveé," and their "droits seigneuriaux et féodaux." —*Ibid.*, sec. 27.

[3] Meyer, sec. 36.

against the formation of a close union between the German States in 1814–15, and for some time after.

At this point must be distinguished several uses of the term "sovereignty," the interchanging of which often led to serious confusion, and gave rise to not a little of the current difference of opinion.[1] First, then, by sovereignty was sometimes understood, independence from all other states, international self-sufficiency, sovereignty in the meaning of international law. In this sense, as has already been shown, state sovereignty or even popular sovereignty could be conceded without very much difficulty, and was in fact generally admitted. The people of France, the state as a whole, including ruler and ruled, was recognized as internationally sovereign.

But by sovereignty might also be understood the whole power of the state, the whole force belonging to the political association as such, the might and power of the political community. This is the field upon which the early defenders of popular sovereignty had fought many a battle, and on which the organic theory again waged war. The political power of the state, they held, must be generated by the people as a whole, and not by any individual whose property the state is.

[1] *Cf.* Klüber, *Oeffentliches Recht des teutschen Bundes*, 1817 (1826), 76; Schmitthenner *Grundlinien*, 284. The Germans had at first no word corresponding to sovereignty. *Obergewalt* and *Landeshoheit* signified rather a position of superiority only; *Staatsgewalt* denoted the force of the state, its whole power; *Majestät* the dignity of the State; *Machtvollkommenheit* seemed to denote "plenitudo potestatis" in a somewhat absolute sense; *Souveränetät* at first signified sometimes merely an attribute of the *Staatsgewalt*, but later took the place of the other general terms and now corresponds to the English *sovereignty*, or French *souveraineté*." Compare G. H. von Berg, *Abhandlungen zur Erläuterung des rheinischen Bundesacte*, 1808 (Erster Theil), 286: "In der Freiheit von höherer Gewalt und äusserem Zwang besteht das eigenthümliche der Souveränetät, und wo diese gefunden wird ist der Fürst, er sei auch durch die Verfassung noch so sehr eingeschränkt, wahrer Souverän." K. E. Schmidt, *Lehrbuch des gemeinen deutschen Staatsrechts*, 1821, sec. 40, compares the international independence of the state to the *majestas realis;* the predominant position of the government within the state to the *majestas personalis*.

Again, sovereignty might signify neither international independence, nor the whole power of the state, but have reference to the relation between the ruling organ in the state and the other members, the relation of the king, for example, to the rest of the state. In this sense one spoke of the sovereignty of the ruler or the monarch in contrast to the sovereignty of the people. The underived right to hold the supreme place, to represent the state, to exercise the highest political power, was in this connection termed sovereignty. The king was in this sense sovereign, not because he held all state power, but because he held the highest place among the bearers of power.

One of the most difficult problems of the time was the differentiation of these last two senses in which sovereignty was used, namely, as the whole power of the State and as the highest among the powers. The task was accomplished, however, before the constitutional position of the monarch could be satisfactorily explained.[1]

The whole power of the State (*Staatsgewalt*) was as a rule regarded as a unit. The doctrine of the division of governmental powers was commonly accepted in some form or other, but this was not regarded as in any way equivalent to the creation of new and independent powers. All were contained in the unity of the State, which included all the various classes of political powers. Practically they might be many, but ideally they were one. The king and the legislature might exercise different functions, but the idea was not prevalent that the sovereignty was on this account divided between the different bearers or holders of the power. The essential unity of the supreme power had been conceded in the theory of Kant in dialectic form of

[1] The nature of the sovereignty of the state among states will not be considered here, as it will appear more clearly in the later discussion of the theory centering around the "Federal State."

major premise, minor premise and conclusion. Likewise, under the organic conception the respective functions could readily be allotted to the different organs, legislative, administrative, judicial, without interfering at all with the fundamental organic unity of the sovereign power.[1]

Moreover, the power of the State was regarded as limited in some way or other. The sovereignty was unified, irresistible, sacred, irresponsible, but it was not left wholly without restraint.[2] The most common limitation advanced was that arising out of the essential nature of the State. The sovereignty of the State arises from the fact that it has duties which it must perform, and for the fulfillment of which supreme power is required. Beyond this, however, the sovereignty does not go, or should not go, must transgress its "natural" or ideal limits if it does go. Thus the State might be restricted to the maintenance of law among men in the sense of the Kantian legal-state (*Rechtsstaat*), or it might be regarded, with Stahl, as an institution for the development of moral qualities (*Sittlichkeit*), or for the development of all the higher qualities of human nature (*Cultur-Staat*).[3]

If the limitation were by the purpose of the state, the field would accordingly be expanded or contracted as the idea of the state varied. The sovereign power was by no means

---

[1] Jordan, *Versuche*, 76, on Kantian grounds; Zachariä, K. S., *Vierzig Bücher*, B. III, 89; Maurenbrecher, *Grundsätze*, sec. 30 who terms it independent, irresistible, irresponsible, inappellable, infallible, sacred, eternal. Zachariä, H., *Staatsrecht*, I, 69, gives a like series of attributes. See also Zoepfl, *Grundsätze* sec. 88; Held, *System*, sec. 138; Mohl, *Encyklopädie* (2te Aufl.), 118–19, who uses the terms absolute, indivisible, eternal, all-inclusive. Ancillon, *Ueber Sou, veränetät*, 19, admits the divisibility of sovereignty.

[2] Metternich complained at the Vienna Congress that " in recent times despotic rights, such as one could not demand, had been confused with the term 'rights of sovereignty.'"—Klüber, *Uebersicht*, I, 258.

[3] *Cf.* Holtzendorff, *Prinzipien der Politik.*

conceived as extending over all fields of activity at will. From all sides the limitation of the supreme power was advanced as an essential characteristic of such an authority. These limitations were however ideal rather than actual.[1]

Again, sovereignty was declared to be a specific mark of the State, a necessary and indispensable attribute. There could be no State which was not a sovereign State. This idea was emphasized and reëmphasized from the earlier years of the century down to the beginning of the strife over the Bundesstaat. Ancillon[2] said that the " essence of every political association consisted in the sovereignty." Waitz[3] held that " every true State must be a sovereign State;" Held[4] maintained that sovereignty denotes the specific, free, inde-

---

[1] Ancillon, *Aphorismen*, 40: the rights of the state arise out of its obligations. Zachariä, K. S., *Vierzig Bücher*, I, 121: sovereignty is the idea of the Absolute applied to human relations, but " ein Gott müsste es sein, welcher über die Menschen herrschte, wenn der Staat in der Wirklichkeit mit dem Staate in der Idee vollkommen entsprechen sollte." *Cf.* Zoepfl, I, 93: " Die natürlichen Gränzen der Staatsgewalt sind ihre Pflichten;" Schmitthenner, *Grundlinien*, 287; Held, *System*, sec. 126: " Ihre natürliche Schranke findet sie schon darin, dass sie eine irdische Macht und darin dass ihr Zweck kein anderer als der des Staats ist;" Zachariä, H. A., *Staatsrecht*, 151; Maurenbrecher, *Die d. reg. Fürsten*, 175–76, who finds the limits in the "sittliche Idee;" Escher, H., *Politik*, 1863, 118: The state power is limited by the state-purpose and by individual liberty; Warnkönig, *Rechtsphilosophie*, 208: " Sie sind aber bei jedem Volke durch dessen ganze Gesittung d. h. durch seine religiösen, moralischen und rechtlichen Ueberzeugungen bestimmt, welche auch die Regierung theilt und nicht leicht zu verachten wagt indem sie das moralische Unmögliche zu wollen sich nicht unterfangen wird;" Gerber, *Grundzüge* 29: " Die Staatsgewalt ist zwar dynamisch die höchste Gewalt im Volke, aber rechtlich besteht sie nur innerhalb der Sphäre ihrer Zweckbestimmung oder m. a. W. nur innerhalb des Kreises ihrer rechtlichen Existenz steht der Staatsgewalt die höchste Macht zur Verfügung. Gierke throughout opposed absolute power. *Cf. Das deutsche Genossenschaftsrecht*, 36; Bluntschli, *Deutsches Staatswörterbuch*, IX, 554 (1865).

[2] *Ueber Souveränetät*, 12: " Das Wesen eines jeden politischen Vereins besteht also in der Souveränetät, oder in der Erschaffung eines allgemeinen Willens."

[3] Waitz, *Politik* 8.

[4] *System*, sec. 125–26. Sovereignty is to the state what personal liberty is to man, sec. 125: " Sie bezeichnet das besondere, freie, selbständige Wesen eisen

pendent essence of a State. The primary characteristic of the State, that which distinguished it from all other associations, was with Gierke the possession of sovereign power. Sovereignty, then, in this sense, of the whole force of the political association, was regarded as a unit, as formally absolute but materially limited by the purpose of the State, and as an essential attribute of every political society ranked as a State.

What was, however, the nature of the "monarchical" sovereignty developed during this time? It was not conceded in Germany that the king was an agent, a delegate, an officer of the people. He was still something more than this: he was an active independent force in the political life of the community, and was not willing to accept a subordinate position at the hands of the people, as the rulers in France and Belgium had done. But on the other hand he could no longer maintain the position held before the Revolution; to hold stubbornly to this in the face of popular opinion would have been to lose all. The royal power must in some way be restricted, limited, confined within definite boundaries. Yet the king was not to become an agent of the people, nor was he to remain free to work his own will. The organic theory afforded an easy way of escape from these two extremes. The king became not an *agent* of the *people*, but an *organ* of the *State* conceived as a juristic person. By him and with him there were other organs, in particular the legislature, without which he could not rule, but which in turn could not rule without him. All were held to be organs in the one great and inclusive organism, the State. As the German phrase runs, there is "nichts ohne und nichts gegen den König," nothing without and nothing against the

---

Staats, die lebendige staatliche, durch keinen höheren juristischen Zwang beherrschbare und Alles ihr Angehörige, soweit es ihr angehört, beherrschende Individualität." *Cf. Gerber, Grundzüge,* 22.

king. His word is not always law, but there is no law without his word. Monarchical sovereignty denotes, then, not absolute power, but superior power, the highest power. There is no controlling organ above the king; he is superior legally to all others in the State; he is subject only to all the organs taken together, to the *organism*, of which he is himself the chief organ. His sovereignty is relative, not absolute. It is the possession of the highest, not of all power. The complete sovereignty belongs to the supreme juristic personality, the organically founded State.[1]

In the development of this idea of monarchical sovereignty, the idea of the organic nature of the State and its real personality was of the very greatest service; for until the State was conceived as a possible bearer of the supreme power, it was difficult to see to whom the sovereignty could go, unless to the people, and that on the basis of the contract theory.

The theory of the sovereignty of the State was thus, as it appears, the result of a slow progression from the Revolu-

---

[1] Gerber, *Grundzüge*, 20: "Das Monarchenrecht ist hiernach ein Recht der Organschaft für den Staat;" Gierke, *Grundbegriffe*, 326; Held, *System*, sec. 126: "Er ist souverän durch den Staat und für den Staat, gleichwie selbst das edelste Organ, doch immer nur durch und für den Organismus, Organ ist." See also, *Staat und Gesellschaft*, III, Abschnitt 24, "Verhältniss der Monarchie zum Constitutionalismus," 920: "Der Souverän einer Monarchie kann daher im Staat weder alles, noch nichts sein." Of popular sovereignty he says: "Wenn besser gemeint nur eine jedenfalls irrthümliche Bezeichnung dafür dass der Souverän nicht alles, die rechtliche Ordnung nicht bloss Formales, sondern etwas von Gesammtleben selbst Bestimmtes sein müsse." Zachariä, H. A., *Staatsrecht*, I, 80 ff.; Bluntschli, *Allgemeine Staatslehre* (6te Aufl., 1886), 575; L. v. Rönne, *Das Staatsrecht der preussischen Monarchie*, 1856 (4te Aufl., 1881, I, 132, distinguishes between sovereignty in the sense of international law and that of public law ("im staatsrechtlichen Sinne"). Sovereignty in a third sense as a characteristic of a person or personality denotes the legal position of that one in the state who appears as bearer of the force or power of the State, "Träger der Staatsgewalt." Fichte, I. H., *System*, (1853), II, 2, declares that the great problem is "eine Souveränetät zu schaffen, die dennoch beschränkt genug ist um nicht schaden zu können."

tionary doctrine of popular sovereignty. "People" was not able to win for itself in the German States, a place equivalent to that of Nation or State; it continued to signify the ruled in contrast to their ruler, and hence the doctrine that the people are sovereign was judged as the inversion of the natural political order. The first stage of the advance was the attack on the artificial or contract theory of the State and the substitution of the "natural" theory, that the political society is a growth rather than a conscious construction. With this came the notion of the State as an organism and personality in the Hegelian sense. Then came the work of the historical school, and the marvelous developments of natural science, the legitimate fruit of which was the development of the idea of the State as a living organism in the meaning of natural science, rather than of transcendental idealism. Further there came, out of the study of German political institutions and the influence exerted by the constitutional changes following the revolution of 1848, the doctrine of the actual juristic personality of the State—the idea that the State might become a bearer of legal rights and duties, and that in no fictitious sense. As the position of the absolute monarch was no longer tenable, and the basis of the doctrine of popular sovereignty appeared to be destroyed, it was an easy step to declare the State itself the juristic person *par excellence*, to be the bearer of the sovereign right, exercised through its constitutional organs. The sovereignty of the State in international law had long been recognized; the place of the people as the source out of which all political power arose, had also been conceded; it was, therefore, comparatively simple to see in the State, as newly conceived in the organic and personal sense, the real sovereign. Thus, the organic theory was called upon to save the monarchy from the "people," and it accomplished the task, but only to substitute for "the people," the State as a living organism, and a juristic person."[1]

[1] On the radical concept of sovereignty during this period see Rotteck, C. v. *Lehrbuch des Vernunftrechts und der Staatswissenschaften*, 1829 (here 1840), sec. 18: the sovereignty arises through a contract; sec. 25: the supreme power rests *ideally* with the commonwill (Gesammtwille), *naturally* with the majority of voters, *artificially* with the government; sec. 32: the ideal sovereignty has no limita-tion except that contained in the conception of the power itself (welche aus ihrem Begriffe hervorgeht); sec. 33: the natural has practically no limitation, the artificial may be restrained by the constitution. Welcker, K. T., *Das innere and äussere System der praktischen-natürlichen und römisch-christlich-german. ischen Rechts- Staats- und Gesetzgebungs-Lehre*, I, 1829, an effort to combine the contractual and the organic theories. The inclination here is toward the recognition of personality to both government and "people," and the attribution of the sovereignty to the two as united under the forms of the constitution. See p. 199. Above the law of the constitution stands as sovereign only God and Nature, 204; above the form of the constitution, the government and the nation. *Cf. Die letzten Gründe von Recht, Staat und Strafe*, 1813; also various articles in the Rotteck-Welcker *Staats Lexikon*, especially on *Staatsverfassung*. See Struve, G., *Grundzüge der Staatswissenschaft*, 1847–48, I, 66, 101, 105; in praise of Democracy, Bk. II, 280. *Cf.* J. L. Klüber, *Oeffentliches Recht des teutschen Bundes*, 1817 (here 1826), sec. 3: the sovereignty rests on the basis of consent; sec. 5: "Every sovereignty (Staatsgewalt) has boundaries, either natural or positive (constitutional) or of both kinds." *Cf.* Murhard, Fr., *Die Volkssouveränetät im Gegensatz zu der sogennanten Legitimität*, 1832.

CHAPTER VIII

THE AUSTINIAN THEORY

DIFFERENT from the development in either France or Germany, was the course taken by the doctrine of sovereignty in England. Here the issue of popular sovereignty had long before been fought out, the theory of Locke had been accepted, and the question was never again seriously considered. The monarch had yielded up his pretensions to exclusive sovereignty, and was at best but "King in Parliament," and the efforts made by the monarchs in France and in the German States found no parallel in the English constitutional experience of the nineteenth century. Practically the Parliament was sovereign; the reigning house had its position by virtue of a Parliamentary act; the veto power had not been exercised since 1707; the political vitality and consciousness of the State were best represented in its two legislative bodies. There was no individual or body of individuals which could contend with the power of the King in Parliament. To Parliament there was, legally speaking, nothing inadmissible or impossible; from this point of view it was all-powerful and irresistible. There was no legal or constitutional limitation which could be invoked against it; there was no body which could pass upon the acts of the Legislature; it was the highest organ, the final interpreter in the sphere of politics and law. England was a centralized national state with a definite body possessing the supreme power, and exercising its power untrammeled by the restraints of constitution. The political conditions were therefore favorable to the development of a sharply-defined theory of sovereignty, stating its nature and character in the most precise terms; and, moreover, of a theory framed away from and uninfluenced by the conflict between king and people. The new doctrine was not a defense of the crown, as that of Bodin, or of the people as with Rousseau, or yet an attempt to compromise between the two. The point of view from which the theory of sovereignty had generally been treated was changed and the problems with it. The leaders in the new movement were inspired by a desire to bring greater clearness and precision into that confused mass of English law upon which Bentham made such vigorous assaults. To effect the desired ends there was necessary a principle of legislation and a theory of law, and they were found in Utilitarianism in ethics and Positivism in jurisprudence. From this side the theory of sovereignty was now approached.

The leader in the new movement was Jeremy Bentham, whose ideas on this subject are best expressed in the *Fragment on Government*, 1776. Bentham, in a violent and destructive criticism of Blackstone, rejects the contract theory of the nature of political society, and bases the whole structure on the foundation of Utilitarianism.[1] Men submit to authority, it is argued, not because they have tacitly or expressly agreed to do so, but because they find such a course of conduct more favorable to their interest than the contrary

---

[1] Compare William Paley, *The Principles of Moral and Political Philosophy*, 3d ed., 1786. The religious theory here stated corresponds to the political theory of the Austinian school. Right signifies "no more than conformity to the will we go by."—*Op. cit.*, 48. "All obligation is nothing more than an inducement of sufficient strength and resulting in some way from the command of another."—*Ibid.*, 52. "As a series of appeals must be finite, there necessarily exists in every government a power from which the constitution has provided no appeal, and which power for that reason may be termed absolute, omnipotent, uncontrollable, arbitrary, despotic, and is alike in all countries."—*Ibid.*, 448.

would be. It is not the fulfillment of a promise as such, but the tendency to follow the line leading to the greatest happiness, that produces the submission to society.

The distinguishing mark of a political society Bentham finds in the fact that there exists in the given community a ruling body and a body which is ruled. In his own words: "When a number of persons (whom we may style subjects) are supposed to be in the habit of paying obedience to a person or assemblage of persons of a known and certain description (whom we may call governor or governors), such persons altogether (subjects and governors) are said to be in a state of political society."[1] The degree of obedience may and does in reality differ; perfect obedience is by no means necessary, is in fact impossible; but the existence of habitual command and obedience in some form constitutes the essence of the State. What then, we may ask, is the extent of the power which rests in the hands of the rulers. Has it limits of any kind; if so, of what nature? Legally speaking, declares Bentham, there is and can be no restraint on the power of the sovereign. "The field of the supreme governor's authority, though not *infinite*, must unavoidably, I think, unless where limited by express convention, be allowed to be *indefinite*. Nor can I see any narrower or other bounds to it under this constitution or any other yet freer constitution, if there be one, than the most despotic."[2]

Applying the principles of his favorite system, Bentham maintained that even if the power of the sovereign were theoretically limited, there could be no fixed and certain bounds established apart from those dictated by considerations of utility. True political liberty depends not on any theoretical limitation, but on a variety of circumstances, such as the manner in which the force of the Government is dis-

---

[1] *Op. cit.*, 18, ch. i, 1st ed.   [2] *Ibid.*, 152, ch. iv.

tributed, the frequency and ease of change from governor to governed, the freedom of the press, the liberty of public association.¹

Bentham's position was, then, that the power of the governing body, though practically capable of limitation, through the operation of the causes which determine the degree of obedience, was theoretically outside of any and all limitation or restriction whatever.² It is conceded, however, that there may be a certain limitation on the power of the sovereign "by convention," by express agreement made by the governing body. The cases which Bentham has in mind are, it would seem, those arising between various States, and not within the limits of one State. In these instances there may be restrictions placed on the power of a State in other respects supreme; in other words, there may be a limited *external* sovereignty. Otherwise, reasons Bentham, we must hold that there is no such thing as Government in the German Empire, in the Dutch Provinces, in the Swiss Cantons.³ Bentham regards the sovereignty as internally unlimited from the formal side, practically held in check by utilitarian considerations; externally it may be further restrained by the positive agreements made with other nations.

The successor of Bentham was John Austin, the keenest of English jurists since the time of Hobbes.⁴ On the con-

---

¹ *Op. cit.*, 153: "On the security with which malcontents may communicate their sentiments, concert their plans, and practice every mode of opposition short of actual revolt, before the executive power can be legally justified in disturbing them."

² *Ibid.*, 155: "To say that there is any act they *cannot* do, to speak of anything as being *illegal*, as being void, to speak of their exceeding their authority (whatever be the phrase) their power, their right is, however common, an abuse of language."

³ *Ibid.*, 162 ff.

⁴ On the life of Austin (1790–1859), see the sketch in the preface to the *Lectures* prepared by Sarah Austin. Compare the *Edinburgh Review* (cxiv), 1863; also J. S. Mill, *Dissertations*, III, 206–74. Austin studied on the continent, espe-

tinent Austin exerted no influence, and is practically unknown down to the present time. Even in England, his work was at first but little noticed, and it was only after many years that his theories became influential in determining the direction of English jurisprudence. The work in which the doctrine of Austin was embodied was the *Lectures on Jurisprudence*, first published in 1832.[1] His method was throughout logical and formal, his effort was constantly directed toward obtaining precision in the definition of terms, and then rigid and unyielding deduction of conclusions therefrom—a method recalling in many ways that of the author of the *Leviathan*, whom Austin had occasion more than once to defend. The abstruseness and laboriousness of his style did much to prevent a general acquaintance with or acceptance of Austin's propositions.[2]

As with Bentham, the philosophy of Austin is through and through utilitarian, and the defense of Utilitarianism permeates his work.[3] His theory of ethics is defended with as much, or even with more, enthusiasm than his theory of politics.[4] Like Bentham, he rejects the social contract, the

---

cially in Germany, but seems to have been but little affected by the political theories then current there. Of Kant's *Metaphysical Basis of Law*, he says, " A treatise darkened by a philosophy which I own is my aversion, but abounding I must needs admit with traces of rare sagacity."—*Op. cit.*, II, 972. His judgment on the German theory is still better stated in I, 310.

[1] References here are to the 3d edition, 1869. See also " *A Plea for the Constitution*, 1859; *On the Study of Jurisprudence*, 1863.

[2] Lord Melbourne said, " Austin! Oh, a damned fool! Did you ever read his book on Jurisprudence."—Dictionary of National Biography, II, 266.

[3] The laws of God, if they " were not generally useful, or if they did not promote the general happiness of his creatures, or if their great Author were not wise and benevolent would not be good or worthy of praise, but devilish and worthy of execration."—*Op. cit.*, I, 179.

[4] Austin opposes the principle of the greatest happiness, to that of right or justice in the abstract. " To a multitude of writers who have flourished and flourish in Germany, the following is the magnificent, though somewhat mysterious object

basis of the theories of Hobbes and Locke, and also the contract in the later forms given by the German philosophers: this he describes as "the German contract which never was made anywhere, but which is the necessary basis of political society and government."[1] An original covenant, even as an hypothesis, would suppose, says Austin, "that the society about to be formed is composed entirely of adult members; that all these adult members are persons of the same mind and even of much sagacity and much judgment, and that being very sagacious and very judicious, they are also perfectly familiar, or are at least passably acquainted with political and ethical science."[2] Granted these facts, one might construct a "coherent fiction." Austin inclines to the belief that the constitution of most societies has not been made by a contractual process, but is the result of a process of growth—the work of a long series of authors, composing the original members and many generations of their followers.[3]

Austin's general point of view is indicated in the statement made, that the "philosophy of positive law" is concerned with "law as it necessarily is, rather than with law as it ought to be; with law as it must be, rather than with law as it must be if it be good;"[4] that is to say, with *really possible* law rather than with *ideal* law.

of political government and society, namely, the extension over the earth or over its human inhabitants of the empire of right or justice. It would seem that this right or justice is not a creature of law, that it was anterior to every law, exists independently of every law, and is the measure and test of all law and morality. . . . I cannot understand it, and will not affect to explain it, merely guessing at what it is. . . . I take it for general utility, darkly conceived and expressed. Let it be what it may, it doubtless is excellently good, or is superlatively fair or high (in a breath), is preëminently worthy of praise. For compared with the extension of its empire over mankind, the mere advancement of their happiness is a mean and contemptible object."—*Op. cit.*, I, 310.

[1] I, 334. [2] I, 329. [3] I, 330.
[4] I, 33. The term "philosophy of positive law," Austin says he has borrowed

The starting point in the theory of Austin is his conception of law; this is the foundation upon which was erected the whole superstructure. It is his way of looking at law which determines his attitude toward questions of political science, and particularly toward that of sovereignty. What then was the Austinian notion of law? He defines a law as "a command which obliges a person or persons and obliges generally to acts or forbearances of a class."[1] Law is essentially a command given by a superior to an inferior: God gives laws to man as his superior; men give laws to men as superiors, understanding here by the term superiority, "might."[2] In any case the essence of the law is the command given from the superior to the inferior, and binding by reason of the sanction which the superior is able to attach to it. There are two great classes of law, the divine, set by God for men, and the human law.[3]

Human law is again divided into two classes, namely, positive *law*, properly so-called, and positive *morality*. Both these classes are positive, that is to say, "placed" or "set" by a superior, as already indicated; but in the one case the superior is political, in which event the command given is a positive law proper, and in the other the superior is not a definite and determinate body, and the command given is a precept of morality, not in the true sense a posi-

---

from the German jurist Hugo. See his *Lehrbuch des Naturrechts als einer Philosophie des positiven Rechts*, 1st ed., 1798, a work which seems to have influenced Austin more than any other of the continental treatises. Hugo defines the philosophy of positive law as "Vernunft-erkenntniss aus Begriffen über das, was Rechtsein kann und zwar hauptsächlich über das Privatrechtliche als über das eigentliche Juristische."—*Op. cit.*, 1.

[1] I, 98.   [2] I, 99.

[3] For a discussion of the relation between Rousseau's theory of the general will as the source of law and that of Austin, see T. H. Green, *Principles of Political Obligation*. The current of Green's thought is parallel to that of the German school.

tive law. It is called positive morality in distinction from the true or divine morality; *i. e.*, the law of God.[1]

Of positive law there may be, according to Austin,[2] three kinds, namely the laws given by monarchs or sovereign bodies, as supreme political superiors;[3] those given by men in a state of subjection, as *subordinate* political superiors, that is to say by those persons who are high in the official series, but still lower than the highest; and thirdly by subjects not acting in any official capacity but merely as private persons in pursuance of legal rights, as the "laws" given by a guardian to his ward.[4] In accordance with this classification, Austin rules out altogether the greater part of the "constitutional" law of England, holding that it is not law at all, but, strictly speaking, must be regarded as "positive morality." In particular is this true of the so-called "laws" governing the relations between ruler and ruled. "All constitutional law," says Austin, "is as against the sovereign in that predicament," namely of being in reality not law at all, not positive law in the strictly defined Austinian sense, but merely positive morality.[5] It is admitted, however, that much of this ethical material must be inserted in the "corpus juris" for "reasons of convenience." A knowledge

---

[1] I, Lecture 1. "Of the laws or rules set by men to men, some are established by *political* superiors, sovereign and subject, by exercising supreme and subordinate *government*, in independent nations or independent political societies. The aggregate of the ruler's terms established, or some aggregate forming a part of that aggregate, is the appropriate matter of jurisprudence, general or particular. . . . As contradistinguished to *natural* law. . . . the aggregate of the rules established by political superiors, is frequently styled *positive* law, or law existing by position. . . . Rules which are not established by political superiors are also positive, or exist *by position*, if they be rules or laws, in the proper signification of the term."

[2] I, 101 following. [3] I, 183. [4] *Ibid.*

[5] I, 253; also, I, 274. "I mean by the expression constitutional law, the positive morality, or the compound of positive morality and positive law, which fixes the constitution or structure of the given supreme government."

of it is necessary to a proper understanding of the positive law itself.[1] But logically considered, in the strict analysis in which Austin delighted, the territory of constitutional law should be given over to the realm of ethics. Constitutional law is not given by a superior to an inferior (for reasons that will later appear); it is not stated in the form of a command; it is accompanied by no adequate and effective sanction. It fails therefore to meet the canons of requirement for positive law, and must accordingly be eliminated from the legal category. Law in the Austinian sense, is essentially the effective command of a superior. It is not at all a vague and general impression that something ought to be done, but a definite, precise order necessitating certain "acts or forbearances." Hence customary law or custom is also excluded from the field proper of positive law, for the reason that it lacks those qualities which constitute the Austinian law. Custom is not law in itself, and does not and cannot become law of itself, alone and unassisted. "Considered as moral rules formed into positive laws," says Austin, "customary laws are established by the state."[2] Mere custom cannot constitute a law proper; for, again applying the tests, it is not given by a definite superior, it is not stated in the form of a command, and finally it is not accompanied by an effective sanction.[3] Custom becomes law, in the proper sense of the word, only when declared to be such by the state itself. It is *command*, not *custom* which is the essential element in the existence of law.

With these observations on Austin's general theory of law, we enter on the consideration of the doctrine of sovereignty intimately connected therewith. Closely following

[1] II, 773: "For reasons of convenience, which are paramount to logical symmetry .... in strictness it belongs to positive morality or to ethics."

[2] I, 105; see also 22–24.

[3] On the significance attached to "sanction," see Lecture I.

Bentham, he says, "If a determinate human superior not in a habit of obedience to a like superior receive habitual obedience from the bulk of a given society, that determinate superior is sovereign in that society, and the society (including the superior) is a society political and independent." This is Austin's political society and sovereign. It is to be observed that in his theory, as in that of Hobbes, the sovereign is the *State*, although the political society, the community, includes both sovereign or state, and subject. The community as a whole is not to be taken for the sovereign. "It is," asserts Austin, "only through an ellipsis or an abridged form of expression that the *society* is styled independent."[1] "The part truly independent is not the society, but the *sovereign portion* of the society." Again, and more explicitly; "The State is usually synonymous with the sovereign. This is the meaning which I annex to the term, unless I employ it expressly with a different import."[2] He understood then, by the sovereign, a part of the society, not the whole community itself. This was not unlike the theory of Hobbes and his school, and the doctrine held by certain German writers, already considered, that the king, the government, the ruling body, is the State. These philosophers had used (and were still using) the theory in defense of the royal power against that of the people, and the argument that the king is the State served them well. Austin's exclusion of a part of the community was, however, no part of an argument against the people, but was a step in his effort to secure a definite and determinate sovereign power as the sole source of law.

It is now necessary to enter yet more closely into the consideration of the sovereignty which was the centre of

[1] I, 227. Compare the current German theory used against the doctrine of popular sovereignty.

[2] I, 249.

Austin's system. Particular emphasis is laid upon the following elements in its nature; first the habit of obedience on the part of the subject to the superior, with this addition to Bentham's proposition, that the superior must not be in a like habit of obedience to some still higher authority. Again, the obedience must be rendered by the "bulk" or "generality" of the given society; and finally the obedience must be given to a "determinate" body.

By a "habit" of obedience is understood general and regular submission to a recognized authority. The possibility of exceptions to the rule is by no means excluded, is even expressly recognized. Thus the presence of the allied armies in France for a time in 1814–15, or of the German army in 1871, even though the foreign military power received temporarily the obedience of the "bulk" of the community, did not suffice to make the invading powers sovereign in the political society. The obedience then given was not at all habitual and usual, but on the contrary it was exceptional and extraordinary. It had not the regularity and continuity necessary to constitute a habit of obedience and a sovereignty in the Austinian sense. This "obedience" has, moreover, an external and an internal, a positive and a negative side: positively, the given superior must, to be sovereign, receive obedience from others: negatively, obedience must not be rendered to any other. Austin himself admits, however, that both of these criteria, the negative and the positive, are inadequate. It is, after all, uncertain just what constitutes the "bulk" of any given society; or how long the obedience must be continued in order to be fairly regarded as habitual; or whether we are to estimate obedience by the number of commands executed, or by the importance of those acceded to.[1] Qualitatively and quantitatively the test is imperfect. There may even be, argues Austin, peoples in a state of natural society, not in the habit of obedience to any one, as is the case with certain tribes in North America.[1] It is necessary to conclude, therefore, that the positive test, that of the reception of obedience, is a fallible test. "It would not enable us to determine of every political society whether it were political or natural,"[2] that is to say whether a sovereign were really in existence. On the other hand, the negative test is also insufficient, and would not enable us to tell whether a political society were independent or subordinate. There is no nation wholly independent, no nation which does not at times render obedience to others; no power is wholly and absolutely independent. It seems from Austin's own statement, then, that habitual obedience can be determined at best with the greatest difficulty, and that it does not give an absolutely safe and sure basis upon which to build. It is always incomplete and uncertain. The political society, the sovereign, must always rest upon a human habit. Farther back than this Austin found it impossible to penetrate.

Given the necessary basis of habitual obedience, the most striking characteristic of the sovereignty, as conceived by Austin, was its definiteness and determinateness. As already stated, the sovereign must be a "determinate human superior." What is meant by a "determinate" body? Austin says: "If a body of persons be determinate, all the persons

[1] I, 238.

[2] I, 234. Austin even goes so far as to say that "the definition or general notion of independent political society is therefore, vague or uncertain."—I, 235. Again: "If perfect or complete independence be of the essence of sovereign power, there is not, in fact, the human power to which the epithet sovereign will apply with propriety. Every government, let it be ever so powerful, renders occasional obedience to the commands of other goverments. Every government defers frequently to those opinions and sentiments which are styled international law; and every government defers habitually to the opinions and sentiments of its own subjects."—I, 242.

who compose it are determined and may be indicated." [1] A determinate body in the sense here used may be composed, first of persons indicated by characters or descriptions respectively appropriate to themselves, as for example the various members composing the firm A. B. & C., each one of whom is indicated or determined by characteristics peculiar to himself; [2] or secondly the determinate body may be composed of all the members of a given class or classes, as the King, the members of Parliament.[3] Such a determinate body, formed in either of these two ways, is capable of corporate conduct, "is capable as a body of positive or negative deportment;" [4] whereas an indeterminate or indefinite body, is by its nature incapable of corporate conduct and of either positive or negative deportment. The most essential characteristic of the sovereignty, in the Austinian theory, is its definiteness—that it be clear-cut and concise, readily ascertainable. It must be located in a definite or determinate person or body of persons, who are marked out either by personal or by class characteristics. The Parliament of England is for example such a definite body (though Austin added the electorate), a Roman Triumvirate would satisfy the requirements, a king would of course be unexceptionable. At all events the distinction between ruler and ruled must stand out clearly and distinctly; there must be no doubt as to where the sovereign power really is; it must possess a "local habitation and a name." By easy inference from the

---

[1] I, 191.

[2] I. 191: "The body is composed of persons determined specifically or individually or determined by characters or descriptions respectively appropriate to themselves."

[3] This class "comprises all persons who belong to a given class, or who belong respectively to two or more of such classes. In other words, every person who answers to a given generic description, or to any two or more given generic descriptions is also a member of the determinate body."—I, 191.

[4] I, 193.

statements made, there is no sovereignty in existence, if there is no definite body to whom it can be attributed. The only sovereign recognized is a definite, determinate person or body of persons to whom the rest of the community renders habitual obedience. An association lacking this central body or organ is not yet an independent political society in the Austinian sense. Austin speaks of societies political but subordinate; but by strict deduction from his premises no society is political which is subordinate or dependent—which lacks the definite and determinate sovereign.[1]

The sovereign in the English nation is held by Austin to be the "king, peers and the electoral body of the commons,"[2] which he would regard as a determinate body.[3] This body is in the habit of receiving obedience from the bulk of the society and not in the habit of receiving commands from any other like determinate body, and is therefore sovereign in the community.[4] In the United States the sovereignty rests with the state governments "as forming one aggregate body," understanding however by the government, "the body of citizens which appoints the ordinary legislature."[5] Such bodies as these he regards as determinate, as capable of corporate conduct, and therefore as fitting repositories of the supreme power.

The nature of the sovereignty as discussed by Austin was wholly absolute. The supreme power, whether vested in an individual or a body of individuals considered in their cor-

---

[1] I, 232.   [2] I, 253.

[3] Austin admits two forms of " supreme government," monarchy and aristocracy. —I, 243. He objects to any division of governmental powers except that into "supreme" and "subordinate."—I, 258.

[4] In the consideration of federal governments Austin rejects altogether the "half-sovereign state," declaring that in all cases apparently of such a nature, it would be found that in final analysis, the state in question was either wholly sovereign, or wholly subject, or else an integral part of a political society.—I, 243.

[5] I, 268.

porate capacity, was regarded as "incapable of legal limitation."[1] To say that such an individual or body could be bound by a legal duty, would be equivalent to declaring it subject to some higher sovereign; "that is to say, a monarch or sovereign member bound by a legal duty were sovereign and not sovereign. Supreme power limited by law is a flat contradiction in words."[2] The sovereign is with Austin the source of law, hence above the binding force of its own decrees. The supreme power can be bound by no legal duties or obligations, since there is no power by whom such obligations can be interpreted or enforced. The law giver cannot be *legally* bound by his own law, however great the moral obligation incurred. Austin very tersely states that, "every supreme government is free from legal restraints, or (what is the same proposition dressed in a different phrase) every supreme government is legally despotic."[3] The frequent objection made to this proposition is, he explains, due to a confusion of ideas, arising from the failure to distinguish between monarch and sovereign. But it does not follow that because the sovereign is despotic, legally speaking, that the monarch, the king, is also despotic in the unpopular sense of the term. In a limited monarchy, the head of the government is loosely called a monarch or a sovereign. The power of this ruler or sovereign is not, however, true sovereignty; for it has been and may be subjected to indefinite limitations by the provisions of the positive law, framed by the real ruler. The king in a limited monarchy, the king as found in the modern constitutional state, is not at all a genuine sovereign, possessing legally illimitable, despotic power. The true sovereign is back of the nominal ruler, *i. e.*, in England, the king, peers and the electoral body of the House of Commons. It is this body,

---

[1] I, 270.   [2] *Ibid.*   [3] I, 283.

and not the modern king, in whose hands rests the despotic power, the legally illimitable authority.[1]

Austin is not only ready to say that the sovereign has no legal *duties;* he approaches the question from the opposite side as well, and maintains that the sovereign can have no legal *rights* against its subjects. A legal right, it is urged, involves the existence of three parties; the two claimants and the umpire. But in case of a right of the sovereign against a subject, the sovereign would necessarily constitute two parties; it must be one of the claimants and at the same time the judge between itself and the other claimant—which would be impossible. The sovereign, the real sovereign, not the king, could have no rights against a subject, because to make this possible we must suppose another sovereign over and above the real ruler, which would be contrary to the hypothesis of an independent supreme power. The sovereign can have no legal rights, since there is no law under which such rights can be given, save the will of the sovereign itself. The supreme power has neither *legal* rights nor *legal* duties; for all law, all that is legal, emanates from this very power whose rights or duties are in question. Kant said that the sovereign has rights but no duties as against the subject; Austin carried the proposition out to its logical end, and declared against both rights and duties.

Austin's theory thus destroys the basis of public law in so far as it is regarded as the legal relation between governor and governed. There can be no system of law where there is no possibility of either a legal right or a legal duty. The relations are all *de facto* and in no way *de jure*. As Locke had said long before, basing his proposition on the contract

---

[1] I, 286. See the defense of Hobbes here. "Just or unjust, justice or injustice, is a term of relative and varying import. Whenever it is uttered with a determinate meaning, it is uttered with relation to a determinate law, which the speaker assumes as a standard of comparison."—I, 287.

theory, the government and the people are always in a state of nature in regard to each other; for there is between them no common judge. Here the theory of Locke and that of the positive law agree. Neither is willing to recognize an ultimate system of legal rights and duties; they agree that the relations between ruler and ruled are necessarily matters of fact and not of law. As already seen, Austin refused to constitutional law the character of true law, and consigned it to the domain of ethics; or it might be a "compound of positive morality and positive law," whatever that may mean.[1] The act of the sovereign which violates the constitution "may be styled with propriety unconstitutional; it is not an infringement of law, simply and strictly so-called, and cannot be styled with propriety, illegal."[2] As Austin reasons, the constitution cannot be law, because the sovereign cannot give to the sovereign a binding command; for, by hypothesis, the sovereign itself is the source of all legal obligation.[3] The ruler cannot be bound by rules, though he may accept counsel and advice.

Again, following out his premises, Austin refuses to admit any difference between a *de facto* and a *de jure* government. A sovereign Government, he argues, cannot be looked upon as either lawful or unlawful. "If it were lawful or unlawful in respect of the positive law of its own independent

---

[1] "Where, then, the supreme government is a monarchy, or government of one, constitutional law as against that government is inevitably nothing more than positive morality. Where the supreme government is an aristocracy, or a government of a number, constitutional law as against the members of that government may consist of positive morality, or of a compound of positive morality and positive law."—I, 278.

[2] I, 274.

[3] But, considered severally, the members of the sovereign body may be bound by their own laws.—I, 277. The sovereign in one state may have legal rights against a subject of another state. Thus the Czar of Russia might have legal rights against a British subject under the British law.—I, 297-98.

community, it were lawful or unlawful by virtue of its own appointment, which is absurd."[1] On the other hand, if lawful or unlawful by virtue of the law of another community, "it were not an actual supreme but an actual subordinate Government, which is also absurd."[2] It is useless, in Austin's opinion, to term a Government sovereign *de jure*, without specifying by what law it is or is not supreme. Now the only law by which it can be supreme is its own utterance, its own command, its own will. Hence the Government is really being judged in last analysis by itself, and the expression Government *de jure* only amounts to saying that the Government is legal because it declares itself to be. A sovereign Government, so far as positive law is concerned, is neither legal nor illegal, just nor unjust. Austin does not even agree that "whatever is, is right;" it merely is.

In the same spirit Austin declares that political or civil liberty is, "the liberty from legal obligation which is left or granted by a Government to any of its own subjects."[3] Civil liberty is generally accompanied by a legal right, as its guarantee. Austin concludes that civil liberty is fostered by the very political restraint often considered as destructive of it, "that restraint from which the devotees of the idol liberty are so fearfully and blindly averse."[4] Political liberty is a creature of law, the grant of the sovereign, a result of the legal system of which the supreme power is the source and centre. There is, as Austin reasons, no conflict between sovereignty and liberty, as the latter is dependent upon the existence and activity of the former. The difficulty is not in

---

[1] I, 337. [2] *Ibid*. [3] I, 282.

[4] I, 283. Austin distinguishes between "liberty," and "right." In "liberty" the prominent or leading idea is the absence of legal restraint, while the security or protection for the enjoyment of that liberty is the secondary idea. "Right," on the other hand, *denotes* the protection, and *connotes* the absence of restraint. —I, 336.

seeing how liberty can exist *with* sovereignty, but how it could exist *without* sovereignty.

Such was the Austinian theory of the supreme power, in method and result recalling, though not slavishly following, the work of the great English philosopher of the 17th century, Hobbes. The key to Austin's argument is the concept of law as the command of the sovereign; and in this connection " borrowing the language of Hobbes," he states that " the legislator is he, not by whose authority the law was first made, but by whose authority it continues to be a law."[1] In other words, it is the *sanction* and not the *source* which is to hold first place in the definition of law. Austin's contemporaries, Savigny and the historical school in Germany, emphasized the sources of law. They examined custom, tradition, usage, observance; and the fabric created out of this material they regarded as law. Declaring that law is a growth rather than a product of conscious human activity, they opposed the codification of the German law, and, therefore, antagonized legislative interference with the development of the legal system. This tendency was, as we have seen, in perfect accord with the reaction against the spirit of the Revolution. Austin, on the other hand, was not a defender of the reaction, but supported Bentham's great movement for the codification and clarification of law by the political authorities. He was perfectly willing, anxious even, to foster the development of law by the aid of political interference. So far as legislation was concerned, Austin was a radical, Savigny a conservative. Austin attempted to draw a sharp line between law proper and custom. Custom and usage are not law, he held, until the sovereign speaks. All rules and regulations which lack this sanction are simply excluded from the domain of positive law. Austin distinguishes between the social and the legal or political relations, barring

[1] I, 226.

the former from the field of law. As already shown, the important point is not *how* the rule was made, but by what authority *it is enforced*. On the one side are the rules accompanied by economic, religious, social sanctions; on the other those rules, alone positive laws, which are sealed by the sanction of the supreme political power in the community.[1]

It is to be noted, however, that although Austin denies that custom is law, in the proper sense of the term, and refuses to recognize it in his jurisprudence, it lies, nevertheless, at the basis of his entire system. Custom is not law, it is true, until it is endorsed by the sovereign; but, on the other hand, the sovereign is not sovereign until recognized by *custom*. Habitual obedience, the *custom* of obeying, constitutes the fundamental and essential basis of the political society and of the supreme power. "If a determinate human superior, not *in a habit* of obedience to a like superior, receive *habitual* obedience," etc.; in other words, a habit or custom is at the foundation of the Austinian jurisprudence. Custom does not make law, but it makes the law-maker. The rule of custom ends, however, where the sovereignty begins, and, whenever the habit of obedience is so far developed that a state of political society is reached, containing a definite and determinate sovereign, the reign of custom ceases, except in so far as it must always continue to be the basis upon which the society rests. All else is regulated by the sovereign, whose will is law. Austin did not despise custom utterly. He recognized it once and for all as the source of the sovereign power, and from there on custom has no place as a law-maker. One must have a

---

[1] Compare Bentham's doctrine of the three classes of sanctions, political, religious, moral in *Fragment*, ch. v. See in the same connection, Locke, *Essay on the Human Understanding*, II, ch. 28: "The law of God, of politick societies and the law of fashion or private censure."

starting point, and Austin's is a highly-developed modern state, with a well-established habit of obedience. It might reasonably be asked, however, why the custom which serves as the basis of the sovereignty, as Austin recognizes in his doctrine of "habitual obedience" should not serve equally well as a basis for private law, or why it is inefficient in the creation of constitutional law? The Austinian answer is that a definite doctrine of sovereignty requires the assumption of the existence of a habit of command and obedience in the given community.

The absoluteness of Austin's sovereign recalls that of Hobbes and Kant; the supreme power is by all regarded as "legally despotic"—as by definition incapable of limitation. Austin strenuously insisted upon the impossibility of restricting the sovereign, formally or legally; but "material" limitations are found at the basis of his system. The obedience to the ruler is always habitual, and never perfect; it has its source in the Austinian principle, in the benefits which result in utility.[1] Hence it would follow that when the utility ceased to exist, the obedience would also come to an end, and the sovereignty find its limit. The limitations found by other philosophers in the "purpose of the state," in respect for the "rights of man," in the moral or divine law, are all summed up, or find an equivalent, in the utilitarian principle laid down by Bentham and Austin. Legally the supreme government is absolutely despotic, practically its power depends upon considerations of a utilitarian nature; but back of the legal and into the realm of the practical the Austinian doctrine does not lead us.[2]

[1] "A perception by the bulk of the community of the utility of political government or a preference by the bulk of the community of any government to anarchy. And this is the only cause of the habitual obedience in question, which is common to all societies, or nearly all societies."—I, 303.

[2] With Austin compare G. C. Lewis, *Remarks on the Use and Abuse of Some Political Terms*, 1853. The second edition (1898) is here used. See especially

THE AUSTINIAN THEORY

The theory of Austin, though widely influential, did not escape severe and searching criticism at the hands of English writers. Coming from the study of early forms of society, Maine vigorously attacked the validity of the newly stated doctrine on the ground that it exclusively emphasized a single element in the concept of sovereignty and law, namely that of force. The theory neglects, urges Maine, the great body of historical facts, determining in the first place who the sovereign shall be, and in the second place, how and under what conditions his power shall be exercised; the doctrine is the result of abstraction. "The whole enormous aggregate of opinions, sentiments, beliefs, superstitions and prejudices; of ideas of all kinds, hereditary and acquired, some produced by institutions and some by the constitution of human nature—is rejected by the analytical jurists,"[1] and the eye fixed exclusively on one fact, common to political societies, namely the possession of force.[2] This is, to be sure, a notable characteristic of the state, but by no means the only one, and its insufficiency to

---

chapter v, Sovereign—Sovereignty, 41: "The sovereign power is absolutely unlimited, the sovereign has complete disposal of the life, rights and duties of every member of the community. . . . There is no law which it has not power to alter, repeal, or enact." Wm. Markby, *Elements of Law*, 1871, 3d edition, 1885; T. E. Holland, *The Elements of Jurisprudence*, 1882; *Cf.* E. C. Clark, *Practical Jurisprudence, A Commentary on Austin*, 1883. With Austin's absolute theory it is interesting to compare that of R. v. Ihering in his remarkable work, *Der Zweck im Recht*, 1877, (2nd. ed., 1884–'86, quoted here): The State is "die sociale Organisation der Zwangsgewalt."—I, 307. "Das Zwangsrecht bildet das absolute Monopol des Staats" (I, 378), it is superior to every other power on its territory. Powerlessness is "the mortal sin for which there is no absolution; which the society never forgives nor tolerates."—I, 312. The State is the only source of law or right (*Recht*), I, 320, and is limited only by itself. A state in which complete provision were made against the possibility of an arbitrary act, would lack only one quality—viability (Lebensfähigkeit). "Ausschliessliche Herrschaft des Gesetzes ist gleichbedeutend mit dem Verzicht der Gesellschaft auf den freien Gebrauch ihrer Hände."—I, 421.

[1] *Early History of Institutions*, 1875, p., 360.   [2] *Ibid.*, 359.

explain all is at once evident when we examine a society of the more primitive type. Here it is found that order is maintained and political functions performed, not so much by the command of a determinate sovereign like the English Parliament, as in obedience to "an instinct almost as blind and unconscious as that which produces some of the movements of our bodies."[1] Here the Austinian doctrine can scarcely be applied with any degree of success; its truth would here become nothing more than verbal, since the sovereign has, as a matter of fact, no such power as that attributed to him by Austin. The analytical doctrine, Maine argues, has grown up in sight of the modern territorial state, with its centralized and relatively determinate political organization, and also in view of the intense legislative activity of the supreme political authority,[2] as for example, indeed as *the* example, in the English state, with the English Parliament as its supreme legislature. In highly developed states such as this, it may be said that the Austinian theory is formally true, though only *formally* even here; but where these advanced political conditions do not obtain, in forms of political society less perfectly organized, the doctrine is true only in the most purely verbal sense. The doctrine is applicable to a certain stage of political development only, and to but one side of that development—hence the accusation of excessive abstraction.

Maine's idea was carried still farther by Sidgwick, who agreed in general with the author of *Early Institutions*,

---

[1] *Early History of Institutions*, pp. 392–93.

[2] *Ibid.*, 394. "We have heard," said Maine, "of a village Hampden, but a village Hobbes is inconceivable." "Until the fact existed (the energy of the legislatures), I do not believe that the system of Hobbes, Bentham and Austin could have been conceived."—*Ibid.*, 398. With Maine compare J. A. Lightwood, *The Nature of Positive Law*, 1883, under the influence of the German school, as represented by Savigny. See p. 386. Of importance is ch. xi., on *Modern Theories of Law*.

but found it unnecessary to go back as far as the primitive types of society where Maine had found material for his argument.[1] Even in politically developed societies, it is not true that any and every command the sovereign chooses to lay down, will meet with obedience. Hence it follows, reasons Sidgwick, "that the proposition that the power of the sovereign is not *legally* limited becomes insignificant, since it does not mean that it is not subject to limitations which even lawyers will recognize, but merely that it is not limited by the sovereign's own commands—which no one can ever have supposed it to be."[2] In many modern states, it may be said, moreover, that limits are set to the sovereign through the constitution. If, as in Belgium, there is a constitutional organ back of the ordinary government, then there is to be considered the "actual organ of government whose commands are habitually obeyed" and also the "possible organ whose power is legally unlimited."[3] The active sovereign is legally limited, while the organ legally unlimited is so seldom seen and so seldom acts that obedience to it can hardly be regarded as habitual.[4] Even in a State like England, where the Parliament is checked by no constitutional limitations, there may be found a certain restraint in the control which the electors exercise over the members of the sovereign body. In emphasizing those general forces which tend to deter the existing governmental authority from some courses of action, Sidgwick asserts that there is really, "a certain sense in which the mass of the people, in any country, may be said to be the ultimate depository of political power."[5] This statement is not to be

---

[1] Henry Sidgwick, *The Elements of Politics*, 1891. [2] *Ibid.*, 22.

[3] *Ibid.*, 23. Sidgwick inquires where the sovereign is, in case certain articles in the constitution are unalterable, as Article V. of the U. S. Constitution. Pollock, *First Book*, 260, says that "where there is a rigid constitution, there cannot be one body in permanent or habitual activity which possesses unlimited sovereignty."

[4] Compare Austin's idea of habitual obedience in *op. cit.*, I, 242.

[5] *Elements*, 604.

too literally taken, however, as the purpose is merely to show that the power of the political sovereign is never wholly despotic in its nature, that it is always limited by the general opinion of the community; as Duden said (*supra* p. 71), that the government can never act in opposition to its own basis. This, however, is an idea which Austin himself had never opposed.[1] That all government rests on habitual obedience, and that obedience is determined by motives of utility, was a fundamental proposition in the Austinian theory.

It appears, then, that the effort of the critics has been to show that undue attention has been given by the analytical school to the purely legal side of the sovereignty, and that the great forces working back of the formal law have been comparatively neglected. In line with the German school, best typified by Savigny, they have demanded that not only the sanction of law be studied, but also its source;[2] that not only the actually existing political authority be examined, but also the social and political forces upon which it rests, and upon whose balance its equilibrium depends.

An attempt has recently been made to reconcile the doctrine which emphasizes the sovereignty found in the Government with that emphasizing the sovereignty found outside the Government. The aim is to preserve all that is valuable in Austin's analysis without falling into mere formalism, and on the other hand to recognize the forces which produce sovereignty, without forgetting what the sovereignty really is

---

[1] A. L. Lowell in his *Essays on Government* (1889) attacks Austin, but seems to mistake his position. Thus he says: "if the extent of the sovereign power is measured by the disposition to obedience on the part of the bulk of the society, it may be said that the power of no sovereign can be strictly unlimited," p. 215. Compare Austin, I, 242.

[2] Lightwood says, *Post. Law*, 386: "Sanction is not an essential point in law, any more than physic is essential to health of body." Pollock, *A First Book, etc.*, 27, asserts that "law is enforced by the State because it is law: it is not law merely because the State enforces it."

in studying how it came to be. The leaders in the new movement are A. V. Dicey,[1] and David G. Ritchie,[2] and their advance is made by means of a distinction which is drawn between *legal* sovereignty and *political* sovereignty.[3] The legal sovereign is understood to be the body whose commands are enforceable in the ordinary courts. It is the lawyer's sovereign, the ultimate legal authority, the last source to which law as law can be traced. As Ritchie says, the command of this body is " good law " in the lawyer's sense, although not necessarily " a good law " in the layman's sense.[4] Such a legal sovereign as for example the King in Parliament, is necessarily absolute and irresponsible, so far as the law goes; it is legally irresistible, legally despotic. Whatever its susceptibility to moral influences, or its liability to physical violence, it is nevertheless in the strictly and purely legal sense, *despotic*.[5]

Back of the legal sovereign, however, stands another power; " behind the sovereign which the lawyer recognizes there is another sovereign to whom the legal sovereign must bow." This is the political sovereign, which Dicey says is that body in the state, " the will of which is ultimately obeyed by the citizens of the State."[6] This sovereignty might be located in England in the " body of electors,"[7] or it might be found

---

[1] *Lectures Introductory to the Study of the Law of the Constitution.*

[2] *Annals of the American Academy of Political Science*, I, 385 ff.

[3] Ritchie considers also a third sovereign, the *nominal*. This is, however, merely the representative of the other two and " need not cause a difficulty." He really reverts to Locke to find the triple classification.

[4] Ritchie, *Annals*, I, 407.

[5] *Ibid*, 401. " It is much better that the law in all its harshness and its makers in all their legal irresponsibility should stand out clearly before the eyes of those who are required to obey."

[6] *Law of the Constitution*, 66–67.

[7] Dicey says that the electorate is the political sovereign.—*Ibid.*, 67. Ritchie says, " The ultimate political sovereign is not the determinate number of persons

in the body of public sentiment or opinion to which the legal sovereign itself must ultimately render obedience. No matter what the opinion of the electorate may be, or what the public will may be, legally it possesses no power, it cannot be enforced in the courts of law. Politically, however, it is supreme, it is the source of the legal sovereign, it must ultimately be obeyed.[1] Legally this power has no effective organization, but it stands outside the domain of positive law, ultimately though not immediately determining what that domain shall be. Its "habit of obedience" makes and unmakes sovereigns.

In this theory, then, the Austinian notion is recognized in the legal sovereign, the authority behind which the lawyer as lawyer need not go, and the notion of the historical school in the political sovereign—the true source of the ultimate political authority. Strangely enough, a similar form of compromise was made by Locke in the attempt to reconcile the natural-right philosophy with the English monarchy. Now, however, the problem is not to harmonize popular custom and royal command, but rather custom and command in the abstract; or, if it is preferred, as fundamental facts in the world of political phenomena. The question is no longer how to find a *modus vivendi* for king and people, but how to show most clearly the existence of both the rigid and the flexible elements in the supreme political power. The answer given by Dicey and his school is reached not by dividing sovereignty, statically, as we might say, but rather in a

---

now existing in the nation, but the opinions and feelings of these persons; and of these opinions and feelings the traditions of the past, the needs of the present, the hopes of the future, all form a part."—Ritchie, *Annals*, I, 407.

[1] "The problem of good government," says Ritchie, "is the problem of proper relations between the legal and the ultimate political sovereign."—*Ibid.*, I, 402. Compare Dicey on the balance between the *external* and the *internal* limitations under representative government.

dynamic sense. At any given moment there is a sovereign clothed in the forms of law, supreme within the bounds of law; but this sovereign, even the sphere of law itself, is fixed by the ultimate political sovereign, against whose will the spells of formal law are powerless. The validity of the doctrine depends upon the possibility of a clear distinction between "law" and "politics," between legal and political facts or phenomena.[1]

[1] The attempt to distinguish between legal and political sovereignty carries the discussion back into the field where the science of Society and that of the State meet. Sociologists are naturally concerned with the various forces that operate to produce the phenomena of social control. The description, analysis and explanation of the various social causes, the resultant of which is that "habit of obedience" with which the jurist starts, have been in recent years a frequent subject of sociological investigation. While it is not proposed in this present study to enter into an analysis of these theories, a few works may be cited to show the tendency of sociological thought upon the problems of social control: Herbert Spencer, *Political Institutions*, 1887; F. H. Giddings, *The Principles of Sociology*, 1896, 3d ed., 1899; L. Gumplowicz, *Philosophisches Staatsrecht*, 1877, *Die Sociologische Staatsidee*, 1892; E. A. Ross, *Social Control*, in *The American Journal of Sociology*, Vol. I, II.; E. V. Zenker, *Die Gesellschaft*, 1899.

CHAPTER IX

SOVEREIGNTY AND THE AMERICAN UNION

THE discussion now turns from what has been called the internal side of sovereignty to the external. Thus far, we have considered an isolated State; we now approach the State in its relation to other States or communities purporting to be States.[1] The elements of the problem are now not parties within the easily-discernible limits of one State, as people and king, but States or political societies combined in one greater State or political society—States merging into a greater State. The impetus to the growth of the new body of doctrine was given by the appearance of important forms of State federations, or new States formed through a process of association, and by the necessity of explaining and interpreting these political phenomena. The three most important examples of the new type were the United States of America as organized under the constitution of 1789, the Swiss Union under the constitutions of 1848 and 1874, and the German Empire, under the constitution of 1871, preceded by the North German Confederation of 1867, and the Confederation of 1815. All were developments from earlier forms of association, in which the individual communities had enjoyed, nominally at least, the possession of sovereign prerogatives. All were constructed upon prin-

---

[1] See H. Preuss, *Gemeinde, Staat, Reich*, 1889, especially Parts 1 and 10; Siegfried Brie, *Der Bundesstaat*, 1874; E. Borel, *Étude sur la souveraineté et l' état fédératif*, 1886; Georg Jellinek, *Die Lehre von den Staaten-verbindungen*, 1882; W. W. Willoughby, *The Nature of the State*, 1896, especially chapter x; H. Rehm, *Allgemeine Staatslehre*, 1899.

ciples of compromise, combining as far as possible the autonomy of the members with the supremacy and effectiveness of the union as a whole. They all had a double set of organizations, a double hierarchy of powers; one for the central or federal government and one for the local government. In all, provision was made for the exercise of large powers by the central government, but at the same time the localities were carefully protected in their control over a great field of governmental activity. And in all the relation between central and local authority presented problems of so perplexing a nature as to stimulate greatly the development of theories regarding the nature and location of the ultimate political power.

It is the purpose of the succeeding chapters to trace the movement of the theory of sovereignty formed to fit the new conditions. The body of doctrine first discussed is that developed in the United States, the pioneer in modern Federalism.

Contemporary with the French, German and English theories already discussed, there were interesting and important developments under the conditions prevalent in the New World. Here the course to be taken by the theory was not determined by the necessity of reconciling pre-revolutionary and post-revolutionary political conditions, as in Germany and France; nor was it dictated by the desire for increased definiteness in the science of law, as in England with the analytical school. In America the supremacy of the Revolutionary ideas was theoretically uncontested, and in consequence it was unnecessary to adopt a compromise system such as that which found favor on the continent;[1] and,

[1] The political theory used by the Americans in the Revolutionary struggle was similar to that of the English revolutionists in the 17th century, and best stated by Locke. It was declared repeatedly that all power arises from the people, that all political authorities are their creatures, and that the people retain the right to alter the form of Government at will. See James Otis, *Rights of British Colonists*

there was no demand for the keen and careful analysis which Austin had brought to bear on the problems of jurisprudence.

In the New World the trend taken by the theory was determined by the peculiar political conditions reflected in the unique frame of government under which the Republic was organized in 1789.[1] The constitution of 1789 was the result of a compromise between the claims presented by the advocates of particularism, that is to say of the states as such, and those put forward by the representatives of the nationalistic spirit. Under the influence of particularistic tendencies the states were unwilling to accept the rank of communities wholly devoid of sovereignty, completely under

Asserted and Proved, 1764; *Inquiry into the Rights of the Colonists*, 1765; Samuel Adams, in *The Life and Public Services of S. Adams* by J. K. Hosmer; John Adams, *Dissertation on the Canon and the Feudal Law*, 1765; *Essays on the British Constitution*, 1765; Thomas Jefferson, in the Declaration of Independence, and throughout his *Works*, (Ford's Edition) IV, 362, 465, 473; V, 115; Thomas Paine, in *Common Sense*, 1776. The idea of popular sovereignty was also expressed very forcibly in the declarations made by the various States. See the Massachusetts Proclamation of Jan. 23d, 1776: "It is a maxim that in every Government there must exist, somewhere, a supreme, sovereign, absolute and uncontrollable power; but this power resides, always, in the body of the people, and it never was, or can be delegated to one man or a few, the great Creator having never given to men a right to vest others with authority over them unlimited, either in duration or degree."—*Force's Archives*, IV, 4—834. Compare the Virgina Bill of Rights, 1776, Sec. 2: "That all power is vested in and consequently derived from the people; that magistrates are their trustees and servants and at all times amenable to them;" also Sec. 1, 3, Maryland, 1776, Art. I. IV. of Decl. of Rights where the doctrine of non-resistance is denounced as "absurd, slavish, and destructive of the good and happiness of mankind." A similar assertion was made in other States. The political theory of the time was permeated through and through with the idea of popular sovereignty, and of the essentially fiduciary character of all Government. "We, the people" was the basis of both national and commonwealth constitutions.

[1] See on the period in general: J. W. Burgess, *Political Science and Comparative Constitutional Law;* G. T. Curtis, *Constitutional History of the U. S.;* H. von Holst, *Constitutional History of the U. S.;* J. Story, *Commentaries on the Constitution*, 1833.

the domination of a supreme central organization. Liberty was regarded as essentially local in its nature, and it was associated with the exercise of self-government on the part of the small communities which had long enjoyed a remarkable degree of autonomy. Centralization, on the other hand, was looked upon as hostile to liberty, and as highly favorable to the establishment of tyranny. There should be very little governmental power, it was thought, and that little should be well divided. But, on the other hand, the failure of the Confederation had demonstrated the pressing necessity for the organization of a government with powers of considerable extent. The constitution reflected, therefore, the political facts and the political theory of the time in its peculiar division of powers between local and central governments, and in its failure to define clearly and explicitly the ultimate source of sovereign power.

It is now proposed to discuss the various theories of sovereignty which grew up out of the governmental relations established by the new constitution. Since the so-called "Bundesstaat" has so deeply influenced the political theory of the last half century, and the American was the first modern state of this class, the treatment of the idea here developed appears to be indispensable to a proper appreciation of the recent movement in the domain of political science. It will be found, furthermore, that the American theories, though not often systematic and scientific in nature, have been widely influential in the development of the continental theory—a fact which Europeans themselves have been more ready to acknowledge than the Americans to assert. Nowhere more than in Germany itself, has there been a full recognition of the influence exerted by *The Federalist* and Tocqueville on the other hand, and that of the southern theorist, Calhoun, on the other.[1]

[1] See S. Brie, *Der Bundesstaat;* H. Preuss, *Gemeinde, Staat, Reich;* and the German theorists, Waitz and Seydel.

The idea of a division of the sovereignty appeared even at the time of the contest over the adoption of the constitution.[1] In *The Federalist*, which echoed the dominant sentiment of the day, the peculiar character of the new form of association was thoroughly discussed, and its double nature brought into the clearest light. The new Government, it was urged, is neither wholly federal nor wholly national, but a remarkable combination of the two elements; federal as to the extent of its power, national as to its operation within its sphere; federal and national in respect to the source of its power, federal and national in the method of amendment.[2] The constitution does not abolish altogether the State governments; it makes them "constituent parts of the national sovereignty" and leaves them in possession of "certain exclusive and very important portions of sovereign power."[3] The States will "retain all the rights of sovereignty which they before had, and which were not, by that act, exclusively delegated to the United States."[4] The argument was directed to show that in some way or other the governmental power was divided between the States, whose sovereignty had been explicitly recognized in the Articles of Confederation, and the newly-formed Government. Expressed in a manner confused and sometimes contradictory, there is nevertheless evident the idea that by the terms of the new national–federal constitution, the sovereignty was being divided between the States and the Nation.[5] Neither was to

---

[1] In the letter of the Constitutional Convention to Congress it was stated that "all rights of independent sovereignty" could not be secured to the States under a federal form of government.—*Journal of Congress*, 12, 165.

[2] Number 39.   [3] Number 39.

[4] Number 32. Compare the passages on the divisibility of the ultimate legislative authority, supported by references to the Roman *comitia centuriata* and *comitia tributa*, in no. 34.

[5] See number 20, against a "sovereignty over sovereigns;" number 46, on the people as back of both State and national governments. *Cf. Elliot's De-*

be supreme, both were to be limited. The Confederacy, it was said, failed in its attempt "to reconcile a partial sovereignty in the Union with complete sovereignty in the States;" "to subvert a mathematical axiom, by taking away a part and letting the whole remain;"[1] but in the new constitution no such blunder was to be made. The acceptance of this idea was enormously facilitated by reason of the prevalence of the theory that the Government was at best but an agent or delegate of another power, the real source of authority, the "people."

The idea of the divisibility of sovereignty was early enunciated by the United States Courts, notably in the case of Chisholm *vs.* Georgia (1792). Here the declaration was made that "the United States are sovereign as to all the powers of government actually surrendered. Each State in the Union is sovereign as to all the powers reserved."[2] Succeeding decisions gave expression to the same theory that sovereignty is capable of division and actually had been divided under the American system. The opinions of the Court were permeated with the idea of the division of powers between the States and the Union.[3]

---

bates, II, 356. In the New York Convention Hamilton said: "This is curious sophistry. That two supreme powers cannot act together is false. They are inconsistent only when they are aimed at each other or at one indivisible object. The laws of the United States are supreme as to all their proper constitutional objects; the laws of the States are supreme in the same way. These supreme laws may act on different objects without clashing, or they may operate on different parts of the same object with perfect harmony."

[1] Number 42.   [2] 2 Dallas, 435.

[3] Compare Ware *vs.* Hylton, 3 Dallas, 232 (1796): "The several States retained all *internal* sovereignty and . . . Congress properly possessed the great rights of *external* sovereignty." Cherokee Nation *vs.* Georgia, 5 Peters, 26: "They have in Europe sovereign and demi-sovereign States, and States of doubtful sovereignty. But this State, if it be a State, must be a grade above them all." See McCulloch *vs.* Maryland, 4 Wheaton, 316; Worcester *vs.* Georgia, 6 Peters, 591–92. In 1879, the court said that "when the National government was formed

One of the staunchest champions of the theory of divided sovereignty was James Madison. He maintained that the American Government was neither federal nor national; it was *sui generis,* federo-republican, unique in the nature of its construction, a "nondescript to be tested and explained by itself alone,"[1] an illustration of the adaptability of republican institutions to new and difficult conditions. To his mind nothing was clearer than the proposition that sovereignty may be divided. If it cannot, he urges, then "the political system of the United States is a chimera, mocking the vain pretensions of human wisdom."[2] Or again: "It is difficult to argue intelligibly concerning the compound system of government in the United States without admitting the divisibility of sovereignty." It is here necessary "to abandon abstract and technical modes of expounding and designating its character," and to regard the constitution as a "system hitherto without a model."[4] He found that the sovereignty was divided between the States on the one hand and the Union on the other, so that the whole society was, as he said, divided up into a number of little sovereignties, a condition which is by no means uncommon in the field of international law.[5] Moreover, he declared openly that the main pillar of "nullification" was the assumption that sovereignty is a unit, at once indivisible and inalienable.[6]

---

some of the attributes of state sovereignty were partially, and others wholly, surrendered, and vested in the United States."—Tenn. *vs.* Davis, 10 Otto, 226. T. M. Cooley, in his *Constitutional Limitations* (3d ed., 1874), I, holds that in American constitutional law there is a "division of the sovereignty between the National and State governments by subjects," each authority having, however, "supreme, absolute and uncontrollable power" within its own sphere of subjects.

[1] *Works,* IV, 420–21. [2] *Ibid.,* IV, 61.
[3] *Ibid.,* IV, 394. [4] *Ibid.,* 420–21.
[5] IV. 393.
[6] Frederick Grimke, *Nature and Tendency of Free Institutions,* 3rd edit. 1871 (1st 1848), 527, argued that "when we assert that the sovereignty is inalienable

In De Tocqueville's work on *Democracy in America* (1835), the American doctrine found a form which enabled it to exercise an important influence upon European thought. The idea of a division of sovereignty between the central and the local bodies was accepted in spite of the acknowledged difficulties in the way. " The rules of logic were broken," said he, " and the principle of the independence of the States triumphed in the formation of the Senate and that of the sovereignty of the Nation in the composition of the House of Representatives."[1] He found that there were two separate sovereignties, that of the Union — " an abstract being, which is connected with but few external objects;" and that of the States, which is " perceptible by the senses, easily understood and constantly active."[2] Such a system, however, although feasible for the United States in its isolated position, would be impracticable for the States of Europe. " A people," says De Tocqueville, " which should divide its sovereignty into fractional parts in the presence of the great military monarchies of Europe would, in my opinion, by that very act abdicate its power and perhaps its existence and name."[3] The division of sovereignty

---

or indivisible, we, in effect, impose *limitations* upon the sovereignty, which is a contradiction." He holds that in the United States, sovereignty is divided between the " States united " and the " States severally." — *Ibid.,* 519–20. Nathaniel Chipman, *Principles of Government,* 1833, 142 ff., concluded that there is an external sovereignty vested in the U. S., but no provision made in the constitution for an internal sovereignty. Sovereignty is also divisible: " the opinion formerly entertained that the sovereignty of a state was a sort of indivisible essence, a power absolute, uncontrolled and uncontrollable, has been corrected in modern times. Experience has shown it capable of division."—*Ibid.,* 273. *Cf.* E. D. Mansfield, *The Political Grammar of the United States,* 1834, 520–21.

[1] Bowen's Translation, 1882, I, 148. Sovereignty is defined as "the right of making laws."—I, 154.

[2] I, 214: " The sovereignty of the nation is factitious, that of the States is natural and self-existent, without effort, like the authority of a parent."

[3] I, 218. Compare E. A. Freeman on divided sovereignty, *History of Federal Government,* 1863, 15.

is a fact, but a fact made possible only by peculiarly favorable political conditions. The theory of De Tocqueville exercised a marked influence on the European discussion and doctrine, as will appear in the consideration of the later theory.

It seems correct to say that up to the time when the theory of Calhoun became widely influential, the characteristic American doctrine was that in the United States at least, whatever might obtain elsewhere, the sovereignty had been divided into several portions without the destruction of its life principle. Even Webster conceded that the States were unquestionably sovereign, so far as their sovereignty was not affected by the Constitution.[1] If the idea of double sovereignty seemed without adequate precedent, so was the whole American system without a historical parallel. As democracy seemed impossible until put in practice in America, so with the division of sovereignty. The fact that such a condition was nowhere else to be found did not constitute an argument against its acceptance, but rather was a testimony to the "peculiar adaptability of republican institutions." As already indicated, the progress of this notion of a division of sovereign power was facilitated by the prevalence of the idea of popular as opposed to governmental sovereignty, and by the presence of an idea that the New World had really little to do with the Old World conception of sovereignty. Webster asserted (1833) that the sovereignty of Government is "an idea belonging to the other side of the Atlantic; no such theory is known in North America . . . with us, all power is with the people."[2]

---

[1] *Works*, III., 321.

[2] *Works*, III., 469: "It seems to me, therefore, that we only perplex ourselves when we attempt to explain the relations existing between the general government and the several State governments, according to those ideas of sovereignty which prevail under systems essentially different from our own."

Sovereignty of the Government he denounced as a "feudal idea," inappropriate and unadapted to the needs of the Union. His great rival, Calhoun, was also ready to show that according to the American theory, "sovereignty resides in the people and not in the Government."[1] By neither of them was the ordinary administration or Government regarded as the genuine ruler, but merely as the agent or creature of the true ruler. It was this very idea which made it possible to talk about the division of the sovereignty, and consequently to quiet the contention between the States by constantly referring to that uncertain quantity, "the people."[2] There was really a very complicated problem to solve, since it involved the antithesis of people and Government, as well as that of State and Union.[3] When the contest between nationalism and particularism entered the acute stage, however, the doctrine of two sovereignties was less easy to maintain. The difficulty concealed behind the complicated governmental machinery and behind the ambiguous "people"

---

[1] *A Disquisition on Government* (1851), 139. His contention is that the "people" is the people of the several States, this being the only people known at the adoption of the Constitution. Nathan Dane, *General Abridgment and Digest of American Law*, 1823–29, vol. IX., Appendix, holds that sovereignty may be indivisible by "a people standing alone as in Russia or France," but in "a family political connexion," like the United States, we "give and distribute almost ad infinitum delegated powers, or what is vaguely called sovereignty." See sec. 8. It also appears that "though the nation is sovereign, the power of the general government is limited, and so, strictly and accurately speaking, is no sovereign."—*Ibid.*, sec. 18. On the omission of the term sovereignty in the Constitution, see sec. 35.

[2] See the argument of James Wilson, in the Pennsylvania Convention, *Elliot's Debates*, II., 504, against the charge that the Constitution would transfer sovereignty from State to general *government;* also, *The Federalist*, No. 46: "The Federal and State governments are, in fact, but different agents and trustees of the people, constituted with different powers and designed for different purposes."

[3] In 1885, Philemon Bliss, *Of Sovereignty*, wished to eliminate the concept of sovereignty from the Federal State and, in fact, from all States. *Cf.* p. 173: "It suggests personal supremacy, and ignores the true province of the magistrate;" p. 175: "Justice is the only true sovereign." See especially Lectures VII. and XII.

became apparent, and the compromise doctrine received the criticisms of both parties to the conflict.

Both the traditional contract theory and the doctrine of a divided sovereignty were energetically attacked by the leaders of the Southern movement; one was contrary to the logical basis of slavery, and the other to that of secession. It was John C. Calhoun who formulated the political theory of the particularistic party, giving to it a shape decidedly different from that of the earlier days. His doctrines were adopted by the champions of the cause of state's rights, who followed his argument even to the conclusion of war. Calhoun repudiated altogether the idea of a contract between individuals to form a political society, and preferred to base his theory upon the social and political nature of man. Men are not born equal, he says, and the state of nature is purely hypothetical and fictitious.[1] Government is not a matter of choice, but a necessity. "Like breathing, it is not permitted to depend on our volition."[2] Government is organized in obedience to a purely natural instinct, and no preliminary state of nature need be presumed to account for its existence among us.[3]

Having rejected the time-honored social contract, Calhoun made light work of the theory of a contract between the States.[4] He started with the thirteen sovereignties of the

---

[1] *A Disquisition on Government*, 58. See also, *A Discourse on the Constitution and Government of the U. S.*, 1851; also his *Works*.

[2] *Disquisition*, 8, also 56–57; *Works*, III, 507–12. Compare Thos. Cooper, *Lectures on Political Economy*, 1826. Here it is held that the law of nature "consists of systems fabricated by theoretical writers, on a contemplation of what might be usefully acknowledged among men as binding on each other." See p. 64. *Cf.* p. 362: "That which society refuses to acknowledge or sanction is not a right: it has no character of a right."

[3] Jellinek misinterprets the position of Calhoun in stating that he was under the influence of the ordinary contract theory. See *Staatenverbindungen*, 189.

[4] There were various applications of the contract theory to the relations between

Confederation, and declared that they had never divested themselves of their inherent quality as independent states. They were sovereign at the outset, and sovereign they continued to be. Calhoun refused the compromise theory already noticed, by the terms of which the sovereignty was divided between the States and the Nation, each party being given only limited powers. Tested by his keen, though narrow logic, the division of the supreme power presented insurmountable difficulties, and he was unable to see how such a separation could possibly be made. As he reasoned, sovereignty was "an entire thing—to divide is to destroy it."[1] Sovereignty, he asserts, is in its nature indivisible. "It is the supreme power in a State, and we might just as well speak of half a square, or half a triangle, as of half a sovereignty."[2] It must be one, or it is not at all; there is no possibility of a political organization consisting of a half-sovereign State or a number of half-sovereign States on the one hand, and a half-sovereign government on the other; there cannot be a State partly sovereign and partly not sovereign. The State must be either wholly and absolutely

the States. Tucker thought the Union formed by a contract similar to the social contract, except that the parties in this case were States instead of individuals. See *Tucker's Blackstone*, 1803, Appendix to Vol. I, Note A. Compare James Wilson, *Works*, I, 539; Madison, *Works*, IV, 63. Webster and Story declared that the Constitution was formed by individuals rather than States, and was really not a *compact*, but a *law*. Thus Story says of a State constitution, that it " is no further to be deemed a compact than that it is a matter of consent by the people, binding them to obedience to its requisitions. It binds them as a supreme rule ordained by the sovereign power, and not merely as a voluntary contract entered into by parties capable of contracting and binding themselves by such terms as they may choose to select."—II, sec. 349. On the general idea of the nature of the Constitutional contract, see an excellent article in *The American Historical Review* (April, 1900), by A. C. McLaughlin, entitled *Social Compact and Constitutional Construction.*

[1] *Disquisition*, 146.

[2] *Works*, II, 232. Speech on the Force Bill.

supreme, or is altogether and entirely subject; it cannot be half one and half the other. Calhoun recognized no middle way, he admitted no compromise, such as that suggested by the *Federalist*, by the courts, by Madison and by others during the first half century of the Union's existence. With rigorous logic, he urged the unity and indivisibility of the supreme power. The States were originally sovereign; they had not *wholly* given up this characteristic quality; they could not *partially* surrender it by a division of the power in various portions. The conclusion was that the Union was an association of States, each of which possessed in final analysis all the attributes of sovereign power.[1]

Although Calhoun refused to concede that the sovereignty itself was capable of division, he was nevertheless willing, in view of the peculiar structure of the federal government, to make certain explanations, if not concessions. It is true that the supreme power itself, the essential and vital principle in the State, cannot be divided; in strict logic this is inconceivable and impossible. There is a distinction, however, between the sovereignty itself and the powers or attributes belonging to it; between the sovereignty as the essential principle of the State and the exercise of the powers emanating from the sovereignty, as for example the legislative power and the executive power. These do not constitute the sovereignty itself but are merely certain sides of it, certain of its qualities. Now these powers or attributes may be divided without impairing the unity and integrity of the principle which lies back of them. Hence the States might cede to the general government the right to exercise certain

---

[1] Calhoun's attempt to distinguish between a mere "confederacy" and a "federal government" involved him in difficulties. Thus he said: "A federal government, though based on a confederacy, is to the extent of the powers delegated, as much a government, as a *national government* itself. It possesses to this extent all the authorities possessed by the latter, and *as fully and perfectly*."—*Disquisition*, 163.

functions which belong to the community in its sovereign capacity, as had been done in the formation of the Federal Union; but this delegation does not in any way amount to the cession of sovereignty, or to the relinquishment of any part thereof. What has been given up in such a case is not the power or principle itself, but only a temporary right to the exercise of the same; not the sovereignty, but the conditional right to exercise sovereign attributes. A State may be willing for some reason or other to allow the general government in a Union to wield certain of its powers, as the right to declare war and peace, and may actually grant the right to use such powers. Such a transfer is not, however, equivalent to an abandonment or alienation of the sovereignty of the State. This principle is something beyond powers such as those enumerated here. Sovereignty is not —and here is really the essence of Calhoun's argument—the sum of all these various powers, but on the contrary they must be regarded as emanations or outgrowths from the supreme power. Sovereignty is something integral, indivisible, unified, deeper than all the forms of its manifestation. It is not legislative, executive, or judicial powers, not their sum, or aggregate, but the vital principle of the State, out of which all these powers arise and on which they rest.

Such was the reasoning by which the illusion of sovereignty as divided between the central Government and the States was dispelled, and the alternative of national or State sovereignty presented in the most uncompromising style. Calhoun's doctrine became the political dogma of the particularistic party; it was pressed with the most rigid and unyielding logic and led straight to the trial of arms in the Civil War. After the close of the struggle, the doctrine of Calhoun was restated in defense of the Southern cause. Sage[1] compared

[1] *The Republic of Republics, or American Federal Liberty*, by P. C. Centz (Bernard J. Sage), edit. of 1881 (first ed., 1865), page 305. *Cf.* p. 583: "Sovereignty . . .

the sovereignty to will, or to a mental unity which cannot be broken up or disintegrated, which must be whole, if it is to be at all. It is really the life and soul of the State, and can no more be divided than can life itself, and remain life. A similar position was taken by Jefferson Davis,[1] the President of the Confederacy, and Alexander H. Stephens,[2] both of whom defended the unity and indivisibility of the sovereignty.

Not wholly unlike the theory of Calhoun, in certain of its features, was the doctrine upon which the justification of the nationalist cause was finally made to rest. The idea of a contract between States similar to that between individuals in the formation of political society was given up, and the structure of political theory in general was put upon foundations other than those of the Revolutionary philosophy. The tendency manifested in the European development already discussed was also manifested here. Furthermore, there was with the nationalists, as with Calhoun, the refusal to compromise the question of sovereignty by an admission of the possibility of its division between various parties, and the unqualified declaration in favor of the supremacy of one of the parties, in this instance the nation. Joseph Story early distinguished two senses of the term sovereignty, in such a way as to obviate the difficulties inherent in the idea of a double supremacy. He observed that "by sovereignty in its largest

---

can be nothing less than the life and soul of the State, in point of importance;" p. 306: Sovereignty is not a mere sum of rights and powers. See his criticism of erroneous theories of sovereignty in chap. VI.

[1] *The Rise and Fall of the Confederate Government*, 1881.

[2] *A Constitutional View of the Late War Between the States*, 1868–70. Sovereignty is "that innate attribute of the Political Body so possessing it, which corresponds with the will and power of self-action in the personal body, and by its very nature is indivisible, as much as the mind is in the individual organism," II, 22; also I., 488. Compare *A Brief Inquiry into the True Nature and Character of our Federal Government*, by A. P. Upshur, 1840, a review of Story's *Commentaries*.

sense is meant supreme, absolute, uncontrollable power, the *jus summi imperii*, the absolute right to govern."[1] But the term, he showed, is also used in another and more limited sense, signifying "such political powers as in the actual organization of the particular State or nation are to be exclusively exercised by certain public functionaries without the control of any superior authority." In this sense, he continues, the sovereignty "may be of a very limited nature. It may extend to a few or many objects. It may be unlimited as to some, it may be restrained as to others." In this use of the term, sovereignty is not the ultimate political power, but that which "under the given form of organization" is exercised "without the control of superior authority." From this point of view it is easy to regard sovereignty as theoretically divisible and as actually divided between the States and the Union, understanding that the "absolute right to govern" still remains in its original unity and integrity. Sovereignty in the limited sense is divided; in the broader sense it remains one.

A great impetus to the nationalist movement was given by Francis Lieber in the *Manual of Political Ethics*, 1838–39, and *Civil Liberty and Self-Government*, 1853,[2] where the doctrine of sovereignty was strongly stated and its intimate relation to the nation made clear. Sovereignty is defined as "the right, obligation and power which human society or the State has to do all that is necessary for the existence of man in society."[3] It is the natural outgrowth

---

[1] *Commentaries*, sec. 207, 208. See Story's views on the contract theory, which he accepted in a very qualified sense only.—Sec. 327.

[2] See also *Miscellaneous Writings*, 2 volumes, containing, " What is Our Constitution—League, Pact or Government ?" 1860–61; *Nationalism and Internationalism*, 1868.

[3] " It is the basis of all derived, vested or delegated powers, the source of all other political authority, itself without any source, imprescriptible in the nature of man. Prima et summa civitatis vis et potestas."—*Political Ethics*, I, 216 (2d ed., 1875).

of the society, as essential to the community as the right to breathe is to a man. It constitutes the vital principle of the State, is inseparable from its existence; to conceive of its alienation by the State is impossible. As Lieber says, it cannot be alienated any more than the trees can delegate the right to sprout.[1] Nevertheless, the sovereignty is not to be taken as an absolute and unlimited power, since absoluteness either in society collectively or in any individual is inadmissible. Absolute power presupposes a right to absolute obedience, to which no merely human authority can claim title.[2] Despotism is despotism, whether it comes from prince or from people.

The most significant part of Lieber's theory is that as to the location of the supreme power. Sovereignty is considered as a fact with which the individual as such has nothing to do; it is on the contrary the function of the society as a whole. It belongs to the community in its organic capacity;[3] it must be socially and organically construed. The doctrine that the supreme power rests with the "people," in its turn resting upon a contract, is no longer satisfactory; the real basis is the great organism which the society itself constitutes. In the fact of organic unity, he says, lies the chief difference between the nation and the people. "People" signifies merely "the aggregate of the inhabitants of a terri-

---

[1] *Political Ethics*, I, 219.

[2] *Ibid.*, I, 181. "Vox populi, vox Dei," cannot be endorsed. "In active politics and in the province of practical liberty, it either implies political levity . . . . or else it is a political heresy, as much so as vox regis, vox Dei would be."—*Civil Liberty and Self-government*, p. 408 (3d ed., 1877). Compare *Miscell.*, II, 129.

[3] *Pol. Ethics*, I, 219. It appears that there are three ways in which the sovereignty of the society is manifested, through *public opinion,* through the *creation of law,* and finally by means of what is termed *power.* The greatest emphasis is placed upon public opinion, which is "the aggregate opinion of the members of the State, as it has been formed by practical life."—*Pol. Ethics*, I, 223. "Public opinion is the continued sovereign action of society."—*Ibid.*, 226.

tory without any additional idea, at least favorable idea."[1] "Nation," on the other hand, implies a homogeneous population, inhabiting a coherent territory; a population having a common language, literature, institutions, and "an organic unity with one another, as well as being conscious of a common destiny."[2] Here was for the nationalists a doctrine more easily defensible than that of the sovereignty of the people in the indefinite contractual sense. The sovereign power which Calhoun said did not exist outside of the individual States was found now in the nation organically considered. The nation was glorified and exalted until it became itself a real existence, an actual entity, a body to which the supreme power might easily be attributed. On this basis the Unionists finally rested their cause, and on this ground were made those defenses of the Union which appeared in the years immediately following the Civil War. The argument was carried back of governmental forms, back of the written Constitution, so long a popular idol, to the primary source of power, the nation itself as the real bearer of the sovereignty, the true fountain of all governmental authority, local or central. In this way reasoned Jameson,[3] Brownson,[4] Hurd,[5] Mulford,[6] Pomeroy.[7]

With this school, the tendency is to assert the nation as a whole as against any of its parts, or even the sum of its

[1] *Miscellaneous Writings, Nationalism and Internationalism*, II, 228.

[2] II, 228. See II, 157.

[3] John A. Jameson, *A Treatise on Constitutional Conventions: Their History, Powers and Modes of Procedure*, 1866. See also, *Political Science Quarterly*, V, 193.

[4] O. A. Brownson, *The American Republic*, 1866.

[5] John C. Hurd, *The Theory of our National Existence*, 1881; *The Union State*, 1890.

[6] E. Mulford, *The Nation*, 1870.

[7] J. N. Pomeroy, *Constitutional Law*, 1868. Compare S. G. Fisher, *The Trial of the Constitution*, 1862.

parts; to go back of written documents, if necessary, to the authority that wrote or can rewrite them. Thus, it is urged by Jameson that "sovereignty resides in the society or body politic, in the corporate unit resulting from the organization of many into one, and not in the individuals constituting such unit, nor in any number of them, as such, nor even in all of them, except as organized into a body politic and acting as such."[1] The Nation is regarded as "a people bound together by common attractions and repulsions, into a living organism." [2] Brownson held that the sovereignty rests with "the people or the collective body," in a modified organic sense.[3] Under the acknowledged influence of writers such as Hegel, Stahl and Bluntschli, Mulford defended the Nation in the most approved German style. To him it appeared as an organism, not as an artificial construction; moreover as a "conscious" organism, as a "moral" organism, and finally as a "moral personality." Political sovereignty he interprets as "the assertion of the self-determinate will of the organic people;" while "the people in its wholeness, in its normal and moral relations, in its conscious unity, constitute the nation." [4]

While these defenders of the Union agreed in vesting the sovereignty in the Nation, as opposed to the individual

---

[1] *A Treatise, etc.*, 4th ed., 1887. Sovereignty is taken in the Austinian sense as "the person or persons in the State to whom there is politically no superior."—Sec. 18. It is inalienable, indivisible, *etc.*—Sec. 22.

[2] *Ibid.*, Sec. 30.

[3] Brownson's work is written from the Catholic standpoint. He holds that "political authority is derived by the collective people or society *from* God, *through* the law of nature."—*Op. cit.*, p. 133. He finds that by the unwritten constitution the "people" are sovereign, but that by the terms of the written constitution there is really no sovereignty, the governmental powers being divided between the local and the general governments. See ch. XI. *Cf.* p. 65: Society is "an organism, and individuals live in its life as well as it in theirs." See also, p. 221.

[4] *The Nation*, passim.

States, as such, there was not entire harmony of opinion as to what part the States were to play in this great body, now endowed with all the attributes of sovereignty.[1] Jameson maintained that the nation is "a political body one and indivisible, made up of the citizens of the United States, without distinction of age, sex, color, or condition in life."[2] This is the ultimate source of political power, out of which all authority flows. Generally and regularly the sovereignty is exercised, it is true, through the individuality of the groups called States, but back of these States there is another power, by which theirs may be limited and restrained, namely the sovereignty of the nation as just described.[3] If the nation outgrows the political system under which it operates, it has still the sovereign right (*i. e.* revolutionary right) to construct new and different forms. To the sovereign all things are possible.

On the other hand, the necessity of the recognition of the States as integral parts of the Union was not less strongly urged. Brownson, although defending the sovereignty of the nation, declared that the political or sovereign people of the United States exists as States united, and only as united States. That is to say, the true sovereignty is the people as organized in the States.[4] In the same spirit, Hurd contended for the recognition of the "States

---

[1] W. A. Dunning, *Essays on the Civil War and Reconstruction*, pp. 99 *et seq.*

[2] *Treatise*, sec. 57. "Modes and instruments . . . merely indicate how sovereignty or exercised, refer, in short, to systems of government established by the sovereign, or conceived to be within its competence to establish."—Sec. 55.

[3] *Ibid.*, sec. 55. There are two modes in which sovereign powers may be exercised, the *regular* and the *irregular.*—Sec. 56. The latter is the field of "possible exercise"—"a field of indeterminate extent, commensurate with the needs of the sovereign body as determined by itself." Compare Mulford, *The Nation*. See the case of Luther *vs.* Borden, 7 Howard, 1, with the argument on the legality of the "popular" government of Rhode Island in 1842.

[4] *American Republic*, p. 219.

united;" "the people," he says, "or the nation holding sovereignty as distinct from the States or the politically organized people of the States, was therefore not even a myth, unless there can be a myth without any mythical history."[1] Since the Civil War, however, it may be held that the former relations have changed, and sovereignty is vested at present in the "aggregated millions, the inorganic people, the nation as a mass."[2]

In any case the ultimate repository of political power was found to be the nation and not the separate, individual States. And it was a nation conceived as the result, not of a purely voluntary contract, but of a more or less unconscious evolution, which obtained recognition as the bearer of the supreme power. The *Union* was something above the individual, above the State, superior to all restraints, even those of the constitution. The idea did not in general, however, attain the degree of abstraction which was reached in Germany, during the contest between king and people. In America the State could not become the demi-god which Hegel had worshipped and his followers after him. It sufficed to establish the doctrine that the ultimate deciding power was not the prerogative of any one commonwealth in the Union, but belonged to the great body, the organism as it was termed, above all the individuals and all the States of which the Union was made up.

[1] *The Theory of our National Existence*, 113.

[2] *Ibid*, 353. Hurd's theory is decidedly Austinian in its nature. There is necessary in every society a supreme power, "limited only by conditions of physical existence" (p. xxi), extending to "all possible action of men in respect to others;" indivisible "in the hands of its ultimate possessors." (xxii). The possession of sovereignty must be regarded, not from the point of view of law, constitutional or otherwise, but from that of fact. "Sovereignty cannot be an attribute of law, because, by the nature of things, law must proceed from sovereignty. By the pre-existence of a sovereignty, law becomes possible; or, law exists in the exercise of sovereignty."—*Ibid.*, 97.

The progress of the American theory under the influence of the federal system may be summarized, then, as follows. Aided by the prevalent notion that sovereignty belongs to the people rather than to the government, the idea of a divided sovereignty was developed, becoming, as in the thought of Madison, a fundamental characteristic of the American system. In the contest between nationalism and particularism, however, this compromise was rejected by both sides. Calhoun and the Southern school advanced the doctrine that sovereignty is essentially one and indivisible—must exist in its integrity or not at all, the conclusion drawn being to the advantage of the individual States. On the other hand, the nationalists began to distinguish between sovereignty in the narrower sense, that is to say the governmental sovereignty, which is capable of division, and sovereignty in the broader sense, the ultimate sovereignty which is indivisible and which rests with the "people." At the same time "people" came to signify less an artificial aggregation, but more and more something organic in its nature, possessing a real existence of its own—a nation.

The results of the American development finally took scientific form at the hands of J. W. Burgess, in *Political Science and Comparative Constitutional Law* (1892.) Sovereignty is here conceived as the "original, absolute, unlimited, universal power over the individual subject and over all associations of subjects;"[1] as an essential quality of the State, indeed the most indispensable mark of statehood. "Really the State cannot be conceived without sovereignty: *i. e.*, without unlimited power over its subjects; that is its very essence."[2] There is no other power, no association or

---

[1] *Political Science, etc.*, I, 52. *Cf.* review of Laband's *Staatsrecht*, in *Pol. Sci. Quarterly*, III., 123.

[2] *Pol. Sci.*, I., 56.

organization which can be conceived as limiting the State in its control over its subjects, for the authority which could exercise such power would itself be sovereign. It is true that the State may abuse its unlimited power, and wrong the individual under its control; but the national State is after all "the human organ least likely to do wrong."[1] Moreover, this unlimited power on the part of the State necessitates no apology to civil liberty for its existence, since this very power is the real guarantee of and security for individual liberty; and hence the more completely and really sovereign the State is, the truer and securer is the liberty of the individual.[2]

The strongest objection to the recognition of the absoluteness of sovereignty arises, it is pointed out, from the general failure of publicists to distinguish clearly between *State* and *Government*.[3] One fears to place unlimited power in the hands of the ordinary Government, and failing to distinguish between this and the State, declares against supreme power in general. In strict analysis, however, the "Government is not the sovereign organization of the State. Back of the Government lies the constitution, and back of the constitution the original sovereign State which ordains the constitution both of Government and liberty." Recognizing the fact that the sovereignty belongs not with the ordinary Government or administration, but with the State in supreme organization, the admission of the character of the ultimate power presents fewer and less formidable difficulties. This double organization is a feature in which American public law has advanced

---

[1] *Ibid*, 57. "For the present and the discernible future, the National State appears to be the organ for the interpretation, in last instance, of the order of life for its subjects."—*Ibid.*, 55.

[2] *Ibid.*, 56.

[3] Compare Lieber, *Political Ethics*, 245; Brownson, *The Am. Rep.*, 174–75; Willoughby, W. W., *The Nature of the State*, 1896, 8, 206 n.

beyond that of the States of Europe, since here is to be found an organization of the Government in its local and central branches, and then, above these Governments, the organization of the State in its supreme and all-controlling capacity.[1] It is to this ultimate organization, and not to the ordinary organs of Government, that sovereignty really belongs.

From the principle that sovereignty is a unit it follows that the so-called Federal State is an impossibility, as there is either one supreme State over subordinate communities, or there are several independent States under a common government.[2] It is possible that there may be created a Federal Government; but a Federal State is impossible. What seems to be such is usually a single State, formed from many States and allowing these members a prominent place in the newly established government. Sovereignty, it is argued, "is entire or not at all," and what remains to the former States is only "the residuary powers of government," by no means equivalent to sovereignty or any portion thereof.[3]

Thus on the basis of the distinction between the State in its ultimate and in its ordinary organization, the recognition of both the unity and the absoluteness of the supreme power is greatly facilitated. This is true of the unity, since the sovereignty rests with the State, while the governmental powers may be divided among the organs of the government; and of the absoluteness, since it becomes evident that the State itself, and not the everyday government, is the body to which political omnipotence is attributed. The

---

[1] See *Pol. Sci.*, I, 57; I, 142, ff.

[2] *Ibid.*, I, 77 ff.; II, 5, ff.

[3] *Ibid.*, II, 7. "It requires patient reflection and successful discrimination to attain a point of view from which it is clearly seen that there can be no such thing as residuary sovereignty."

government may be limited at will in favor of individual liberty by the State, which marks out the limits of the government and the individual. Against the State there is of course no guarantee possible, but as already seen, the national State is the safest repository for irresponsible power.[1]

[1] Compare Woodrow Wilson, *The State* (1892); *An Old Master and Other Political Essays* (1893). A distinction is drawn between "the powers and processes of governing on the one hand," and "the relations of the people to those powers and processes on the other."—*Essays*, 80. Sovereignty is the power of "framing and giving efficacy to laws."—*Essays*, 81. It is none the less sovereignty, because limited by the degree of obedience accorded it. The sovereign organ of the State is found to be the "law making organ."—*Essays*, 95. It is held that the individual States of the Union still preserve the character of genuine States, although their "sphere is limited by the presiding and sovereign powers of a State superordinated to them. . . . They have *dominion;* it has *sovereignty.*" —*Essays*, 94. Compare W. W. Willoughby, *An Examination of the Nature of the State*, 1896, who understands by sovereignty "the supreme will of the State" (p. 280), and denies the possibility of a non-sovereign State, p. 244. Sovereignty must be located in a *political* body, and not in the general will, opinion or sentiment of the community. "Those persons or bodies are the sovereigns who have the legal power of expressing the will of the State. . . . We leave to the sociologist or practical politician, the examination of the nature and force of Public Opinion."—*Ibid.*, 293–94. Or, as elsewhere stated: "All organs through which are expressed volitions of the State, be they parliaments, courts, constitutional assemblies, or electorates, are to be considered as exercising sovereign power, and as constituting in the aggregate the depository in which the State's sovereignty is located."—*Ibid.*, 307. State and sovereignty are considered to be almost identical. "In fact, it is almost correct to say that the sovereign will is the State, that the State exists only as a supreme controlling will."—*Ibid.*, 302.

CHAPTER X

FEDERALISM AND THE CONTINENTAL THEORY

WE have now to consider the development of the theory of sovereignty in another connection, namely in relation to the two great types of Federal Government on the continent, Germany and Switzerland. There the progress of ideas was similar to that already observed in America, but was accompanied by far greater refinement of analysis and much more philosophic method of treatment throughout.[1] The long-protracted struggle over the so-called internal sovereignty in the German States was not yet ended, when there began another and still more complicated contest over a different aspect of the problem. The occasion of the first contest had been the necessity of an adjustment of the system of public law to the new order of things introduced by the Revolution, and the result had been the formulation of the doctrine of the sovereignty of the State. The new task was the adaptation of the doctrine of sovereignty to the peculiar relations to one another sustained by the several States under the closer form of association adopted. There was now involved, not the relation of king or Government to people, but that of State to State or community to community. Moreover, a further complication arose from the fact that the organs of local government were introduced into

---

[1] See the works already cited, page 158; and also Otto Gierke, *Althusius*, Pt. II, chap. v, Die Idee des Foederalismus, coming down to the 19th century; Albert Hänel, *Deutsches Staatsrecht*, 1892; Laband, *Das Staatsrecht des deutschen Reiches*, 3d ed., 1895.

the number of elements to be considered, thus still more embarrassing the publicists in determining the proper position of the newly aggregated "States."[1]

The historical basis for the theories here considered was found in the formation of closer union between the States in Germany and a similar process in Switzerland. The German Confederation, composed originally of forty States, was formed in 1815.[2] By the constitution itself the union was expressly termed an "international association" (völkerrechtlicher Verein), and the prerogatives of the separate States were carefully reserved. It was a "Staatenbund," as was the American Union under the Articles of Confederation. Attempts to form a more intimate union, notably that of 1848–49, proved unsuccessful, until a crisis was reached in the war of 1866. The events of this year resulted in the union of twenty-two States in the North German Confederation of 1867,[3] in which the supremacy of the Union was asserted with greater distinctness. This was followed by the formation of the German Empire under the constitution of 1871. The Swiss constitution underwent a number of changes during the century, of which the general tendency was toward a more intimate association.[4] Yet the exclusive supremacy of the Union was not recognized, and the constitutions of 1848 and 1874 contained the significant sentence; "The Cantons are sovereign in so far as their sovereignty is

---

[1] In 1857–63 appeared the work of Gneist on *Das heutige englische Verfassungs und Verwaltungsrecht*, and in 1865–68 that of Stein, *Die Verwaltungslehre*, marking the rise of interest in local self-government. A little later came Gierke's work on the Genossenschaft.

[2] See Die Bundesakte, June 8th, 1815; Die Wiener Schlussakte vom 15 Mai, 1820.

[3] The Constitution could be amended by a majority vote in the Reichstag, and a two-thirds vote in the Bundesrath; by the Constitution of 1871, fourteen negative votes in the Bundesrath are sufficient to prevent an amendment.

[4] See Bluntschli, *Geschichte des schweizerischen Bundesrechts*.

not limited by the Federal Constitution, and as such, exercise all rights which have not been delegated to the Federal Government."[1]

During the earlier years of the existence of the German Confederation, there was a general opinion that it was to be construed as an association of sovereign States.[2] Those members which had but recently come into the possession of sovereignty were naturally desirous to retain it undiminished. Under the influence of the movement for German unity, however, there was a tendency to concede the possibility of a diminution or limitation of the sovereignty in some way.[3] This was, in fact, a condition precedent to the success of any attempt to unite the German States; for an effective union of sovereigns was difficult to organize and maintain.[4]

In 1853, there emanated a new theory from the historian

[1] Const. of 1848, Article III; Const. of 1874, Article IV.

[2] Under the old Empire there was ample occasion for the formulation of theories as to the nature of state associations. As early as 1661, Lud. Hugo, in *De statu regionum Germaniæ et regimine principum, etc.*, declared the sovereignty in the Empire divided between the central and the local states. Pufendorf, *De Statu Imperii Germanici*, 1667, denied this, but was driven to declare that the Empire was not a regular form of state at all, but must be looked upon as a " monstrum." Preuss says: "So haben diese ersten Kämpfer in diesen Streite eine bleibende prototypische Bedeutung."—*Gemeinde*, 17.

[3] See Brie, *Der Bundestaat; cf.* Welcker, *Staatz-Lexikon*, Artikel *Bund* (1836), III, 86; Rotteck, *Lehrbuch des Vernunftrechts*, III, 152; Bluntschli, *Geschichte des Schweizerischen Bundesrechts*, 1849, I, 518. But see Stahl: *Die deutsche Reichsverfassung*, 1849.

[4] See the Frankfurter Reichsverfassung, Art. I, sec. 5 : " Die einzelnen deutschen Staaten behalten ihre Selbständigkeit, soweit dieselbe nicht durch die Reichsverfassung beschränkt ist; sie haben alle staatlichen Hoheiten und Rechte, soweit diese nicht der Reichsgewalt ausdrücklich übertragen sind." In the movement of 1848, there was, on the one hand, a contest between people and king, popular versus monarchical sovereignty; and on the other, particularism versus nationalism, state versus national sovereignty. It was, therefore, necessary to regard the supreme power in both its internal and its external phases—a condition which enormously increased the difficulties of interpretation. As will be seen, there was developed a theory of sovereignty adapted to each case.

and publicist, Georg Waitz.¹ To the existence of a Bundesstaat, he asserted, it is necessary that a definite portion of the political functions of the association be given up to the charge of the individual members, and another portion placed under the care of the body as a whole. The central government and each member of the association has its own organization; each has its own particular sphere of operations. Within the limits of its own sphere, one is as independent in the exercise of its power as is the other. "Now this independence," urged Waitz, "may not inappropriately be called by a name customary in Political Science, sovereignty."² Although it may seem that in a federal State the sovereignty of members must be limited, it must also be observed that " only the *extent*, not the *content* of the sovereignty is limited, and this for the one as well as for the other."³ In other words, the sovereignty of the undivided States, though it may be limited in its range of action, is as perfect and complete within this range, as if without any restraint whatever in the field of its activity.⁴ The power is irresistible and supreme, *as far as it goes*. The sovereignty is to be considered, it appears, qualitatively rather than quantitatively. The question is not how far does the power extend, if it is sovereign, but in what manner is it exercised within the given limits. The sovereign need not be very extensive, but it must be intensive. Thus, the local or State

---

¹ *Allgemeine Monatschrift.*

² "Mann kann diese Selbständigkeit mit einem in der Politik üblichen Namen nicht unpassend Souveränetät nennen." *Grundzüge der Politik*, 1862, p. 162.

³ "Nur der Umfang, nicht der Inhalt der Souveränetät ist beschränkt und jener für die eine Staatsgewalt so gut wie für die andere."—*Ibid.*, 166.

⁴ Waitz really distinguishes between Staatsgewalt and Souveränetät. The former is "die Einheit der in dem Staat vorhandenen (lebenden) Kräfte oder Vermögen; andere Ausdrücke die man für die Staatsgewalt oder ähnlich wie Staatsgewalt gebraucht, haben eine andere Bedeutung, oder führen irre: Majestät, Souveränetät des Staates, Obrigkeit, Regiment."—*Ibid*, 17.

government may be just as much sovereign in its sphere, whatever that is, as the central or federal government in its; and both, as Waitz reasons, may be sovereign, that is to say, independent of control, in the limits of same State. There is, therefore, no contradiction involved in the statement that there may be two sovereigns in the State: if we understand by this two independent political powers, each supreme in its own particular sphere. If sovereignty is independence in a certain sphere, then one is as much sovereign, or independent, as the other. The negative quality of independence need not be the monopoly of one, but may be shared by many.

The ingenious theory of Waitz was widely influential, and succeeded in obtaining the endorsement of publicists such as Mohl,[1] Schulze,[2] Blumer,[3] Treitschke,[4] and others. Mohl still defended sovereignty in the earlier style, as absolute and indivisible, eternal and all-inclusive; nowhere was there to be found a stronger statement of its character. Yet, he was ready, nevertheless, to concede that there is one exception to this sweeping rule, and that is found in the case of a Bundesstaat. Here a part of the functions of the State is under the care of a number of subordinate organizations, while the remainder belongs to a higher, unified whole, the central

[1] Robert v. Mohl, *Encyklopädie der Staatswissenschaften*, 1872, 2d ed., 118 ff.

[2] *Einleitung in das deutsche Staatsrecht*, 1867, 207: "Nur da ein Bundesstaat vorhanden ist, wo die Souveränetät nicht dem einen und nicht dem andern, sondern beiden, dem Gesammtstaate und dem Einzelstaate, jedem innerhalb seiner Sphäre zusteht." See the retraction in his *Lehrbuch*, 1881, I, 39.

[3] J. J. Blumer, *Handbuch des schweizerischen Bundesstaatsrechtes*, 1863–64, I, 147.

[4] *Bundesstaat und Einheitsstaat*, 1864, in *Historische und Politische Aufsätze*, II. In the same year with Waitz, H. A. Zachariä, in *Deutsches Staats- und Bundesrecht* (2te Aufl., 1853), found in a Bundesstaat "Selbständigkeit oder Unabhängigkeit (s. g., Souveränetät) der Einzelstaaten in Betreff aller in die Sphäre der Staatsgewalt gehörigen Gegenstände, insoweit sie nicht in Interesse der Gesammtheit der Reichs- oder Bundesstaats-Gewalt überwiesen sind."—I, 94.

government.¹ In this case the States associated (*Gliedstaaten*) lose a part of their sovereignty and there is found beside the power of the State (*Staatsgewalt*) the higher power of the Union (*Bnndesstaatsgewalt*).²

The concept of a State with many sovereigns remained for a time the dominant one in the explanation of the true character of Federal State. This new concept was regarded as offering a solution for the difficulties necessarily accompanying that conflict between nationalism and particularism which was the permanent obstacle in the way of German unity and strength. With this idea as a basis it seemed possible to obtain all the advantages of unity without sacrificing the independence of the several States.³ If there might be many sovereigns in one State, the honor of all might be satisfied.

The source from which the theory was derived has already been made apparent in the discussion of the American doctrine. The work of De Tocqueville appeared in 1835, and it was under the influence of his statement of the federal system in the United States that the idea of Waitz was evolved. As he himself said: "Most of all Tocqueville's clear sighted exposition of the North American constitution instructed me." ⁴ The theory was, however, not Tocqueville's own, but the formulation of ideas already long in existence. It was, in fact, the familiar compromise theory of the American federal State that was applied by Waitz and his followers

---

¹ *Encyklopädie*, 118 ff.   ² *Ibid.*, 119.

³ *Ibid.*, 43. Schulze spoke in similar terms of the sovereignty.—*Einleitung*, 162.

⁴ *Allgemeine Monatschrift*, 1853, p. 496. See quotations from Tocqueville, 500, 501, 504. Waitz says that "den eigentlichen Fortschritt in dem Verfassungsleben der Völker überhaupt hat Amerika eben durch seine Bundesverfassung gemacht. Hier ist, wie wir zeigten, ein neues Princip grossartig durchgeführt. Die Weisheit seiner Staatsmänner hat nicht auf dem Wege theoretischer Betrachtung, sondern in praktischer Erfassung dessen was das Bedürfniss forderte, Grundsätze aufgestellt die eine allgemeine Bedeutung haben."—*Ibid.*, 530.

to the German problem. The reign of the new doctrine was, however, of short duration. Speculation was soon turned into another channel by the new course of political events, and though the idea of a limited sovereignty remained, it was no longer generally accepted.[1] The formation of the North German Confederation and of the German Empire did not proceed along lines favorable to the sovereignty of the States or to a division of sovereignty; but on the contrary emphasized the supremacy of the Confederation and later of the Empire. As Bismarck said: "It could not have been our aim to establish a theoretical ideal of a federal constitution in which, on the one hand, the unity of Germany should be permanently guaranteed, and on the other free play be given to every particularistic tendency. Such a philosopher's stone, if it is to be found, we must leave to the future."[2] The widespread con-

---

[1] Compare Rüttiman, *Das nordamerikanische Bundesstaatsrecht verglichen mit den politischen Einrichtungen der Schweiz*, 1867, I, 70–71 : " Ebenso ist der Ausspruch dass eine Theilung der Souveränetät zwischen der Union und den Staaten unmöglich, eine leere Behauptung die nicht nur jeder Begrundung ermangelt sondern auch durch die Erfahrung widerlegt wird." Karl Gareis, *Allgemeines Staatsrecht*, 1883, 31-32, concedes that sovereignty cannot be divided, but favors the use of the term "limited sovereignty." Will is *limitable*, he argues, though it is not at all divisible. J. B. Westerkamp, *Staatenbund und Bundesstaat*, 1892, maintains that sovereignty is neither illimitable nor indivisible. " Die Prämissen (Vollkommenheit, Einheit, Untheilbarkeit der Staatsgewalt) waren doch erst zu erweisen. . . . Uebrigens folgt aus den eben angeführten Namen nur die Unabhängigkeit von einer andern menschlichen Macht innerhalb des Bereiches, den die betreffende Gewalt hat, und das Recht der Selbstbestimmung innerhalb dieses Bereiches."—*Op. cit.*, 109. In his *Preussisches Staatsrecht*, I, 71, Bornhak finds that, considered positively as a sum of rights and powers, the sovereignty may be regarded as divisible. In this sense both Empire and the individual states are sovereign.—*Ibid.*, I, 73.

[2] Bezold, *Materialen der deutschen Reichsverfassung*, I, 117; Dubs, J., *Das öffentliche Recht der schweizerischen Eidgenossenschaft*, 2nd ed., 1878 (1st, 1877): " Man kann Grenzen eben so gut wie in Raum nach Materien oder nach andern, idealen Gesichtspunkten ziehen so dass man in solcher Weise verschiedenen Souveränetäten doch eigene Gebiete anweisen kann."—Pt. II, 24. Brie, S., *Theorie der Staatenverbindungen*, 1886, 25, refers to limited (eingeschränkte) and

viction that in the new union the sovereignty rested with the Empire itself, to the exclusion of the States of which it was made up, led to the rejection of Waitz's theory and to the formulation of a new principle better adapted to the political facts of the time.

In the new doctrine evolved, sovereignty was regarded from the point of view of the power of the community to fix the limits of its own jurisdiction; as the phrase ran, to determine its own "competence." There is no longer satisfaction with the idea that the States operate peacefully, each in its own sphere; but the further question is raised: Who has power to mark out the limits for the States? Who or what power determines these "spheres" in which Waitz had said the States might be each sovereign? If there is a power which fixes the limits of activity for both state and federal authority, is not this power to determine the boundaries, to fix the competence of the federal and local governments, the real essence of the much disputed sovereignty? Already in 1868 it had been argued by Georg Meyer, that a State must be in a condition to make whatsoever it chose an object of its activity, "in other words, be able to determine its own jurisdiction."[1] He had further urged that the community lacking such power was neither true State nor proper sovereign. Hence he drew the conclusion,[2] that the power to determine the limits of jurisdiction is an essential mark of sovereignty.

---

unlimited sovereignty. In the German Union, the Federal State is sovereign, but Prussia still retains its sovereignty.—*Ibid.*, 112. Karl v. Stengel in *Schmoller's Jahrbuch*, 1898, vol. 22³, 82, on *Staatenbund und Bundesstaat*, also admits the idea of a limited or relative sovereignty.

[1] *Grundzüge des norddeutschen Bundesrechts*, p. 3.

[2] "Ein Bund ist niemals souverän, mag er in der Form des Bundesstaates oder in der des Staatenbundes auftreten: es fehlt ihm stets ein nothwendiges Erforderniss der Souveränetät, die selbständige Bestimmung der Sphäre seiner Thätigkeit."—*Ibid.*, 24. The North German Union is limited in this respect and therefore not properly sovereign.—*Ibid.*, 56–57.

Four years later, after the formation of the German Empire, the same idea was reiterated with greater emphasis. Meyer declared that where there exists any power whatever which may constitutionally take away the powers of the individual States in an association, then it must be held that these States "are no longer sovereign, not even limitedly sovereign."[1] This, he found, was the case in Switzerland, North America and Germany, in all of which there is a supreme power, the "constitution-making power," which is superior to both central and State Governments.[2] This is alone the sovereign power, that is to say, it alone is able to determine the limits of activity for all authorities within the State. Likewise did Haenel argue for "Kompetenz–Kompetenz" as the characteristic feature of the notion of sovereignty.[3] No person or association in the State can be said, so runs the reasoning, to be able to extend or expand the field of its legal activity at will. They are all legally limited by some other and superior body. The sovereign alone has the power to do whatsoever it wills, to choose its own field of operation, to limit itself and to be limited by no superior. The city, for example, or the organ of local government, may have its jurisdiction expanded or contracted or wholly removed. It does not determine its own *legal competence*, but is subject to the will or command of another. The sovereign State, however, sees above itself no organization to which it is legally liable, no body which can

---

[1] *Staatsrechtliche Erörterungen über die deutsche Reichsverfassung*, 1872, 6. He excepts those states which possess certain rights not to be taken away without their consent. These, says Meyer, may be looked upon as still sovereign "in ganz beschränkter Weise."—*Ibid.*, 82.

[2] *Ibid.*, 7: "Diese Gewalt ist nicht etwa die Bundesgewalt......es ist vielmehr eine ganz besondere Gewalt, die verfassungsgebende."

[3] Albert Haenel, *Studien zum deutschen Staatsrechte*, Part I, 1873; *Die vertragsmässigen Elemente der deutschen Reichsverfassung*, Part II, 1888; *Deutsches Staatsrecht*, 1892.

by a legal or constitutional process determine the limits of its jurisdiction, no legal superior to whom it owes obedience.[1] Just here is to be found the essential and indispensable mark of sovereignty. " In this legal power of the State over its competence lies the first requisite of self-sufficiency, the kernel of its sovereignty." [2] The heart of the sovereignty of a State is, then, the " legal self-determination of its jurisdiction " (die rechtliche Selbstbestimmung seiner Kompetenz) ; the legal power, not the mere physical force, to say where it shall act and how it shall act. Lack of a legal superior constitutes sovereignty; the existence of such a superior is consistent with subordination only. In the German Empire, for example, what organ has the legal power to define its own limits; the individual State or States, or the Empire itself ? Applying his criterion, Haenel finds that the true sovereign is the Empire, inasmuch as it possesses the undisputed power to change its competence or jurisdiction as it will, since it has, in his own phrase, "the legal power of self-determination." [3] Acting in a wholly legal and constitutional way, the Empire may, as it chooses, increase its own powers, diminish those of the individual States, and determine their respective fields of governmental activity.

In like manner, Laband rejected the earlier theory of Waitz, and stigmatized the idea of the double-sovereignty as a chimæra. The national life, he held, can no more be torn in two and continue to be life, than that of the individual man.[4] States are either sovereign or non-sovereign; there is

---

[1] *Studien* I, 148: "So gilt von allen Personen im Staate in jedem Sinne der Satz, Niemand kann sich selbst seine Kompetenz erweitern, aber er trifft nicht zu für den Staat selbst."

[2] " In dieser Rechtsmacht der Staates über seine Kompetenz liegt die oberste Bedingung der Selbstgenügsamkeit, der Kernpunkt seiner Suveränetät."—I, 149.

[3] I, 240.

[4] *Das Staatsrecht des deutschen Reiches*, 1st ed., 1876–82; 2d, 1894; 3d, 1895.

no such a thing as a half, divided, diminished, dependent, relative sovereignty; but only whole sovereignty or no sovereignty.[1] By sovereignty he understands the power to determine the limits of jurisdiction for the community. Determine in whom this power lies, he says, and you determine where the sovereign power is. If limits for a State can be fixed by a power external to it and able to act without its consent, though still within the bounds of the existing law, the sovereignty of that State is simply at an end. There is no middle ground possible, since the community either has supreme power or has it not, and no compromise such as that suggested by Waitz and his school is admissible.[2] As a matter of law the Empire is sovereign, the States are subordinate and non-sovereign, and there is no division of the supreme power possible in theory or existent in fact.[3]

A modification of the Kompetenz-Kompetenz theory has been made by the Austrian publicist, Georg Jellinek.[4] His position is that while, so long as the community is considered internally, the sovereignty may consist in the legal power of a State to determine its own competence, yet from

---

[1] *Das Staatsrecht*, 2d ed., 15: "Das Kriterium der obersten, höchsten Gewalt besteht darin, dass sie nur sich selbst bestimmt und von keiner andern Gewalt rechtlich verpflichtende Vorschriften empfangen kann."

[2] 1st ed., I, 65. "Es giebt keine halbe, getheilte, verminderte, abhängige, relative Souveränetät, sondern nur Souveränetät oder nicht Souveränetät."—3d ed., I, 65, 66.

[3] 1st ed., I, 93. Treitschke changed front in 1874. See *Preussische Jahrbücher* xxxiv, on *Bund und Reich*. "The dualistic theory of the two sovereignties of the federal state stands in open contradiction to the public law of the two federal states of the present," 526. The essence of sovereignty is found "in der Kriegsherrlichkeit und in der Befugniss des Staates den Umfang seiner Hoheitsrechte selber zu bestimmen," 527. The Empire is sovereign, but Prussia with its veto over all constitutional amendments has not lost its sovereignty, 539.

[4] *Die rechtliche Natur der Staatenverträge*, 1880; *Die Lehre von den Staatenverbindungen*, 1882; *Gesetz und Verordnung*, 1887; *System der subjektiven öffentlichen Rechte*, 1892; *Ueber Staatsfragmente*, 1896.

an international point of view, this criterion appears to be insufficient.[1] This is seen clearly in the case of the suzerainty of one State over another, as that of Turkey over Bulgaria, in which case neither the superior nor the subordinate power has the right to change the limits of its legal competence with reference to the other. It seems that if " Kompetenz–Kompetenz" were made the test, neither Bulgaria nor Turkey would be sovereign, since neither can of its own will alter the limits set; so in the relations of Hungary with Croatia and Slavonia, as fixed in 1868.[2] Here the test fails, and no sovereign is discoverable, since the power to determine the limits of jurisdiction belongs to none of the communities in question. To Jellinek it seems preferable, therefore, to emphasize the manner in which a State may be legally bound, rather than its power to determine its legal competence. It is not necessary that a State be able to alter positively the boundaries of its jurisdiction, but merely that it cannot be legally bound except by its own will. If the State can be obligated by itself only, and by no other power, then we must say that it is in the possession of sovereignty. "Obligation *exclusively* through its own will," says Jellinek, "is the juristic mark of the sovereign State."[3] Other associations may be bound or obligated by a will not their own, as the city or the local community, but the sovereign State can be bound solely by its own will.[4] Sovereignty is therefore defined by Jellinek as "the characteristic of a State, through which it can be legally

---

[1] *Staatenverbindungen*, 29.   [2] *Ibid.*, 30.

[3] *Staatenverbindungen*, 34: "Ausschliessliche Verpflichtbarkeit durch eigenen Willen ist das juristische Merkmal des souveränen Staates."

[4] Jellinek argues throughout that the promises made by a state give rise to a real and genuine *right;* that if this be not true, neither constitutional nor international law is possible.

bound only by its own will."[1] Sovereignty is the power of exclusive legal self-determination. That State and only that State is sovereign, all of whose acts are determined in accordance with its own legal or constitutional forms, whose acts are all consequences of its own legally expressed will. Thus, as long as a State is bound merely by its own agreement or contract, it must be regarded as "legally self-determinate," in contrast to a body which is bound whether it wills or not.[2] Moreover, out of this idea of "legal self-determination," says Jellinek, come all the other attributes connected with the supreme power. From this follows the right to determine the competence of the State, from this the customary body of concrete rights, from this the indivisibility of the sovereignty, from this its permanence.[3] These qualities may all be derived from the primary concept of the power of exclusive obligation through one's own will.

Another argument in support of Jellinek's position is found in the possibility, under the new form of definition, of limiting the power which must otherwise appear as unlimited. As ordinarily considered, sovereign power is absolute and unlimited power; but if regarded as a right to exclusive self-determination, we do not shut out the idea of limitation altogether, but only that of limitation by another than one's own will. The sovereign power is limited, but only by itself, and in Jellinek's system this self-limitation may create perfectly good right.[4] Sovereignty is therefore regarded not as

[1] *Staatenverbindungen*, 34: " Souveränetät ist demnach die Eigenschaft eines Staates kraft welcher er nur durch eigenen Willen rechtlich gebunden werden kann."

[2] "Juristisch muss vielmehr, jeder Staat sofern und solange er nur durch einen Vertrag verpflichtet ist, was auch durch diesen seine politische Stellen werden möge, als souveräner Staat angesehen werden."—*Staatenverbindungen*, 55.

[3] *Staatenverbindungen*, 34, 35.

[4] Well stated in *Die rechtliche Natur der Staatenverträge*, 27 : " In every con-

limitlessness (Schrankenlosigkeit), but as the "possibility of self-limitation" (die Möglichkeit der Selbstbeschränkung),[1] with the emphasis on the "self." It is in the nature of the State that it should be limited (in Jellinek's sense of the term), but it is also in the nature of the sovereignty that it should be limited only by itself, by its own voluntary act, through the recognized organs of the State. "What could be maintained until now," says Jellinek, "only in spite of the sovereignty and against the sovereignty, can now be explained only through the sovereignty and out of the sovereignty." [2]

The new doctrine of sovereignty, then, whether as "Kompetenz–Kompetenz" or as "exclusive legal self-determination," replaced the earlier idea of a double sovereignty. The events of 1867 and 1871, the formation of the constitution for the North German Confederation, and still more that of the constitution of the Empire, made almost untenable the juristic position that there may be many sovereignties or many half-sovereignties within the limits of Germany. The proposition that the Union, the Empire, was the true sovereign and the only sovereign obtained general

crete act of will lies a limitation of the will.......Therefore every act of will on the part of the State is a limitation of the will of the State.......The State does not cease to will what it has once fixed as the content of its will, until a contrary act of will has annulled the first."

[1] *Staatenverbindungen*, 36. Haenel criticises Jellinek's proposition as being true only in the general sense that "all human will is in last instance determined by itself."—*Staatsrecht*, sec. 16.

[2] With Jellinek, compare H. Rosin, "*Souveränetät, Staat, Gemeinde, Selbstverwaltung*," in Hirth's *Annalen*, 1883, against "Kompetenz-Kompetenz," and in favor of "legal self-determination." Georg Liebe, *Staatsrechtliche Studien*, 1880, 10: "The sovereignty of a State does not consist in the fact that the State can in general do what it wills, but that in its legal capacity (Rechtsfähigkeit), in the capacity to determine its legal competence, it is *in general*, and in its capacity to act (Handlungsfähigkeit) *only so far*, limited as it wishes to limit itself." See also *Zeitschrift für d. g. Staatswissenschaft*, 1882.

recognition among publicists; the individual States were no longer able to maintain their claims to sovereignty, either in fact or in law. There was a constitutional power in article 78, to which they owed obedience.[1] But if sovereignty must be given, why, it was asked, is it necessary that statehood be surrendered with it? There is but one sovereign, is there also but one State? If there cannot be a *semi*-sovereign State, can there not be a *non*-sovereign State? In other words, is it not possible to separate sovereignty from statehood, to maintain that sovereignty is not an essential mark of the State?

Down to this time, as has been shown, sovereignty and statehood had been inseparably bound together; sovereignty had been regarded as the life and soul of the State, as its most essential and indispensable attribute. Whatever else the State might be, it was at all events and before all things a sovereign organization. From the time when the State emerged from the chaos of feudal conditions, its most characteristic element had been the possession of the supreme power. Bodin said: "The State is a just Government of many families with their common property and with sovereign power." Following him, political theorists had again and again built their systems of political science upon a like foundation: whatever else the State might be, it was supreme, it wore the crown and wielded the sceptre. Even more, in Germany itself there had been developed an exalted and majestic idea of the State by Hegel and his successors, and the long contest between king and people had ended with the general recognition that neither party was supreme, but that the only proper bearer of the sovereign power was this very *State*. But now the particularism of the members of the German Empire demanded however that either sov-

---

[1] Prussia retains a veto on all amendments to the constitution, and the states with reserved rights cannot be constitutionally deprived of them.

ereignty or statehood be assigned to them. The former quality they could no longer possess; the latter they could retain only by the divorce of the two concepts, sovereignty and statehood. Thus, in response to a demand of the former States for continued recognition, the idea of the non-sovereign State was formed.

The first step in this direction was taken by Georg Meyer (1872).[1] He announced that Bodin's idea of the State could lay no claim to universal application for all times and peoples, that it was not fitted to become the basis of political science. The true foundation for a system of modern politics must be found, not in the idea of the sovereign State, or of sovereignty as with Bodin, but in the political community (Gemeinwesen) in general, and aside from considerations of sovereignty or non-sovereignty. "State," he argued, may be used in two senses, either as having reference to a centralized State (Einheitsstaat) or to a member of a greater political society, along with other associated communities or States.[2] In the first instance, that is, in the case of a centralized State, we have a sovereign political entity, in the common use of the term; in the second instance the States possess only a limited governing power, and may or may not be sovereign, according to the nature of the union of which they are a part. If the political society is organized in the form of a confederacy, the members are fully

---

[1] *Staatsrechtliche Erörterungen*, 8: "Der Staatsbegriff Bodins kann daher eine allgemeine Gültigkeit für alle Zeiten und Völker nicht beanspruchen ...erscheint der Begriff des Staates nicht geeignet die Grundlage der politischen Wissenschaft zu werden. Mann muss vielmehr von dem allgemeinen Begriff des politischen Gemeinwesens ausgehen." With Meyer compare Mohl, *Encyklopädie* (1872), II, sec. 13, denying that sovereignty is an essential mark of the state.

[2] *Lehrbuch des deutschen Staatsrechts*, 1878, 2, 3: "Staaten in diesem Sinne sind niemals in vollen Umfange souverän. Die Frage ob sie ein beschränkte Souveränetät besitzen, kann nicht allgemein, sondern nur auf Grund eines concreten politischen Verbandes beantwortet werden."

sovereign still; if in the form of a Federal State, the possession of sovereignty may be a matter of doubt, but even if sovereignty is really lost, they remain as truly States as before the formation of the union.¹ "States," declares Meyer, "are those political communities which have the authority to perform political functions independently, that is, according to their own laws, and to regulate their constitution independently, that is, by their own laws." ² They may be either sovereign States, that is, "such as are subjected to no higher power, or they may be non-sovereign States, that is, those over which a superior political society has a limited government." ³

Laband also agreed to the possibility of a non-sovereign State. There are political communities, he claims, which although not sovereign, nor half-sovereign, nor relatively sovereign, are none the less entitled to the name of State. They possess a "non-sovereign political power," consisting in the fact that they can, "in their own right, and not on the basis of mere delegation, establish binding rules of law" (Rechtsnormen).⁴ They may have governmental rights,

[1] There are, it appears, two distinguishable elements in the idea of sovereignty, namely, that of independence (Unabhängigkeit) and that of absoluteness (Unbeschränktheit). In international law a State is sovereign when it has independence; in the sense of constitutional law, when it is unlimited by any other person on its territory.—*Lehrbuch*, 10.

[2] *Lehrbuch*, 4th ed., 1895, 8: "Staaten sind demnach alle diejenigen politischen Gemeinwesen, welche die Befugnisse besitzen, politische Aufgaben selbständig d. h. nach eigenen Gesetzen zu erfüllen und ihre Verfassung selbständig d. h. durch eigenen Gesetze zu regeln."

[3] *Ibid*.: "(a) welche keiner höheren Gewalt unterworfen sind; (b) welche einem höheren politischen Verbande eine beschränkte Herrschaft zusteht."

[4] "Autonomie als ein juristisch relevanter Begriff setzt daher eine nicht souveräne öffentliche rechtliche Gewalt voraus, der die Befugniss zusteht, kraft eigenen Rechts, nicht auf Grund blosser Delegation verbindliche Rechtsnormen aufzustellen."—*Staatsrecht*, I, 108, 1876. *Cf. Haenel Studien*, I, 63: "Nicht der Einzelstaat, nicht der Gesammtstaat sind Staaten schlechthin, sie sind nur nach der Weise von Staaten organisirte und handelnde politische Gemeinwesen."

although lacking sovereign power; they have State powers, although these are not sovereign State powers. The whole situation is summed up by Laband in the following way: " It is enough to show that when a number of States, formerly independent, come together in a Union, so that they have above them a superior power, nevertheless there can remain to them an abundance of governmental rights in their own name, of duties in the regulation of the community, and of means for their forcible execution. If these governmental powers belong to them in their own right, that is, not through delegation or transfer from the sovereign power that is superior to them, and if they can make these rights good according to their own independent will and execute them, they cease to be sovereign, but do not cease to be States."[1]

In the same path follows Jellinek, who admits the existence of political communities which govern, which give binding commands, which possess these powers, moreover, in their own right, yet are, despite all this, merely non-sovereign States.[2] The essential mark of the State is that it rules or governs, but this the non-sovereign may do as well as the sovereign. The essential point is that this be done in one's own right, and by this phrase Jellinek means that the right be "legally uncontrollable." Neither the source from which the right is derived, nor the manner in which it may be taken away is bound up in the idea of independent right. It is enough that under the existing legal order this right cannot be legally taken away.[3]

---

[1] *Staatsrecht*, 3d ed., 1895, 1–67. See *Staatsrecht*, 2d ed., 1894, 17: "Man kann also nach Gerber's zutreffenden Ausdruck die Souveränetät als eine Eigenschaft der vollkommenen Staatsgewalt bezeichnen; aber ein wesentliches Element des Staatsbegriff ist sie nicht."

[2] *Lehre von den Staatenverbindungen*, 36.

[3] *Ibid.*, 42: "Eigenes Recht ist rechtlich uncontrollirbares Recht," referring at

FEDERALISM AND CONTINENTAL THEORY

Even Gierke, who worked so effectively for the development of the theory of the sovereignty of the State as a juristic person, in order to reconcile the claims of king and people, is disposed to admit the possibility of a non-sovereign State. He refuses to consider those theories " which rob either the German Empire or the German individual States of their quality as States."[1] Since the Federal State exists as a State formed from associated States, the idea of the State must be so framed that it will remain applicable even in such a case. As a matter of fact and of law, these States exist, and political theory has no right to dispute their reality and possibility. Gierke starts from the proposition that the sovereignty, though the supreme and indivisible power, may nevertheless, as is generally recognized, be held in common by several organs. Thus the king is no longer the exclusive holder of the sovereignty, but has by his side other organs, such as the Legislature and the Judiciary. So, in the Federal State, reasons Gierke, there is a supreme and indivisible power, which is held in common by a number of parties, that is, the individual States and the central State.[2] None of these alone, but all taken together, are the real bearers of the sovereign power. In this association, however, the formerly sovereign States, though losing their sovereignty, retain their statehood; they all possess a share of the State-power (Staatsgewalt) which is exercised independently of

---

this point to Cooley's definition of sovereignty as "uncontrollable power." Non-sovereign States " sind Staaten, denn sie herrschen d. h. sie stellen aus eigenem Entschluss und eigener Macht die Unterthanen unbedingt bindende Normen auf. Ihre Hoheitsrechte stehen ihnen zu eigenem Rechte zu, d. h. sie sind nicht aus der aktuellen Rechtsphäre des souveränen Staates abgeleitet."—*Gesetz und Verordnung*, 201.

[1] *Schmoller's Jahrbuch*, 1883, 1159–60.

[2] " Der Gesammtstaat und die Einzelstaaten in ihren Zusammengehörigkeit bilden das Subjekt welches sonst in einer einzigen Persönlichkeit entsteht."—*Ibid.*, 1168.

the others; they are juristic persons knowing no superior, and must fairly be regarded as genuine States.

The German theory of a divided sovereignty and of the half sovereign state was early attacked in the most vigorous style by a partisan of state-sovereignty. As Waitz had been influenced by *The Federalist* and De Tocqueville, the champion of the states, Max Seydel, was indebted to the theory formulated by John C. Calhoun. Seydel assailed, root and branch, the theory of the Federal State and the prevalent doctrine of sovereignty attached thereto.[1] All so-called Federal States, he said, are in fact either simple States or associations of sovereign States; there are no combinations of States which are partly sovereign and partly non-sovereign: for a State is either sovereign or it is not at all.[2] It is conceivable that a State should not fulfill all its functions, but a State which not only does not, but cannot do this, because limited by another, would be an absurdity—in the happy German phrase, an "Unding."[3] The idea sometimes urged, that sovereignty is a merely relative matter, he denounced as equivalent to the "bankruptcy declaration of the idea of the Federal State" (die Bankerroterklärung des Bundesstaatsbegriffs).[4] The attempt to divide or compromise the sovereignty merely shows the inherent weakness of the whole conception. In reply to the argument that in the Federal State only the extent, not the content, of the sovereign power is limited, Seydel asserted it to be "exactly the content of the sovereignty that it has no definite extent;"[5] in other

[1] *Tübinger Zeitschrift für die gesammte Staatswissenschaft*, 1872, on "*Der Bundesstaatsbegriff.*" Also *Grundzüge einer allgemeinen Staatslehre*, 1873.

[2] *Tüb. Zeitschrift*, 208. Seydel quotes Calhoun, 198.

[3] "Ein Staat der dies gar nicht thun darf, sondern darin durch einen anderen beschränkt ist, ist ein Unding."—*Ibid.*, 205.

[4] *Ibid.*, 207.

[5] *Ibid.*, 202: "Es ist gerade der Inhalt der Souveränetät dass sie keinen bestimmten Umfang hat, ebenso wie dies der Inhalt des Eigenthumsrechts ist."

words, the essential nature of sovereignty is that it be in no direction limited, that a free field of activity be opened to it in every direction.[1] The content of the sovereignty, as Seydel would have it, is the impossibility of any theoretical limitation of its extent. His position is that sovereignty is indivisible in its nature, and that is an inseparable attribute of the State: from this vantage point he argued against the existence of the Federal State, and in favor of the unimpaired sovereignty of the original States. Although his polemic against the Federal State was unsuccessful, he showed clearly enough the impossibility of a divided sovereignty, and early rendered the position of Waitz's school almost untenable.[2] Written from a particularistic standpoint, his work really facilitated the advance of an idea nationalistic in nature.

The idea of sovereignty as a characteristic mark of the State has not of late found many active defenders, yet has not wholly lacked partisans. In particular Zorn[3] has protested against the idea of a non-sovereign State. He declares that "sovereignty is the first and highest conceivable mark of the State."[4] Where the sovereignty fails, there no State is to be found; they must always be found in combination; one cannot exist without the other.[5] The school of

[1] *Ibid.*, 191: "Man muss alle denkbaren Befugnisse ausüben können, aber man muss sie nicht ausüben."

[2] With Seydel compare Hagens, *Staat, Recht und Völkerrecht*, 1890.

[3] *Das Staatsrecht des deutschen Reiches*, 1880; in the *Zeitschrift für die gesammte Staatsw.*, 1881, on *Streitfragen des deutschen Staatsrechts;* Hirth's *Annalen*, 1884, *Neue Beiträge zur Lehre vom Bundesstaat.*

[4] Hirth's *Annalen*, 475: "Souveränetät ist die Möglichkeit der eigenen Rechtssetzung ohne höhere Kontrole. Ist die letztere Möglichkeit die spezifische Eigenschaft des Staates, so ist damit zugleich erweisen, dass Souveränetät ein essentiales Begriffsmoment des Staates ist."

[5] Compare Held, *Grundzüge*, 1868, 328: "Was die Gewalt und Verwaltung des Staates von jeder andern Gewalt und Verwaltung juristisch unterscheidet ist gleichfalls nur die staatliche Souveränetät." Lasson, A., *System der Rechtsphilosophie*, 1882, 391: "Souveränetät ist also die wesentliche und unterscheidende Eigen-

thinkers who support the doctrine of the inseparability of sovereignty and statehood seems, however, unable to make headway against the widespread theory of the non-sovereign State.

It appears, then, that the result of the German constitutional and political development has been the evolution of a theory of sovereignty as the power of determining legal competence, or as the faculty of legal self-determination. The new conditions presented for solution a problem different from that of the period when the idea of a divided sovereignty flourished. The question then was: How shall the co-existence of the separate States and the central State be reconciled? How shall the various States operate within the limits of one and the same political society? The answer was: By a division of the subjects upon which the several sovereigns operate; to one belongs this function, to another that, yet each within his own particular and proper sphere is equally sovereign, equally supreme. As the idea was expressed: "It is the extent, not the content of the sovereignty which is limited." But with the events of 1866-71 the conception of sovereignty underwent as great a transformation as did actual governmental conditions. It was now held that sovereignty is really the power of marking out the bounds of jurisdiction or competence (Kompetenz–Kompetenz), the power to determine in last resort the field or the subjects over which the State will act; or in the later form of statement, the power of exclusive legal self-determination. The sovereign not only must be supreme in its sphere, but must be able to say what its sphere shall be.

schaft des Staates und sie besteht in der vollkommenen Unabhängigkeit eines Willens gegenüber dem Willen eines anderen Staates." Lasson holds that sovereignty is really applicable to international relations only.—*Ibid.*, 392-93. Borel, E., *Étude*, 77 and following, defends the sovereignty of the State. He is particularly influenced by the difficulty of distinguishing between the non-sovereign State and the local administrative bodies.

As Seydel said against Waitz's theory, "it is the content of sovereignty that it be able to determine its extent." Manifestly, under such an interpretation, there can be but one sovereign in any given political society, for there could not be two powers each capable of drawing the boundary lines at will. Hence the claim that the members of the German Empire were individually sovereign lost its foundation. But the question was at once proposed: Though sovereignty has vanished, does not statehood still endure? And the response was: Though there can be but one *sovereign* in a given political society, there may be many *States* within one Federal State. If the former sovereign State cannot continue sovereign, it can at least remain a State. That is to say, the idea of a non-sovereign State, or so to speak, a semi-State, has been made the successor of the idea of a relative or semi-sovereignty. The State possesses the power to govern, but not the sovereign power; it rules, but not supremely.

At this point, however, arises a difficulty of the most serious nature, namely, the distinction of the State as thus conceived from the city or local community. In view of the increased and increasing importance of these smaller units in government and administration, they become serious rivals of the non-sovereign State. They too are in possession of governmental rights, they too establish law and compel obedience to it.[1] How shall the State deprived of its sovereignty be distinguished from the organ of local government, with its growing importance as a political unit? The answers given have been of so discordant a nature as to show the seriousness of the difficulty. On the one hand, the mark of distinction has been found in the circumstance that the State possesses power to govern " in its own right," as

---

[1] See the review of Laband in *Political Science Quarterly*, III, 123, by Professor Burgess. *Cf.* Willoughby, *Nature of the State*, ch. x.

opposed to the delegated or derived right which the organ of local government has. So reason Laband[1] and Jellinek.[2] Other theorists have rejected this idea, contending that the local organ also governs "in its own right," and have found the distinction [3] in the nature of the functions performed; those of the community being local in character, while those of the State are national in nature.[3] Again, it has been held that the difference between State and locality consists in the fact that the latter cannot be a subject of international law;[4] or again, by Preuss, in the fact that only the State possesses the "Gebietshoheit," the essence of which is the legal power to alter the territorial basis of the political society.[5] Thus opinions are still diverse and no settled con-

[1] *Staatsrecht*, 3d ed., 1895, I, 62.

[2] *Staatenverbindungen*, 40. In the work, *Ueber Staatsfragmente*, 270, a distinction is found in the fact that the non-sovereign State would, on the removal of the control exercised by the sovereign State, become sovereign "ohne weiteres." Thus Bulgaria is a non-sovereign State and on the removal of its superior would at once become sovereign, whereas Canada is only a colony and would require a reorganization before becoming sovereign. Jellinek, 300, proposes a new term "Land," by which is to be understood "die Zwischenform......die zwischen Provinz und Provinzialband einerseits, und Staat anderseits sich einschiebt." Canada is really a "Bundesland," "ein aus der Föderation von Ländern entstandenes Gesammtheit, ein Staatsfragment, das wiederum aus Staatsfragmenten besteht."—*Ibid.*, 307. Austria is ranked as a "Länderstaat."—*Ibid.*, 308. G. Meyer, *Staatsrecht*, 1895, 7, finds that the will of the State over the organ of local government is "legally unlimited," whereas the State itself has a field in which it is legally unlimited, namely in the performance of certain political duties, and in the determination of the State's organization. Compare an article *Ueber den begrifflichen Unterschied zwischen Staat und Kommunal-Verband*, by W. Rosenberg, in *Archiv für öffentliches Recht*, 1899, 328–70.

[3] S. Brie, *Theorie der Staatenverbindungen*, 1886, 13–14. H. Rosin, *Souveränetät, Staat, etc*, 1883, Hirth's *Annalen*, 291. O. Meyer, *Einleitung*, 2nd ed., 1884, 28. Gierke also criticises the "eigenes Recht" as a mark of distinction between State and community (*Schmoller's Jahrbuch*, 1883), although rejecting Rosin's criterion of distinction.

[4] Stoeber, P., *Archiv für öffentliches Recht*, 1886, 638.

[5] *Gemeinde, Staat, Reich*, 406, "Die rechtliche Fähigkeit einer Gebietskörperschaft sich selbst wesentlich zu verändern."

clusion has been reached. The element of sovereignty having been eliminated from the State, there seems to be no characteristic mark remaining to distinguish the non-sovereign State from the local unit of government, at least none upon which there is anything like a general agreement.[1]

It appears, then, that the German school accepted the theory of sovereignty in a limited sphere, but under the influence of political events soon rejected it as illogical and impossible. The indivisibility and the illimitability (formal at least) of the sovereignty have been generally maintained, but its indispensability as a mark of the State has been abandoned. The indivisibility of sovereignty has been purchased at the price of sovereign statehood. There could not be two sovereigns in one State, but there has been found room for two States and one sovereign.

The last consequences of the new development are seen in the attempt to eliminate altogether the idea of sovereignty from the concepts of political science. This is the work of Hugo Preuss in a recent suggestive study.[2] The notion of sovereignty—by which is understood absolute power, Bodin's "absolute and perpetual power of a State"—is assailed as inconsistent with the existence of modern public law. It is incompatible with international law, since an absolute power can be in no way bound by its agreements with other States; the sovereign remains as free after contracting as before, and

---

[1] Compare in this connection the review of Laband by J. W. Burgess in the *Pol. Sc. Quarterly*, III: "If sovereignty in the federal system be exclusively in the Union, then it seems to me that this makes the Union the only real state, and that the only distinction between the separate states and the municipalities lies in the fact that while the municipalities derive their authority from the states in a positive and definite manner, the states derive their power from the Union in a permissive and general manner." Also, *Political Science Quarterly*, I, on "*The American Commonwealth.*"

[2] *Gemeinde, Staat, Reich als Gebietskörperschaften; Versuch einer deutschen Staatskonstruktion auf Grundlage der Genossenschaftstheorie*, 1889.

there is no basis left upon which a structure of international law may be erected. Again, sovereignty stands opposed to the idea of the Federal State, since it necessitates the sacrifice either of the Federal State altogether, or of the independent position of its members. The conception of sovereignty is, moreover, hostile to any system of constitutional law, inasmuch as it excludes the notion of reciprocal rights and duties on the part of the State, thus arraying itself against any possibility of a body of law. Finally, it is unfavorable to the recognition of legal personality to the local organizations or communities, being incompatible with personality in any other association than the State itself.[1] "Sovereignty is," says he, "a negative legal idea, that is, the technical expression for a conception of law and the State; an idea which, outside the boundaries of private law, recognizes no relations of independent personalities, but only the sovereign will of the omnipotent State."[2] The idea of sovereignty may have been eminently adapted to the days of the absolute State, when the doctrine was enunciated by Bodin, but with the modern constitutional State (Rechtsstaat) it is wholly at variance.[3] The absolute State, he reasons, was an exclusive society *(Exclusiverband)*, recognizing no person above it, and admitting the existence of none beneath it.[4] In contrast to this, the modern State, the constitutional State, shows an extended series of "social persons," from the family up to the Empire, all associated in a complicated system of reciprocal rights and duties. Preuss is led, there-

[1] *Gemeinde, Staat,* etc., 118 ff.   [2] *Ibid.,* 133.

[3] Preuss endeavors to show throughout that his conclusions are logically deduced from Gierke's premises.

[4] *Ibid.,* 111: "Der souveräne Staat und die romanistische absolute Person sind korrelate Begriffe. . . . . In so analoger Weise haben sich beide Begriffe ausgeprägt und dieses ihr gemeinsames Gepräge in ein Wort gefasst, heisst. Souveränetät. Das ist das ureigene und eigentliche Wesen dieses Proteus unter den Begriffen."

fore, to conclude that the idea of sovereignty is wholly inconsistent with the modern idea of public law, and must consequently be stricken out from the categories of political science.[1]

The concept of sovereignty disposed of, there remains in its place the idea of authority (Herrschaft),[2] which is the characteristic relation of a society as a whole to its members; a relation which is possible only in an organic union or association of various persons. One will is ranked above another will only when standing in the relation of the whole to a part. This is seen even in the family, and runs through the whole series of legal persons. It is common to the community, the State, the empire, to all forms of corporate existence. There is involved no idea of absolute, unlimited, exclusive powers, but a reciprocal organic relation of a wholly different nature. But while all these " social persons," such as the family and the community, possess the governing power, there still remains to the State one distinguishing characteristic. This is found in the " Gebietshoheit," which is the " legal capacity of a " Gebietskörperschaft " to alter itself essentially."[3]

Closely connected with the theory arising out of the federal relation is that which is found in the field of international law. Here the complexities due to the various

[1] *Ibid.*, 135, 36.

[2] " Das charakteristische Verhältniss, in welchem die Gesammtpersonen des Sozialrechts zu ihren Gliedpersonen stehen." . . . " Eine Herrschaft d. h. die aus eigner Macht fliessende Ueberordnung eines Willens über andere ist erst denkbar, sobald die Personen aus dem Nebeneinander gleichen Individuen heraus und in das Verhältniss organischer Eingliederung eintreten. . . Ein Wille ist einem andern einzig dann, aber auch dann immer übergeordnet, wenn er zu ihm im Verhältniss des Ganzen zu seinem Theile steht."—*Ibid.*, 181.

[3] " Sie ist die rechtliche Fähigkeit einer Gebietskörperschaft, sich selbst (bezw. auch die in ihr enthaltenen engeren Gebietskörperschaften) wesentlich zu verändern (bezw. aufzulösen)."—*Ibid.*, 406.

combinations made between States have occasioned yet more embarrassment than those presented by the Federal State. The case of the Ionian Islands, of Turkey in its relations with Bulgaria and Roumania, of France and Madagascar, of England and the Transvaal, and the numerous other forms in which great and small States have been united, present enormous difficulties of interpretation.[1]

The march of empire has so stimulated diplomatic subtilty in the production of treaties into which either sovereignty or subjection may be read, that abstract theory has scarcely been able to classify the new relations as fast as they have been created. Where one governmental organization has the supervision of external relations, as was the case of France and Madagascar, what shall be said of the protected party? Is it sovereign or not? Under the relations established between England and the Transvaal by the agreement of 1884, could the latter be classed as a sovereign State or not? What shall be said of the status of a political society situated as is modern Egypt? Advancing in this direction, one is brought face to face with problems that seem to defy solution by the processes of ordinary logic, yet there must be some solution given; one must have at the very least a name for the situation, even if there is no real explanation forthcoming.

As a practical way out of difficulties such as those just suggested, the authorities in international law have been generally inclined to admit the divisibility of sovereignty, and the possibility of a non-sovereign State. The doctrine was early announced by J. J. Moser, who found that certain States, as those in Germany, were subject in some directions, yet at the same time supreme in others, and therefore desig-

---

[1] See F. von Holtzendorff, *Handbuch des Völkerrechts*; W. E. Hall, *A Treatise on International Law*; Conrad Bornhak, *Einseitige Abhängigkeitsverhältnisse unter den modernen Staaten*.

nated them as half-sovereign States.[1] Objection was made by Vattel, who declared the sovereignty to be, properly speaking, one and indivisible; but the doctrine reappeared and has remained in almost uncontested possession of the field.[2]

Thus Martens finds that a State generally enjoys perfect sovereignty (souveraineté parfaite), which means that in those things which concern its constitution and its civil government it need not receive laws from any stranger. There may be found, however, States which, "either because of a lack of certain rights which are a part of public law, or because of their obligation to recognize above them a legislative power, foreign and supreme, are called, although improperly, half sovereigns."[3] Klüber holds that if a State is dependent on the power of another State in the exercise of any essential right of sovereignty, even though independent in the exercise of other essential rights, it is to be classed as dependent or half-sovereign.[4] Halleck says that "many European States . . . have their sovereignty limited and qualified in various degrees either by the character of their internal constitution, or by the stipulations of unequal treaties of alliance and protection."[5] Wheaton admits the existence of the non-sovereign State, although openly confessing that "the denomination of semi-sovereign States is an apparent solecism in terms; as no State can properly be considered at once sovereign and subject, so no State

---

[1] *Beiträge zu dem neuesten europäischen Völkerrecht in Friedenszeiten*, Theil I, s. 506. Moser finds " ganz keinen Anstand . . diese mittlere Gattung zwischen Souveränen und Unterthanen mit dem ganz wohl passenden Ausdruck von halbsouveränen zu belegen." Cited by Jellinek, *Staatenverbindungen*, 39.

[2] *Le droit des gens*, 1778, tom. i, liv. i, ch. i.

[3] *Précis du droit des gens moderne de l'Europe*, 1831, sec. 16 (1st ed., 1788).

[4] *Europäisches Völkerrecht*, 2d ed., 1851, p. 28.

[5] *International Law*, 65.

can, with strict propriety, be considered as half or imperfectly supreme."¹ Pradier-Fodéré says that metaphysically there ought not to be half-sovereign States, but historically, there have been and there may be again.² Rivier, in the same spirit, declares that " utility, necessity even, have compelled the admission of imperfect sovereignty."³ Holtzendorff marks off perfect from imperfect sovereignty by a distinction which is similar to that between the whole and the half-sovereignty.⁴

From the standpoint of international law, sovereignty is really regarded as signifying the independence of a State from other States. No community is wholly independent of all other political societies, and hence there is really none that is absolutely sovereign. Now the concrete test of the State's independence is its possession of certain powers or faculties necessary to enable the community to assume its " equal station " in the family of nations. When a State asks for admission to the circle of sovereigns, the international lawyer inquires first of all into the political powers which the applicant possesses. In other words, sovereignty is really re-

---

[1] *Elements of International Law*, 3d ed., 1846, p. 67.

[2] *Traité de droit international public*, 1885, I, 159.

[3] *Principes du droit des gens*, 1896, I, 79: " Le droit des gens se plie aux exigences de la vie internationale, qui le crée et la consacre. . . . L'utilité, la necessité même, a fait admettre l' existence d' une souveraineté imparfaite, à laquelle on a donné le nom, nullement irréprochable, de mi-souveraineté." Compare Bluntschli, *Das moderne Völkerrecht*, 3d ed., 1878 (1st, 1867), p. 90. Heffter, A. W., *Das europäische Völkerrecht*, 6th ed., 1873 (1st, 1844): " Halbsouveränetät ist zwar ein überaus vager Begriff, ja beinahe ein Widerspruch in sich," but must be admitted none the less, p. 40. C. Calvo, *Le droit international théorique et pratique*, 4th ed., 1887 (1st, 1867), I, 171. Phillimore, *Commentaries on International Law*, 2d ed., 1871, I, 98–99.

[4] Franz v. Holtzendorff, *Die völkerrechtliche Verfassung und Grundordnung der auswärtigen Staatsbeziehungen*, 1887, sec. 24. He remarks that "neben der *effectiven* Halbsouveränetät giebt es eine im Sinne des Völkerrechts fictive Halbsouveränetät;" as that possessed by the Indian tribes in the U. S.

garded as a sum of powers, a collection or aggregate of governmental faculties, the possession of which will entitle the bearer to recognition in a sovereign capacity. These powers are of such a nature as that of making war and concluding peace, of negotiating treaties with other powers, of regulating the internal administration, of independent legislation.[1] For the purposes of international law sovereignty is regarded as the aggregate of these powers, rather than as an indivisible principle out of which they all emanate. Hence, being a sum or mass of rights, a part may be taken away without wholly destroying the sovereignty. The sovereignty may be less perfect, but it is still sovereignty. One State may yield up to another the care of its internal relations, its military defence, or even a part of its internal administration, without forfeiting its claim to recognition as in some sense sovereign. There are degrees of completeness in the possession of the essential rights of statehood. Certain prerogatives may be ceded without the least impairment of sovereignty; a continuance of the process may result in the reduction to a status of semi-sovereignty; and a still more serious transfer may result in the total forfeiture of the claim to sovereignty. The idea of sovereignty is throughout a relative one. The nature of international relations, indeed, forbids us to emphasize the absoluteness of any one State at the expense of the others; since no one community can be regarded as

[1] Holtzendorff, sec. 2, says that a State must have power to carry on war (Kriegsführung) and to establish its own constitution (die Macht eigener Verfassungsgebung); otherwise one must speak " von einen mehr oder weniger unvollkommenen oder unvollendeten Machtzustand." Rivier, *Principes*, I, 52, finds that a State is sovereign "lorsqu' il est indépendant de tout autre État dans l' exercice de ses droits internationaux à l' extérieur et dans la manière dont il vit et se gouverne à l' intérieur." Phillimore, *Commentaries*, I, 98–99, says: " States which cannot stand this test, which cannot negotiate or declare peace or war with other countries without the consent of their protector, are only mediately and in a subordinate degree considered as subjects of international law." See Oppenheim, *System des Völkerrechts*, 102.

wholly independent of the other members of the society of nations. By some writers it has been held that there are in reality two distinct sides to the problem of sovereignty, namely, the international or external and the purely internal. External sovereignty relates to the position of the State among other States: internal to the relation between the State and all other persons or associations within its territory. The essence of the external or international sovereignty is consequently independence in relation to sovereigns, while that of internal sovereignty is supremacy in relation to subjects. In the sense of international law, said Klüber, we understand by sovereignty "merely the independence of a State from the will of all other States."[1] Wheaton discovered an internal sovereignty, "which is inherent in the people of any State, or vested in its ruler by its municipal constitution or fundamental laws;"[2] and on the other hand an external sovereignty which "consists in the independence of one political society in respect to all other political societies." A similar distinction is made by other thinkers, e. g., Pradier-Fodéré,[3] Heffter,[4] Ullman,[5] and notably by Georg Meyer[6] and Rehm.[7] From

[1] *Europäisches Völkerrecht*, 2d ed., 1851, 23: "Im engern oder Völkerrechtlichen Sinne versteht man unter Souveränetät bloss die Unabhängigkeit eines Staates von den Willen aller anderen Staaten."

[2] *International Law*, 6th ed., 1863, 1846, 20–21: "This is the object of what has been called internal public law, droit public internal, but which may more properly be termed constitutional law."

[3] *Traité*, I, 160.

[4] *Völkerrecht*, 6th ed., 1873, 40.

[5] *Völkerrecht*, 1898, 41.

[6] *Staatsrecht*, 4te Aufl., sec. 6. Woolsey, T. D., *Introduction to the Study of Int. Law*, 6th ed., 1899, distinguishes between "independence" and "sovereignty," sec. 37. W. E. Hall, *A Treatise on Int. Law*, 4th ed., 1895, finds two classes of rights belonging to the State, namely, "independence" and "sovereignty," sec. 10.

[7] H. Rehm, *Allgemeine Staatslehre*, 63. See his defense of "Halbsouveräne-

this point of view, the distinguishing characteristic of sovereignty is found in the independence of the will of other States, while the internal aspects of the case are almost wholly ignored. The two sides of the State's existence are distinguished, and its external and internal relations regarded as separable. Hence it may follow that a community may be sovereign internally, that is, supreme over all persons and associations on its territory, but non-sovereign or semi-sovereign in relation to other political societies. Or on the other hand, a State may be sovereign externally and yet lack the internal sovereignty, as in the case of a confederacy. For example, Madagascar might be sovereign internally only, the German Confederation of 1815 sovereign externally only, though the one lacked control over its relations with other powers and the other control over the persons on its territory.[1] Thus the State from one point of view is sovereign, from another subordinate. Where independence in relation to other States is lost, there may remain control over internal affairs; or where complete control over internal affairs is wanting, there may be independence internationally. A complete sovereignty would, of course, include both the external and the internal sovereignty; but the absence of one

tät," p. 69: "Das Wesen der Souveränetät liegt in der Unabhängigkeit ... So mag man die relative Unabhängigkeit anderer Staaten auch Souveränetät nennen, aber nie die Souveränetät schechthin, sondern eben Halbsouveränetät. ... In dem Worte Halbsouveränetät ist (dagegen) ausgedrückt: es fehlt diese Souveränetät; es liegt etwas der Souveränetät *Nahes*, aber es liegt weniger als Souveränetät vor."

[1] Jellinek, *Staatenverbindungen*, 23 ff., protests vigorously against the idea of external and internal sovereignty, declaring that what is called external sovereignty is merely a reflex of the internal supreme power, and that the two sides of the state's activity cannot be thus divided. Holtzendorff, p. 2, points out that the external and internal sovereignty are in practical unity and stand in reciprocal relation. *Cf.* Held, *Grundzüge*, 322: "So wäre eine Unterscheidung der Souveränetät nach aussen und nach innen, oder eine doppelte Souveränetät, eine völkerrechtliche und eine staatsrechtliche, ein juristisches Unding."

does not necessarily work the destruction of the other, and the State may still live on, relatively or half-sovereign.

In international law, then, sovereignty is primarily the independence of a State among States. This independence is indicated by the possession of certain rights which afford a criterion of the existence or non-existence of sovereign power. Sovereignty being equivalent to a sum of powers, the loss of a part of these does not destroy its existence, and there is consequently room for the recognition of a semi-sovereign State. The great authorities on international law have not failed to find in this division of sovereignty a logical contradiction, even an apparent absurdity, but in view of the perplexing conditions to be interpreted and construed, no other way of escape seems open. The half-sovereign State may be "almost a contradiction in terms," an anomaly, a passing phenomenon, even " a bastard political society;" but it persists in its troublesome existence. International relations, it is reasoned, must when presented be accounted for and explained; and in these nicely graded forms of transition from sovereignty to subjection, the doctrine of the half-sovereign State is of invaluable practical service.

CHAPTER XI

CONCLUSION

IT is now in order briefly to resume the development made in the theory of sovereignty during the period which has been under discussion. Starting with the political theory of the Reaction, we noticed the various lines along which the attack upon the Revolutionary doctrine of popular sovereignty was conducted. Here was considered the doctrine of Kant and his school, the course taken by the religious reactionaries, and the patrimonial system constructed by Von Haller. In all of these schools there was found not so much a discussion of the nature of sovereignty, as a general denial that it was vested in the "people," as the Revolutionists had understood the term. Thus Kant denounced the "right of revolution;" De Maistre and Stahl defended "divine right;" Haller asserted the property right of the ruler to the government. In the same connection came the compromise theory which prevailed for a time in France, namely, the doctrine that sovereignty is not a creation or possession of man at all, but, on the contrary, exists only in pure reason or justice. After 1830 appeared the theory of the sovereignty of the general reason, in place of the general will which had been in earlier days so much emphasized, and this general reason was found to be embodied in the government of the State. Later a more democratic idea was given expression in the declaration of the sovereignty of the nation, regarded in a broader sense, as the general body of the citizens.

Contemporary with this movement was the important development in Germany from the idea of the sovereignty of the people to that of the State. Owing to the fact that it identified "people" with the governed class as opposed to the governors, and that it was, furthermore, associated with the eighteenth-century contract theory and the excesses of the Revolution, the doctrine of popular sovereignty was unable to stand against the attacks of the reactionary school. At this juncture there came into the foreground an exalted idea of the State shaped by Hegel. This idea was soon organically interpreted at the hands of various publicists of the "natural science" school, and later the idea of the State as a real juristic person, that is, as a bearer of legal rights and duties, rose to prominence. The result was that sovereignty was finally attributed to the State, viewed in its organic-personal character, while at the same time, the monarch was assigned to a position and dignity still nominally sovereign, but in a secondary and subordinate sense only. He now became the highest organ in the State; though superior to all others, he was, nevertheless, merely an organ, having beside him other organs, and above him the organism as a whole.

During this time there had been in England a growth of theory uninfluenced by any conflict between crown and people, but due to the desire to simplify the English system of law, and render it more definite and precise. In view of the legal omnipotence of the English Parliament, the doctrine was developed that sovereignty must be located in a determinate body of persons, and must bear the character of legal absolutism. In this same connection there was marked out a distinction between what is called legal sovereignty and political sovereignty. The legal sovereign is the final and determining power, so far as the legal order or system goes; the political sovereign is that body in the community, the will of which is ultimately obeyed; one is characterized as the lawyer's sovereign, the other that of the layman. The commands of the legal sovereign may be enforced in the ordinary courts of law, while those of the political sovereign are capable of some less direct sanction, as through the electorate or by means of the controlling power of public opinion.

In another direction there was developed a body of doctrine in relation to the "external" side of sovereignty, and in that field of its activity in which are involved the relations between States, or between communities of questionable statehood united in federal form. In America, there came into existence the idea of a division of the supreme power between federal and local governments, each of which was found to be fully supreme, but only within its proper sphere. The dominance of this theory was soon broken, however, by assaults directed from the standpoint of both individual State and Nation. First, the separate States declared for the indivisibility of sovereignty, and later the supporters of the Union proclaimed the Nation in a certain organic sense to be the real bearer of the undivided sovereignty. A later development, made in view of the extraordinary body back of the Government of each commonwealth, and a similar body back of the local and federal Governments, resulted in a general distinction between State and Government, with the attribution of original sovereignty to the former, and simply derived powers to the latter. It was also held that there should be not only a theoretical distinction between State and Government, but in addition a separate organization of the State provided for in every well-ordered constitution.

Likewise the continental forms of federalism induced the growth of theories as to the nature of sovereignty. Transmitted by De Tocqueville, the idea of a double sovereignty was at first accepted as a satisfactory solution of the problems presented by the "Bundesstaat." But under the influence of altered constitutional conditions, in which German national sovereignty appeared in a clearer light than before, this theory was abandoned, and another developed. This took the form of the "Kompetenz-Kompetenz," the idea that sovereignty consists essentially in the power of the State to determine at will the limits of its own competence or jurisdiction. The distinguishing characteristic of the supreme power was held to be the capacity to mark out independently the metes and bounds of its own activity. Even this doctrine was deemed too positive, however, and there appeared a modification of the idea to the effect that sovereignty consists merely in the power of a community to be legally bound solely through its own will. A State may not be able to extend the bounds of its jurisdiction at pleasure, yet if its acts are all determined by its own will and it cannot be legally bound by the will of another, the possession of sovereignty must, none the less, be conceded. These new doctrines were attended, however, by important changes of view as to the nature of the State. The historic theory that the State and sovereignty are inseparably united was found to be no longer applicable to modern political conditions, and the idea of a non-sovereign State was widely adopted as the easiest way of escape from the difficulties of constitutional and juristic construction presented by federalism. Finally, the idea of sovereignty having been torn from its intimate connection with the State, it has been urged that the concept of sovereignty has really no place in modern political science and should be banished from juristic nomenclature altogether.

Again, there was developed a theory of sovereignty in the field covered by international law, without especial reference to federal forms of association. Here it is seen that the relations between States involved in the protectorate, suzerainty and other like forms of association, are of so complicated a nature as to make the application of the ordinary rules almost impossible. Sovereignty is hence conceived as independence of a State from other States, as something essentially relative in its nature. It is, therefore, freely admitted that there are States which are imperfectly, or, as the phrase goes, half-sovereign, as well as those which are fully sovereign. The ideas of the divisibility of sovereignty and the existence of the semi-sovereign State are generally conceded to be illogical in strict analysis, but none the less held necessary for the purposes of international law.

From the internal point of view, the development of the theory shows a decided movement away from the idea of monarchical sovereignty. In Germany, the supreme power has been located in the State, conceived in a very abstract form; elsewhere, the nation, or the people, is regarded as sovereign, though considered in a less speculative way than is the German "Staat." But sovereignty as the prerogative of a single individual, or even as the attribute of a few, has ceased to obtain theoretical defense. There is a monarchical sovereignty still, but it is generally nominal or titular, or, at best, includes only the right to be the highest among the representatives of the State. Yet when one inquires more closely into whose hands the right of kings has passed, there is by no means a unanimity of opinion. Is it some organ of government, or the government in general, or the constitutional convention, or the electorate, or the nation or State organically or personally conceived, or the whole mass of the State's population inorganically regarded—public opinion, sentiment, or will? Where is this ultimately controlling power, and how shall we communicate with it? To this it may be said that the modern theory — especially the English theory—shows a marked tendency to distinguish between the legal or governmental sovereignty and the extra-legal or, as it is sometimes called, political sovereignty—one, the sovereign within the acknowledged limits of the field of government, the other, the power that ultimately defines these very boundaries; one is sovereign inasmuch as, and in so far as, habitual obedience is rendered to it; the other, in that it may or may not render this habitual obedience on which the legal sovereign rests. Yet even here the question is raised whether the power that has no legal or governmental organs of expression may properly be termed *political;* whether the potentiality of becoming political control is rightly designated as a political force, when existing in an inchoate condition.

From the external point of view—the relation between States, or communities claiming to be States—the difficulties of interpretation have been found enormous. In international law the doctrine of the semi-sovereign State reigns supreme. In relation to the Federal State, a double sovereignty, a limited sovereignty and the non-sovereign State have all been presented as bases upon which the difficulty might be settled. The first two of these, the double sovereignty and the relative sovereignty, have been generally rejected, but the idea of a non-sovereign State still flourishes in Germany. Despite the energy and the ingenuity with which this doctrine is defended, it would seem, however, that with the continual growth of national sentiment and the decline of particularistic feeling, the theory of statehood without sovereignty will subside, and the union of State and sovereignty be re-established.

In regard to the *nature* of sovereignty, there are two points which have been particularly emphasized during this period. In the first place the indivisibility of sovereignty has been, with the exception of a short time in America and Germany, generally recognized. The writers during the reaction against the Revolutionary theory were inclined to emphasize the unity of the sovereignty as much as Rousseau had done. The conflict between king and people ended, not by a division of powers between them, but by a recognition of the essential unity of the ultimate power in the hands of people, nation or State. Modern constitutionalism has rated highly the utility of a division of governmental powers, but it has not tended to show that the sovereignty itself is capable of such a division. The legislative, administrative and judicial functions are not regarded as militating against the essential and ultimate unity of the principle from which they emanate. Not even in the haziness that has obscured the Federal State has the principle of a divided sovereignty been able to maintain the ground it won, but it has been driven out and replaced by the conception of the one and indivisible sovereignty resident in the State. In the United States the logic of Calhoun, in Germany that of Seydel—both particularists—so damaged the idea of divided sovereignty that it has not since recovered its lost prestige.

Again, as to the *absoluteness* of sovereignty. In this direction there has been a general tendency to admit the impossibility of placing limitations on the sovereign power, formally at least. There have been found various restrictions in the nature of the State, in the general principles of righteousness, in considerations of a utilitarian nature; but none of these can be regarded as political limitations. It is generally agreed that there is no other political power capable of limiting the sovereign, else by hypothesis that limiting power must itself be sovereign. And here again neither Constitutionalism nor Federalism has operated against the strength of the idea. The king is no longer absolute, the ordinary Government is no longer unrestrained, but, nevertheless, the power that organizes the constitution, that can add to or subtract from it, is as unlimited and irresistible as ever. And this fact has been generally recognized in political theory. Also in relation to the Federal State, the drift of opinion has been toward the denial of the possibility of a relative or limited sovereignty. Despite the temptation to the recognition of a mere diminution of sovereign power on the entrance of a State into a Federal Union, the opposite principle has clearly triumphed. The State is "legally despotic," and the old maxim is still applicable to it: "The king can do no wrong."

We may summarize as follows the different senses in which the term sovereignty has been and is employed:

I. Sovereignty may designate the position of privilege held by the monarch in a State. In the modern constitutional State, the sovereignty of the king either is merely titular, or at the most denotes a pre-eminent position in the hierarchy of the constitutional organs of the State. "Monarchical Sovereignty" is in its best estate a position of constitutional superiority, not of complete supremacy.

II. Sovereignty may have reference to the relation of the State to the individuals or associations on its territory. The State, as the organization for the purpose of social control, determines what ends it will follow out and what means it will devote to these purposes, and forcibly compels the execution of its plans. This power is the vital principle of a political society; it is universal, absolute, indivisible, continuous. This is sovereignty conceived as the supremacy of the State over the individuals or associations of individuals on the given territory.

Under this head are to be distinguished again several significations of the term: (*a*) Sovereignty may refer to that power which in a given government or constitutional order has no governmental or constitutional superior. Thus the English Parliament possesses a governmental sovereignty. (*b*) Sovereignty may refer to the power of the State in an ultimate organization, back of the ordinary government even. This is not the supreme power under any given *constitutional* organization, but the power that determines what this constitutional order shall be. Such a body is a Constitutional Convention in the United States. (*c*) Sovereignty may signify that power in the given State or society the will of which is ultimately obeyed,—that body which if not adequately organized in the ordinary government or in the extraordinary government will, when occasion demands, create for itself means through which its supreme will may find expression. If the pressure of public opinion cannot accomplish this, then a way will be made by fire and sword.

III. Sovereignty has been regarded as the relation of a State to other States. In this sense, the term signifies the independence or self-sufficiency of a political society as against all other political societies. From this point of view, sovereignty might be termed international autonomy or independence.

These various and widely divergent uses of the term may not be right and proper uses; it is not contended here that they were good, but merely that they were or are. Keeping in mind the points of view from which the idea of sovereignty is ordinarily approached, it becomes easier to understand the bearings of the controversies that have arisen and to appreciate the drift of the present development. Illustrations of this are frequent during the period here considered. Thus in the doctrine of Kant there were two concepts of sovereignty, partially distinguished, the ideal sovereignty of the State (II), and the *de facto* sovereignty of the monarch (I). The interchange of the two made of a revolutionary theory a bulwark of reaction.

In the same way the theory of divine right which, really meant that the sovereign power of the political society (II) comes from God, was interpreted to mean the authorization of established dynasties (I). When the defenders of monarchy declared that the king was sovereign (I), they did not mean that he was sovereign in the sense in which the nation is sovereign (II), and they were willing to admit that the people were sovereign as constituting the material out of which the political power arose. What the crown wanted was a position of governmental pre-eminence (I). On the other hand the advocates of popular sovereignty, particularly in Germany, meant that the will of the people ought to be so organized as to ensure that it be ultimately obeyed (II, c), and they were not necessarily in conflict with constitutional monarchy. But the road to the adjustment of the two ideas was a long and tortuous one. Again, those who maintain that in every political society there is a determinate body which is legally despotic (II, a), do not mean that it is actually omnipotent either externally or internally. So far as law goes, it is sovereign; but law does not go the whole way. On the other hand, those who adhere to the sovereignty of the general will or of public opinion, sentiment, reason (II, c), do not mean that this sovereign is at any given moment organized to express the will of the State (II, a); they mean that it is to be obeyed, not immediately, but ultimately. Again, when, as in the recent American theory, it is held that the State is absolute in its sovereignty (II, b), this does not signify that the ordinary government has supreme and irresistible power, but that this attribute belongs to the ultimate organization of the State. The control exercised by the government and the sovereign majesty of the State are to be distinguished.

In the field of federal and international relations an understanding of the concepts of sovereignty entertained does much to clear up the confusion and contradiction so generally in evidence. Here it is seen that those who admit a half, double, limited, or relative sovereignty do not mean by sovereignty the control of the State over all subjects or associations thereof (II), but conceive it merely as the *independence* of the State externally (III). At the same time those who hold that sovereignty must be either complete or not at all, do not mean that the State is wholly unlimited in its relations with other States, but that there is no body to which effective control over a sovereign State may be attributed. There may be control, but not of so regular a nature as to constitute political control. Where there is political control, the sceptre of some State must be broken, its sovereignty destroyed.

These, then, are illustrations of the various concepts of sovereignty, and their frequent confusion. The dogmatist should show which is the proper point of view; in a historical study it is sufficient to indicate the various ways in which the subject of sovereignty is approached, and to emphasize the importance of knowing the path that is followed by each school of theorists.

BIBLIOGRAPHY

GENERAL WORKS.

Bluntschli, J. K. Geschichte der neueren Staatswissenschaft. 3te Aufl., 1881.
Janet, P. Histoire de la Science Politique. 3ème édit, 1887.
Michel, H. L' Idée de l' État, Essai critique sur l' Histoire des Théories sociales et politiques en France depuis la Révolution. 3ème éd., 1898.
Pollock, Fr. An Introduction to the History of the Science of Politics, 1895.
Graham, Wm. English Political Philosophy from Hobbes to Maine, 1899.
Mohl, R. v. Geschichte und Literatur der Staatswissenschaften, 1855-58.

SPECIAL WORKS.

Ahrens, H. Das Naturrecht oder die Rechtsphilosophie. 2te aufl., 1846-50.
Ancillon, Fr. Ueber Souveränetät und Staatsverfassungen, 1815.
——— Ueber den Geist der Staatsverfassungen, 1825.
Austin, John. Lectures on Jurisprudence, 1832. 3rd edit. 1869.
Baader, Fr. v. Evolutionismus und Revolutionismus, 1834.
——— Grundzüge der Societäts-Philosophie, 1837.
Bähr, O. Der Rechtsstaat, 1864.
Barante, de. Questions constitutionelles, 1849.
Bentham, J. Fragment on Government, 1776.
Bierling, E. R. Zur Kritik der juristischen Grundbegriffe, 1877-83.
Bliss, Philemon. Of Sovereignty, 1885.
Blumer, J. J. Handbuch des schweizerischen Bundesstaatsrechts, 1863-64.
Bluntschli, J. K. Psychologische Studien über Staat und Kirche, 1844.
——— Allgemeine Staatslehre, 1852.
Böhlau, H. Rechtssubjekt und Personenrolle, 1882.
Bonald, de. Théorie du Pouvoir politique et réligeuse dans la Société civile, 1796.
——— Essai analytique sur les Lois naturelles de l' Ordre social, 1800.
——— Législation Primitive, 1800.
——— Pensées, 1817.
Borel, E. Étude sur la Souveraineté et l' État fédératif, 1886.
Brie, Siegfried. Der Bundesstaat, 1874.
——— Zeitschrift für privat und öffentliches Recht, 1883, on Lehre von den Staatenverbindungen.
——— Theorie der Staatenverbindungen, 1886.
Brownson, O. A. The American Republic, 1866.

Burgess, J. W. Political Science and Comparative Constitutional Law, 1893.
    Pol. Sc. Quarterly, I, III.
Calhoun, J. C. A Disquisition on Government, 1851.
——— A Discourse on the Constitution and Government of the United States, 1851.
Calvo, C. Le Droit international, 1867.
Centz, P. C. The Republic of Republics, 1865.
Chipman, Nath. Principles of Government, 1833.
Clark, E. C. Practical Jurisprudence, 1882.
Coffinières, A. S. G. Traité de la Liberté individuelle, 1828.
Constant, Benj. Principes Politiques, 1815.
——— Réflexions sur les Constitutions et les Garanties, 1814–18.
Cooley, T. M. Constitutional Limitations. 6th ed., 1890.
Cousin, V. Cours d' Histoire de la Philosophie au dixhuitième Siècle, 1839–40.
——— Cours de Philosophie, 1828.
Dane, Nath. General Abridgment and Digest of American Law, 1823–29.
Daunou, P. C. Essai sur les Garanties individuelles que réclame l' État actuel de la Soci té, 1819.
Davis, Jefferson. The Rise and Fall of the Confederate Government, 1881.
Dicey, A. V. Lectures Introductory to the Study of the Law of the Constitution, 1885.
Dubs, J. Das öffentliche Recht der schweizerischen Eidgenossenschaft, 1877.
Duden, Gottfried. Ueber die wesentlichen Verschiedenheiten der Staaten, 1822.
Escher, H. Politik, 1863.
The Federalist, 1787–88.
Franz, K. Vorschule der Physiologie der Staaten, 1857.
Fries, Jakob. Philosophische Rechtslehre, 1803.
Fröbel, J. System der socialen Politik. 2te Auflage, 1847.
Gareis, C. Handbuch des öffentlichen Rechts, 1883.
Gerber, C. F. von. Ueber öffentliches Recht, 1852.
——— Grundzüge eines Systems des deutschen Staatsrechts, 1865.
Giddings, F. H. Principles of Sociology, 1896. 3d ed., 1899.
Gierke, Otto. Das deutsche Genossenschaftsrecht, 1863–81.
——— Die Grundbegriffe des Staatsrechts in *Zeitschrift für die gesammte Staatswissenschaft*, 1874.
——— Die Genossenschaftstheorie und die deutsche Rechtssprechung, 1887.
——— Johannes Althusius, 1880.
——— Review of Laband in *Schmoller's Jahrbuch*, 1883.
——— Deutsches Privatrecht, I, 1895.
Göschel, Fr. Zerstreute Blätter, 1832–37.
Green, T. H. Principles of Political Obligation.
Grimke, Fr. Nature and Tendency of Free Institutions, 1848.
Guizot, F. P. G. Du Gouvernement répresentatif, 1816.
——— Du Gouvernement de France depuis la Réstoration et le Ministère actuel, 1821.

—— Histoire de la Civilisation en Europe, 1828–30.
Haenel, Alb. Studien zum deutschen Staatsrecht, 1873–88.
—— Deutsches Staatsrecht, 1892.
Hall, W. E. A Treatise on International Law, 1880.
Halleck, H. W. International Law, 1861.
Haller, L. v. Handbuch der allgemeinen Staatenkunde, 1808.
—— Restauration der Staatswissenschaft, 1816–34.
Hegel, G. W. F. Grundlinien der Philosophie des Rechts, 1821.
—— Encyklopädie der philosophischen Wissenschaften, 1817.
Held, Jas. System des Verfassungsrechts, 1856.
—— Staat und Gesellschaft, 1861–65.
Hello, C. G. Du Régime constitutionel, 1827.
Holland, T. E. The Elements of Jurisprudence, 1882.
Holtzendorff, Franz v. Die völkerrechtliche Verfassung und Grundordnung der auswärtigen Staatsbeziehungen, 1887.
Hugo, Gustav. Lehrbuch des Naturrechts, 1798.
Hurd, J. C. The Theory of our National Existence, 1881.
—— The Union State, 1890.
Ihering, R. v. Der Zweck im Recht, 1877.
Jameson, J. A. A Treatise on Constitutional Conventions, 1866.
Jarcke, C. E. Vermischte Schriften, 1839.
—— Prinzipien-Fragen, 1854.
Jellinek, Georg. Die Lehre von den Staatenverbindungen, 1882.
—— Gesetz und Verordnung, 1887.
—— System der subjektiven öffentlichen Rechte, 1892.
—— Ueber Staatsfragmente, 1896.
Jordan, Sylvester. Allgemeines Staatsrecht, 1828.
Kant, Im. Vom Verhältnisse der Theorie zur Praxis im Staatsrecht, 1793.
—— Zum ewigen Frieden, 1795.
—— Rechtslehre, 1797.
Klüber, J. Oeffentliches Recht des teutschen Bundes, 1817.
Krause, C. C. F. Abriss der Philosophie des Rechts, 1828.
Krieken, A. T. v. Ueber das Wesen der sogennanten organischen Staatstheorie, 1873.
Laband, Paul. Das Staatsrecht des deutschen Reiches, 1876. 3te aufl., I, 1895.
Lammenais, H. F. Essai sur l' Indifférence en matière de Réligion, 1817.
—— Le Livre du Peuple, 1838.
Lasson, A. Princip und Zukunft des Völkerrechts, 1871.
—— System der Rechtsphilosophie, 1892.
Leo, Heinr. Studien und Skizzen zu einer Naturlehre des Staats, 1833.
Lerminier, J. L. E. Philosophie du Droit, 1832.
Lewis, G. C. Remarks on the Use and Abuse of some Political Terms, 1853.
Liebe, G. Staatsrechtliche Studien, 1880.
Lieber, Francis. Manual of Political Ethics, 1838–39.

―――― Civil Liberty and Self-government, 1853.
―――― Miscellaneous Writings, 1881.
Lightwood, J. A. The Nature of Positive Law, 1883.
Madison, James. Works.
Maine, H. Early History of Institutions, 1874.
Maistre, Jos. de. Étude sur la Souveraineté, 1794–96.
―――― Considérations sur la France, 1797.
―――― Essai sur la Principe générateur des Constitutions politiques, 1807.
―――― Du Pape, 1817.
Markby, Wm. Elements of Law, 1871.
Martens, Fr. v. Völkerrecht, 1883.
Martens, G. F. de. Précis du Droit des Gens moderne de l' Europe, 1788.
Maurenbrecher, Romeo. Grundsätze des deutschen Staatsrechts, 1837.
―――― Die deutschen regierenden Fürsten und die Souveränetät, 1839.
Meyer, Geo. Grundzüge des norddeutschen Bundesrechts, 1868.
―――― Staatsrechtliche Erörterungen, 1872.
―――― Lehrbuch des deutschen Staatsrechts, 1878.
Mohl, R. v. Encyclopädie der Staatswissenschaften. 2te Aufl., 1872; 1te, 1859.
Mulford, E. The Nation, 1870.
Müller, A. Von der Nothwendigkeit einer theologischen Grundlage der gesammten Staatswissenschaften, 1819.
Phillimore, R. J. Commentaries on International Law, 1871–74.
Pollock, Fr. A First Book of Jurisprudence, 1896.
Pomeroy, J. N. Constitutional Law, 1868.
Preuss, H. Gemeinde, Staat, Reich, 1889.
Rehm, H. Allgemeine Staatslehre, 1899.
Ritchie, D. G. Darwin and Hegel, 1893.
Roenne, L. v. Das Staatsrecht der preussischen Monarchie, 1856.
Rosin, H. Souveränetät, Staat, Gemeinde, Selbstverwaltung, in *Hirth's Annalen*, 1883.
Rotteck, K. v. Lehrbuch des Vernunftrechts, 1829–36.
Savigny, R. Fr. v. Vom Beruf unserer Zeit für Gesetzgebung und Jurisprudenz, 1814.
―――― System des heutigen römischen Rechts, 1839.
Schelling. System des transcendentalen Idealismus, 1800.
―――― Methode des akademischen Studiums, 1803.
Schleiermacher, Fr. Ueber die Begriffe der verschiedenen Staatsformen, 1814.
―――― Staatslehre. Posth.
Schmitthenner, Fr. Grundlinien des allgemeinen oder idealen Staatsrechts, 1845.
Schulze, H. System des deutschen Staatsrechts, 1865.
―――― Einleitung in das deutsche Staatsrecht, 1867.
Serrigny, D. Traité du Droit Publique des Français, 1846.
Seydel, Max. Der Bundesstaatsbegriff in *Tübinger Zeitschrift*, 1872.
―――― Grundzüge einer allgemeinen Staatslehre, 1873.

Sidgwick, Henry. The Elements of Politics, 1891.
Sismondi, J. C. L. Études sur les Constitutions des Peuples libres, 1836.
Stahl, F. J. Philosophie des Rechts, 1830-33.
—— Das Monarchische Princip, 1845.
Stein, Lorenz v. Verwaltungslehre, 1865-84.
—— System der Staatswissenschaften, 1852-56.
Stephens, A. H. A Constitutional View of the late War between the States, 1868-70.
Story, Jas. Commentaries on the Constitution, 1833.
Tocqueville, Alexis de. Démocratie en Amérique, 1835.
Treitschke, H. v. Bundesstaat und Einheitsstaat in Historische und Politische Aufsätze. B. II, 1864.
—— Bund und Reich in *Preussische Jahrbücher*, 1874.
Tucker, St. G. Blackstone, 1803.
Wagner, J. J. Der Staat, 1815.
Waitz, Geo. Grundzüge der Politik, 1862.
Warnkönig, L. H. Rechtsphilosophie als Naturlehre des Volks, 1839.
Welcker, K. T. Rechts-Staats-und Gesetzgebungslehre, 1829.
—— Die letzen Grunde von Recht, Staat und Strafe, 1813.
Webster, Daniel. Works.
Westerkamp, J. B. Staatenbund und Bundesstaat, 1892.
Wheaton, Henry. Elements of International Law, 1836.
Willoughby, W. W. The Nature of the State, 1896.
Wilson, James. Works.
Wilson, Woodrow. An Old Master and Other Political Essays, 1893.
Woolsey, Th. D. Political Science, 1877.
Zachariä, H. A. Deutsches Staats- und Bundesrecht, 1841.
Zachariä, K. S. Vierzig Bücher vom Staate, 1820-32.
Zoepfl. Grundsätze des gemeinen deutschen Staatsrechts, 5 auf., 1863.
Zorn, Philip. Das Staatsrecht des deutschen Reiches, 1880-83

VITA

THE writer of this dissertation was born at Hopkinton, Iowa. He was graduated from Lenox College in 1893 with the degree of A. B.; in 1893–94, he taught in the public schools in Iowa. He attended Iowa University in 1894–95, receiving there the degree of A. B. in 1895; in 1895–96, he was instructor in Lenox College. In 1896–98, he was a student in the School of Political Science in Columbia University. He received here the degree of A. M. in 1897; in 1897–98 was University Fellow in Political Philosophy. In 1898–99, he was a University Lecturer on Political Theory, and in 1899–1900 a student in the University of Berlin and in Paris.

The writer's major work in Columbia was in Political Theory under the direction of Professor Dunning. His minors were American History under Professors Burgess and Osgood, and Constitutional and Administrative Law under Professors Burgess and Goodnow. He has also taken courses under Professors Munroe-Smith, Seligman, Giddings, Clark, Robinson and Butler.